John Wodehouse Audubon, son of the famous artist-naturalist, joined the California Gold Rush to cure a lingering malaise, a popular idea of the times being that a rigorous trip through the American West would surely toughen the body and heal the spirit. Homesick and lonesome, he spent a miserable Christmas Day of 1849 in San Francisco in which he remarked on the total absence of female companionship but failed to mention in his diary that the center of town burned up the night before. Only a few fragments of his drawings were saved, among them, this vignette of mining life and San Francisco which bears the legend, "Rain, rain, and more rain . . ."

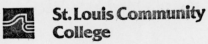

MIRROR
OF THE DREAM

MIRROR OF THE DREAM

An Illustrated History of San Francisco

T.H. WATKINS
AND
R.R. OLMSTED

Designed by John Beyer

Scrimshaw Press   San Francisco 1976

Library of Congress Cataloging in Publication Data

Olmsted, Roger R   1928–
  Mirror of the dream.

    1. San Francisco—History.   I.   Watkins, Tom H.,
joint author.   II.   Title.
F869.S3045   979.4'61   76-18168
  ISBN 0-912020-44-X

The Scrimshaw Press
6040 Claremont Avenue
Oakland, California 94618

San Francisco is the genius of American cities. It is the wild-eyed, all-fired, hard-boiled, tender-hearted, white-haired boy of the American family of cities. It is the prodigal son. The city which does everything and is always forgiven, because of its great heart, its gentle smile, its roaring laughter, its mysterious and magnificent personality. . . . It seems delirious with energy, incoherent because of the many things it has to say, broken-hearted with sorrowful memories. You walk through the streets of the city and feel its loneliness, and you wonder what memory is troubling its heart.

——WILLIAM SAROYAN

CONTENTS

The Images

CONTENTS

The Chapters

Louis Choris, an artist with the Russian exploring expedition that put into San Francisco in September of 1816, saw the Indians of Mission Dolores celebrating the Christian God in their own fashion.

A SITE WITHOUT A CITY

IN THE NORTHEAST CORNER of Golden Gate Park, otherwise a monument to the wonderful changes that can be wrought by men who have a visionary purpose, stands a little copse of stunted, windblown oaks—a thoughtfully preserved remnant of the original climax vegetation of the windswept peninsula that became the city of San Francisco. Some of the Indians who lived in the hills of Oakland and Marin and San Mateo must have known these oaks. They were a people who seem to have been fond of excursions, for we know something of their making of tule canoes in which to cross the bay, but there certainly was little to keep them long on the desolate hills hereabouts. The natural setting of San Francisco is magnificent only to a people with a dream and a purpose associated with a whole world of geopolitics and commerce, and only in this setting of the mind could the site of San Francisco acquire a meaning and a history. To the thoroughly practical folk who occupied the Bay Area for thousands of years before the white man, San Francisco was not even a particularly nice place to visit.

This is not to malign the Indians as insensible to matters other than daily comfort. Their culture appears to have involved a highly developed spiritual life, and the ease of living in the mild climate of the central coast gave ample scope to the development of a speculative turn of mind. Elaborate creation myths were central to the Indian philosophy, as were the cultural histories of their tribelets. Their minds tracked back to earlier times, to people even earlier than themselves. They spoke of their speculations as dreams, and their dreams ran backwards. They could not cope with the Spanish mentality, and if the Americans could scarcely think of them as people at all, the regard must have been mutual.

It is certainly fair, if harsh, to ignore the Indians in a history devoted to the city of San Francisco, as we do here, but what of the Spanish and Mexican periods that figure so largely in previous histories of the city? In point of fact neither the Spaniards nor the Mexicans built so much as a town at San Francisco, though a mostly American village did appear late in the Mexican period.

"Thus was our curiosity satisfied concerning the Spanish town and settlement of St. Francisco."

The ubiquitous bulrush, called tule by the Spaniards, gave the Indians of the San Francisco region these surprising watercraft.

Thus the history of Spain and Mexico at the site of San Francisco is but a prologue to the history of the city. It is the story of why San Francisco Bay was so long in being found and why a city did not get built. It is a story of dreams and goals as well as physical conditions and chance.

If Spaniards sailed west across the Atlantic in the time of Columbus with the notion that their voyages might return the kind of profits realized by the Portuguese in the East, their discoveries almost immediately forced revision of their goals. The Indies which they discovered, they seized, to the benefit of the crown and those of aggressive intention and the right connections. Cortez was given the chance to raise the horizons of Spanish adventures from mere exploitation to outright looting, and the development of the New World became a quick scramble for plunder—a story to be repeated in American California, but under different conditions and with different overtones and consequences.

Cortez himself was on the way to California a dozen years after his spectacular conquest of central Mexico. Politics, however, were running against the great conquistador, and geography worked heavily against the success of the expeditions that set out. The land that came to be called Alta California was beyond easy or natural reach. The Sea of Cortez and the shores of Baja California were dead ends as approached from the south, leading only to remote and barren lands; the ultimate trail to California rightly earned the title *el Camino del Diablo*. The northward navigation of the Pacific shore was opposed by adverse winds in summer and was dangerous in winter and as time and practical endeavor would show, California was effectively further from Mexico City than Mexico City was from Seville.

Nevertheless, as early as 1542 Juan Rodriguez Cabrillo had sailed north well past the latitude of San Francisco, and while he missed the entrance to San Francisco Bay, he did discover the good harbors at Monterey and San Diego. This excursion was not followed up, and may well be considered the last push toward California generated in the era of Cortez. Sebastian Cermeño, the captain of a Manila Galleon, attempted in 1595 to survey the coast the easy way, from north to south, in the course of his voyage homeward across the Pacific. The attempt was ill-timed, however, and he was trapped and wrecked in November by a southerly gale at the north rim of a little bay he named for Saint Francis. This "San Francisco Bay" was the outer bay, the bight between Point Reyes and Pedro Point. Cermeño and his crew almost certainly would have discovered the great inner bay had they not had at hand the easy means of escaping their predicament—a large knocked-down launch which they had brought along to assist in surveying the coast and its harbors. In this they proceeded south to Mexico, close inshore, but crossing such important ports as San Francisco and Monterey from point to point. Thus, little profit came from what could have been an epic of discovery.

Sebastian Vizcaíno, an adventurer in search of pearls and other such loot, was the next white visitor to the Alta California coast. He rediscovered the harbor at Monterey in January of 1603. The date is significant in that at such seasons of the year, when southerly storms sweep the coast, only Monterey, of all the "outside" ports, is a safe haven for the mariner. Vizcaíno's justifiably glowing description of Monterey Bay marked that spot in the consciousness of Spanish officialdom for nearly two centuries; in effect, it defined the Spanish view of California, for it was assumed that, except for Monterey, there was nothing in the area that deserved interest. And Spain, riven by difficulties on the European continent during all this time, had neither the energy nor the incentive to waste itself on colonization efforts whose only justification was the

The hunters of the hidden strait showed Choris how their fathers had stalked the elk of far Marin.

presence of the fine harbor of Monterey. With no booty and no trade to speak of, California lay undisturbed, discovered but not yet known.

The Russians began to exhibit an interest in the coast in the middle of the eighteenth century. Spain, so embroiled in European politics that its government displayed outright and well-founded paranoia, found the energy to decide, under its new Bourbon kings, that the colonization of California was indeed necessary for the preservation of its New World empire. So it was that Visitador-General José de Gálvez was authorized to initiate the first colonization effort in Alta California in 1768. Captain Gaspar de Portolá was placed in charge of a colonization expedition, part by land and part by sea, in early 1769. While the presidio and mission at San Diego were still in the embryonic stage, Portolá set out to march north, to find the harbor of Monterey and establish a settlement. But Portolá was a foot soldier and spectacularly ignorant of what might constitute a splendid refuge in mariner's terms, and when he encountered Monterey he dismissed it and continued his march north, to discover San Francisco Bay in early November, 1769. Landlubber Portolá inserted in his diary the sour observation that they had "found nothing," but the more perceptive Fray Juan Crespi, the expedition's missionary, scribbled in *his* diary that the bay was "a very large and fine harbor, such that not only all the navy of our most Catholic Majesty but those of all Europe could take shelter in it."

Portolá returned to San Diego and in the spring of 1770 marched north again and established the presidio and mission of Monterey, under the aegis of Fray Junipero Serra. He forthwith fled to Mexico, his duty done. It was not until six years later that another expedition, this one under the command of Captain Juan Bautista de Anza, journeyed beyond Monterey and planted the presidio of San Francisco on a dune-ridden peninsula, together with the Mission of San Francisco de Asís on the edge of a sluggish little slough he called *Laguna de Nuestra Señora de los Dolores.* The year was 1776. Spanish empire had come to the bay of San Francisco within precisely the same years that a group of Yankee merchants, slaveholders, printers, and land speculators were busily forging the outlines of something that would come to be known as the United States of America. But had Spanish empire truly been extended, or was this the merest shadow of empire?

The Presidio at its best—much less than Anza surely envisioned a generation earlier in 1776.

Consider for a moment the distances in time involved. It was 234 years after the voyages of Cabrillo that San Francisco Bay was occupied by the Spanish; when the *San Carlos,* one of the ships of the colonization expedition of 1769, sailed some 1,200 miles against the wind from San Blas to San Diego she was 110 days at sea—as long as an average clippership run from New York to San Francisco by way of Cape Horn 85 years later. And if the distance in time was great, the distance imposed by institutions was even greater. The system of military outposts and missionary settlement, suggested by conditions on the frontier and imposed by the state policy of Spain, offered scant incentive to rapid or adventurous development; rigid and unimaginative licensing procedures discouraged private entrepreneurial efforts. The presidios were nothing so much as a drain on the accounts of the king of Spain; the missions brokered in souls and traded in nothing but supplies to the presidios, even while their cattle herds increased to countless numbers and little purpose.

The golden land lay fallow, and nowhere was it more obvious than in the San Francisco Bay area, as sketched by Captain George Vancouver, Royal Navy, who had, of all things, been sent out to the coast to cast some weight against the Spanish claims to Nootka Sound in British Columbia in 1792. Vancouver was much impressed by the civility of Commandant Sal of the San

Francisco Presidio when he dropped by the port to find out just what kind of show the Spaniards ran, and he was taken by the charm of Señor Sal's wife and the behavior of their children. His enthusiasm, however, did not extend to the settlement as he found it: "We soon arrived at the Presidio, which was not more than a mile from our landing place. Its wall, which fronted the harbour, was visible from the ships; but instead of the city or town, whose light we had so anxiously looked for on the night of our arrival, we were conducted into a spacious verdant plain, surrounded by hills on every side, excepting that which fronted the port. The only object of human industry which presented itself, was a square area, whose sides were about two hundred yards in length, enclosed by a mud wall, and resembling a pound for cattle. On entering the Presidio, we found one of its sides still uninclosed by the wall, and very indifferently fenced in by a few bushes here and there. . . .

"Thus, at the expence of very little examination, though not without disappointment, was our curiosity satisfied conserning the Spanish town and settlement of St. Francisco. Instead of finding a country tolerably well inhabited and far advanced in cultivation, if we except its natural pastures, the flocks of sheep, the herds of cattle, there is not an object to indicate the most remote connection with any European, or other civilized nation.

"This sketch will be sufficient, without further comment, to convey some idea of the inactive spirit of the people, and the unprotected state of the establishment at this port, which I should conceive out to be a principal object of the Spanish crown. . . . Should my idea of its importance be over-rated, certain it is, that considered solely as an establishment, which must have been formed at considerable expence, it possesses no other means for its protection than . . . a brass three-pounder mounted on a rotten carriage before the presidio, and a similar piece of ordnance which (I was told) was at the s.e. point of entrance lashed to a log instead of a carriage; and was the gun whose report we heard the

What progress in this favored land? As Choris saw, the games of the missionized population meant more to them than faint models of European architecture and dress.

evening of our arrival. Before the presidio there had formerly been two pieces of ordnance, but one of them had lately burst to pieces."

A succession of visitors, of Vancouver's period and later, saw at San Francisco a great harbor surrounded by a rich hinterland that neither Spanish nor subsequent Mexican policy and energy could develop. All were impressed by the tens of thousands of cattle that roamed the mission lands of the Bay Area—but of what value were they? Spanish policy strangled potential trade, but even under the more economically enlightened Mexican regime after 1821 a cow was nothing but a two-dollar hide and maybe a dollar's worth of tallow, and worth that only because Yankee traders could smell a dollar 18,000 sea miles from home. San Francisco was beyond the end of the earth that Spain or Mexico could compromise, beyond what they could reasonably colonize or administer.

"Administer" is the key word, for Spanish policy demanded centralized authority, an authority which could not operate effectively at the end of year-old strings. Consider Felipe de Neve, first governor of the Californias: in 1772, he complained, from his adobe house at Monterey, that he had no secretary and spent long hours by candlelight transcribing the five copies of everything that were required by administrative procedure. Five copies of complaints about the tobacco ration; five copies about the punishment of a private who may or may not have raped a neophyte; five copies about damp gunpowder; five copies about the illness of a corporal who wanted to retire; above all, five copies about the state of his own health and the prospects of the honorable termination of his own services. So it went, this quintuplicate dirge of the frontier. The aggressive self-interest involved was that of the clerks in a county courthouse—no matter for sniggering, for there are good clerks and important clerks and civic-minded clerks and our civilization today is largely in the hands of clerks; but after all, clerks do *jobs*, not the kind of work that develops empires.

Whatever the burdens on Felipe de Neve, the greatness of Spanish empire lay elsewhere. So let us listen to the voice of a different breed, the annalists of American San Francisco, writing in 1854: "Better, a thousand times, that the missions and all their two-legged and four-legged *beasts* should be ruthlessly swept away, than that so fine a country, one so favored and framed by bountiful nature for the support, comfort and elevation of her worthier children, should longer lie a physical and moral waste—a blotch on the fair face of creation.

"But another race was destined soon to blow aside the old mists of ignorance and stupidity, and to develop the exceeding riches of the land, which had lain, undisturbed and concealed, during so many ages. The Spaniards had scarcely proceeded any way in the great work—if they had not rather retarded it—when the Anglo-Saxons, the true and perhaps only type of modern *progress*, hastily stepped in, and unscrupulously swept away both their immediate forerunners as effete workers, and the aborigines of the land, all as lumberers and nuisances in the great western highway of civilization. This highway is fated to girdle the globe, and probably, in the course of a few centuries, will join the original starting point in the natal home of the 'Pilgrim Fathers' in old England. The *pioneers* of California are *our* 'Pilgrim Fathers,' and there need be not the slightest doubt but that the empire, or rather the great *union* of peoples and nations in the Pacific will soon . . . rival if not surpass the Magnificent States of the Atlantic. Indians, Spaniards of many provinces, Hawaiians, Japanese, Chinese, Maylays, Tartars, and Russians, must all give place to the resistless flood of Anglo-Saxon or American progress."

The proper placement of the landing spot of Sir Francis Drake's group arouses increasingly lively controversy as the 400th anniversary of the date— 1579—approaches.

Indeed. This resistless flood of Anglo-Saxon progress had been stretched back far enough to include the second navigation of the California coast and the discovery of a "good and fair harbor" in the vicinity of San Francisco. The landing of Francis Drake, privateer extraordinary, is a fact of the year 1579. The precise point at which he landed to overhaul his ship before continuing his round-the-world voyage is not only still in doubt, but agitates local partisans of one theory or another more strongly than ever. The strongest argument against those who insist upon Drake as the European discoverer of San Francisco Bay lies in the plainest seaman's interpretation of what would constitute a good harbor of refuge on the extremely inhospitable California coast. A good harbor would be some shelter in the outer bay, such as Drake's Bay. An excellent harbor would be something like Cabrillo's or Vizcaíno's Monterey. The inner bay of San Francisco would have called forth a full battery of superlatives, not simply the modest praise it received from Drake.

Be that as it may, the main point is that Drake *did* claim the area for England. But England was no better prepared than Spain to colonize the place at that time. The resistless flood of Anglo-Saxon progress had to wait on a real tide rather than a controversial title.

That tide finally came. The founder of Yerba Buena—the town of San Francisco as distinct from the official outposts of the mission and presidio—was an Englishman, W. A. Richardson, who set up shop at this sailor's port of call in 1835. The next year an American, Jacob P. Leese, built the first permanent structure. The building was completed at ten o'clock on the morning of July 4, 1836, and was inaugurated with a grand Independence Day feast, ball, concert, and general debauch attended by the Vallejos, Castros, and all the other Mexican gentry of the Bay Area. The Mexican and American flags flew side by side

A coincidence of lively signifi-cance: the first public gathering at the first permanent building at Yerba Buena was Jacob B. Leese's grand 4th of July affair in 1836.

at the celebration, a portent of what was to come in northern California during the next decade.

What it all came to was simply this: within ten years northern California had an influential American population, and San Francisco was definitely an outpost of Anglo-Saxon men of commerce. As late as 1844 perhaps only fifty persons lived at Yerba Buena; two years later there were maybe two hundred. But the U. S. Navy patrolled the coast and was ready to swoop down on San Francisco quite as rapidly and effectively as Commodore Jones had indeed done in his abortive seizure of Monterey in 1842.

In 1846 Americans were on the move. The numbers involved were not large, as this trans-Mississippi migration started, but they were most significant in their impact on the small populations of Oregon, California, and the Mexican territories that would be taken by force even before it was obvious that they had been taken by right of habitation. At San Francisco, the determinate settlement of that year was the arrival of Sam Brannan and two hundred thirty-five other emigrants from New York. This was essentially a Mormon colonization effort, and it is said that in July of 1846 when Sam saw from the decks of the ship *Brooklyn* the stars and stripes already floating over Yerba Buena, he impiously murmured, "That damned rag again!"

But if Sam Brannan—like other Mormons—had no cause to love the United States, he was still the quintessential American. His company effectively doubled the population of San Francisco and was influential in making the American seizure of northern California more than a military adventure. Many of the Mormons left when Brigham Young called the Latter-Day Saints to the Salt Lake establishment—but Sam stayed at San Francisco, where he cut a swath worthy of a boy who had come of age in the midst of the Ohio land speculations and peculations of 1836 and 1837.

The die had been cast: San Francisco was an American town, outpost of a continental empire of the bourgeoisie, of a people almost as distant from the Spaniards they displaced as from the Indians they finally exterminated. The ruthlessness of Spanish imperial policy was far outdone by the standards of American private interests, and the aggressiveness of a Cortez was more than matched by the ambition of Yankee shopkeepers.

If gold had not been found in American California, God would have been guilty of an omission. Yet San Francisco would still have grown rapidly into an important city, for even the village of Yerba Buena was a concrete expression of the hopes, fantasies, abilities, and energy common to the moving element of the American population. It was entirely appropriate that gold cast loose all restraint upon a temper that was already present, a dream that was already wide-awake.

The history of the American period, therefore, is the true history of San Francisco, the city as distinct from the place. The city as an institution is the very essence of civilization, the mirror of its dream. And nowhere does the reflection of our own civilization gleam more authoritatively than in the successive exposures of the process and purpose, the accident and ambiance that shaped the city of San Francisco—where even today the American Dream flashes back at us every time we take another look.

The utter nothingness of the site of Yerba Buena is brilliantly captured in this view from the Annals of San Francisco *(1854).*

VIEW OF SAN FRANCISCO, FORMERLY YERBA BUENA, IN 1846-7
BEFORE THE DISCOVERY OF GOLD

WE THE UNDERSIGNED HEREBY CERTIFY THAT THIS PICTURE IS A FAITHFUL AND ACCURATE REPRESENTATION OF SAN FRANCISCO AS IT REALLY APPEARED IN MARCH 1847

J. D. Stevenson
COMMANDING 1ST REGT OF N.Y. VOLS. IN THE WAR WITH MEXICO.

Gen. M. G. Vallejo

George Hyde
FIRST ALCALDE DIST. OF SAN FRANCISCO 1846-7

Although this lithograph of San Francisco at the beginning of 1847 was not made until the 1880s, it faithfully delineates each house and street of the town nestled at the head of Yerba Buena Cove when the water came up almost to Montgomery Street. In the foreground are the Portsmouth and other ships of the Pacific Squadron.

Chapter I

DESTINY'S VILLAGE

JUST BEFORE DAWN on July 1, 1846, a group of twenty men climbed aboard the launch of the United States trading barque *Moscow*, anchored in the little harbor of a wood-and-water stop called Sausalito, some twelve miles north across San Francisco Bay from the village of Yerba Buena. Most of the men were bearded. Most were young, though their faces were weathered like aging mahogany and their clothing hung as patched and tattered as it would have on any indigent in New York City's Five Points. In command of this ragged crew was Lieutenant John C. Frémont, of the United States Topographical Engineers. For more than a year, Frémont and most of these men—together with another forty individuals now in camp near Mission San Rafael—had been wandering around the West on Frémont's third official exploring expedition—from St. Louis, Missouri, to the Great Salt Lake, through the biblical desert wastes of Utah Territory (later Nevada), across the splendid upthrust of the Sierra Nevada, up and down the Central Valley of California, up to Oregon's Klamath Lake, and back to the settlements of northern California. At the moment, they were all somewhat vaguely embroiled in the "Bear Flag Revolt," a clownish insurrection against the territory's Mexican government on the part of American settlers in the Sacramento Valley—clownish because on May 12, 1846, President James K. Polk, unbeknownst to the insurgents, had officially declared war on Mexico, rendering their little rebellion irrelevant; clownish because the whole affair, in spite of patriotic bluster and high-minded rhetoric, was probably based on the greedy notion that if a "California Republic" could somehow be pieced together its leaders would be able to get their hands on the vast mission lands the Mexican government had secularized in 1834, lands even now being granted by Governor Pio Pico to his friends and relatives; clownish, finally, because the style of California warfare developed during fifty years of bickering among its Mexican officials (most of whom were in some way related to one another) was more a matter of fiery proclamations and sabre-rattling than of blood and death. (Some doubtless would have thought otherwise: the two Americans killed in ambush

"To this gate I gave the name Chrysopolae."

John C. Frémont, when he was Senator from California in 1850—by then, the glitter of gold had obscured the clownish aspects of his "conquest" of California.

on June 19, the one *Californio* [Mexican-Californian] killed during the "Battle of Olompali" on June 24, and the three combatants murdered by two of Frémont's party, [mountain man Kit Carson and an unidentified French-Canadian *voyageur*,] on June 28.)

Frémont, acting on his own initiative, though at the request of the valley settlers, had taken command of the Bear Flag army, which consisted of some one hundred twenty armed men in addition to his expeditionary force of sixty. For several days this little army had been fruitlessly chasing an even smaller contingent of *Californios* under the command of Joaquin de la Torre all over the region north of San Francisco Bay. De la Torre had escaped the hurrying vengeance of the Americans, who were eager now to accomplish something of import. (How else could they describe all the minor skirmishing as a war of conquest?) That something, Frémont had decided, was a dawn assault on the seventy-year-old Presidio of San Francisco, a fortification that from a slope at the northern tip of the San Francisco peninsula guarded the entrance to the great bay.

So off they sailed on the morning tide in a little commandeered sloop-rigged launch, this group of mountain men become marines. The launch anchored just off the beach below the Presidio, and the assault force jumped over the side and waded ashore through the surf, Hawken rifles and Navy pistols at the ready. When no fire greeted their landing, they scrambled up the hill to the fort, where they found neither a garrison of bloodthirsty *Californios* (there had not been a force kept at the Presidio since 1835) nor even any gunpowder. What they did find was a single unoccupied adobe building, the crumbling remains of two others, some gun emplacements thoroughly eroded by time, weather, and neglect, and ten small seventeenth-century cannons, most of which had not been fired within living memory. Frémont ordered the cannons spiked and the expeditionary force retreated to Sausalito, none the worse for wear but no closer to glory. The next day, he dispatched ten men to the village of Yerba Buena, which they invaded (again without resistance) at high noon, arresting one Robert Ridley, who had been appointed captain of the port by the Mexican authorities, charged with expressing pro-Mexican and anti-Bear Flag sentiments. Ridley was bundled off to Sutter's Fort at New Helvetia (now Sacramento) where the insurgents were keeping all "prisoners of war."

So began and ended the only direct experience with military action that San Francisco has ever known. Frémont's curious amphibious landings and his unwarranted seizure of poor Ridley displayed neither logic nor good sense. Nor would most of the rest of his military exploits in California, though in all fairness it should be pointed out that Frémont was not alone. The whole story of the "conquest" of California, even after it became official, once word of the President's declaration of war reached the Pacific, was a tapestry of incompetence and wretched excess, surely the least elegantly performed action in any theater of any American war before Vietnam. Still, Frémont's assault did occasion something for which he should be remembered with proper appreciation. Sailing back after the landing, he stood at the rail of the boat and contemplated the entrance to the Bay of San Francisco, watched the waves breaking against the rocks of its southern point and the rise of the brown summer hills that loomed up from the sea at its northern point. "Between these points is the strait," he wrote in his *Memoirs*, "about one mile broad in the narrowest part, and five miles long from the sea to the bay. To this gate I gave the name of *Chrysopolae*, or Golden Gate." And it is indeed "Chrysopolae (Golden

Gate)'' that appears on the official 1848 map of his third expedition. If nothing else, Frémont had at least given the future a name.

THE VILLAGE that had received Frémont's attentions so briefly should have been flattered. Yerba Buena was not exactly prepossessing in the midsummer of 1846. It was, in fact, a rather dismal little town, judging by the accounts of the time. It was surrounded on all sides by what a later visitor called ''naked, monstrous sand hills,'' and the only greenery to be found was scattered patches of scrubby brush, much of it that ''good herb'' from which the village had taken its unofficial name. Its inhabitants endured winter winds, summer fogs, occasional sandstorms, and rains that turned the ground to swampland. They spent much of their time scratching at welts and blotches inflicted by the sand fleas that popped from the ground with nearly every step, outnumbering the town's human residents by several million to one. Although surveyed as early as 1839 by Jean Jacques Vioget, a local grocer and tavern-keeper, Yerba Buena had no streets worthy of the name—merely dirt tracks that became muddy sinkholes during the rainy season. The gentle slope above the little scoop out of the peninsula called Yerba Buena Cove held, at most, only fifty buildings of any sort—the most substantial of which were a two-story frame trading post built by Jacob Leese in 1837 and an adobe customs-house built by the *Californio* government in 1844—together with the ram-shackle, fly-ridden ''necessaries'' that perched behind most of them. The town's permanent population, excluding a handful of local Indians and a few Kanaka seamen from the Sandwich Islands (Hawaii), probably did not approach two hundred souls. Aside from Frémont's diminutive exercise in conquest, the most noteworthy event in the village's history up to 1846 had been the suicide in 1845 of William Glen Rae, manager of the Yerba Buena post of the Hudson's Bay Company.

The town was small, but the hopes of most of those who occupied it were not. A brisk, if not particularly consequential, commercial life fluttered in the village, centering, first, on the provisioning of British and American whaling vessels that utilized San Francisco Bay as their principal port-of-call in northern California, second, on the hide-and-tallow trade with merchantmen from New England, and third, on its function as the entrepôt for the agricultural produce of New Helvetia and the few American settlers in the Sacramento Valley. This nascent commerce was dominated by a small clutch of early settlers, chief among them William A. Leidesdorff, a trader and American vice consul; Robert Ridley, captain of the port and operator of a small grog shop (and he who had been captured by Frémont); and merchants William Hinckley, John Fuller, Nathan Spear, William H. Davis, and W. D. M. Howard. (Captain William H. Richardson, who had constructed the village's first building of any sort in 1835, and Jacob Leese, who had erected its second and third in 1836 and 1837, had long since left for other parts—Richardson to his land grant in Sausalito, and Leese to Sonoma, where he was overseeing the affairs of his father-in-law, General Mariano Vallejo.) With no specific evidence to support the theory, these men and a few others like them were nevertheless gearing up for the day when this pinprick of a hamlet would become, inevitably, inexorably, the ''great commercial emporium of the Pacific.''

A minor shift in that direction occurred on July 9, 1846, just a week after Frémont's visit. This time, the visit was official and attended by ceremonies

Jacob P. Leese, the first American merchant of Yerba Buena.

suggestive of the future. On July 8, word had been received of the outbreak of war between the United States and Mexico, and the next morning, Captain John B. Montgomery, whose U.S.S. *Portsmouth* had been anchored in Yerba Buena Cove since late June, led ashore a detachment of some seventy sailors and marines, and marched them up to the customs house on the plaza (later Portsmouth Square), "to the soul-inspiring tune of Yankee Doodle from our band, consisting of one drum and fife, with an occasional put-in from a stray dog or disconsolate jackass," according to the recollections of one of the marines. At the plaza, the marine continued, "we rested on our arms, while the aides of the commander-in-chief disseminated themselves through the town and gathered together some thirty or forty persons of all nations, colors, and languages, and having penned them in the square formed by the soldier-sailors, the captain, putting on all his peculiar dignity, walked up to the flagstaff and gave a majestic nod to his second in command. The first lieutenant gave a similar nod to one of our quartermasters, who came forward, flag in hand, and bent it on the halyards. . . .

"Captain M. [Montgomery] had a proclamation ready prepared, and our first lieutenant now read it to the assembled crowd, and when he finished, gave the signal, and in a moment, amid a roar of cannon from the ship, the hurrahs of the ship's company, the *vivas* of Californians, the cheers of the Dutchmen, and barking of dogs, the braying of jackasses, and the general confusion of sounds from every living thing within hearing, that flag floated proudly up, which has never yet been lowered to mortal foe." The ceremonies of occupation done, Montgomery assigned a troop of twenty-five of his men to the customs house, rechristened it an official U.S. Navy barracks, and marched back down to the beach where the *Portsmouth*'s boats lay waiting.

The observers of this splendid event immediately retired to the town's three saloons to lift a toast. "The houses being on three of the four corners of the square," the marine recalled, "one standing in the door of the barracks could see the maneuvers of each of them. For the first hour, things went quiet enough, but soon the strong water began to work, and such a confusion of sounds could never have been heard . . . as came from these three corners. . . . This pandemonium lasted for some hours, in fact, until sundown, when the commandante sent a guard to warn the revelers that as the town was now under martial law, they must cease their orgies and return to their respective homes."

It seems appropriate, somehow, that Yerba Buena, the embryonic San Francisco, should have begun its second day as an American possession with a monumental hangover.

San Francisco in 1847.

EVENT WAS SUDDENLY piling upon event; the little town was acquiring history. On July 15, 1846, work was completed on a small adobe fortification on a hillock near Clark's Point at the northern end of the cove. The Presidio's cannons—those which Frémont and his men had spiked just two weeks before—were hauled down, drilled out, and installed in the fort (thus, Battery Street). On July 31, the ship *Brooklyn* arrived from New York via Honolulu with 230 men, women, and children. They were Mormons, part of the "gathering of Zion" of 1846, which saw the country of the Saints established in the valley of the Great Salt Lake of Utah. Their leader was Elder Samuel Brannan (twenty-six years old), a state-of-Mainer with a fringe of beard and an eye for the main chance. As far as he was concerned, Zion was right here in California, specifically in Yerba Buena, in spite of the "damned rag" that now flew in Portsmouth Square. To his everlasting disgust, Brannan was never able to convince Brigham Young of that fact, and the Mormon patriarch soon ordered the *Brooklyn*'s emigrants to cross the mountains to Utah with all deliberate speed. (Ultimately, only about one hundred of them would obey the command; Brannan would not be among them.) Most of Brannan's flock still had to work off their passage, and there was no unseemly rush to Utah. Some went up to the hills north of the bay to cut lumber for the suddenly growing Yerba Buena; others went to work in Sutter's Fort at New Helvetia; still others—twenty families in all—hiked up to the Stanislaus River in the San Joaquin Valley to found a short-lived agricultural colony called New Hope. Brannan himself bought a small house at the northwest corner of Portsmouth Square and began casting plans for a general store at Sutterville, the small river landing some three miles below Sutter's Fort, and for a newspaper, using the press and type fonts of *The Prophet*, a Mormon journal he had published in the East, whose equipment had come with him on the *Brooklyn*.

Elder Sam Brannan, leader of the Mormon colony that arrived in the ship Brooklyn.

On August 26, Captain Montgomery appointed Lieutenant Washington A. Bartlett Yerba Buena's first *alcalde* (mayor), an appointment confirmed by an election on September 15. Under Spanish-Mexican law and practice, which for the sake of convenience was temporarily retained, the office was close to despotic. Walter Colton, who had been appointed *alcalde* of Monterey, fretted over the tyrannical nature of the position. "There is not a judge on the bench in England or the United States," he wrote in his diary for 1846, "whose power is so absolute as that of the *alcalde*. . . ." If Bartlett also worried about it, we cannot say. Unlike Monterey, however, whose population was still made up mostly of native Californians, Yerba Buena was an American—or at least, Anglo-Saxon—colony, and its inhabitants expressed no undying fealty to the notion of one-man rule. The almost immediate result was the kind of civic squabbling that would characterize the politics of the town forevermore. On January 30, 1847, Bartlett issued the following decree: "Whereas, the local name of Yerba Buena, as applied to the settlement or town of San Francisco, is unknown beyond the district, and has been applied from the local name of the cove on which the town is built: Therefore, to prevent confusion and mistakes in public documents, and that the town may have the advantage of the name given on the public map, It is hereby ordained that the name of San Francisco shall hereafter be used in all official communications and public documents or records appertaining to the town."

The proclamation, at least in part, was inspired by the recent emergence in the north bay region of the little port town of Francesca, which was conjured into existence by a handful of entrepreneurs (among them former American Consul Thomas Larkin and *Californio* Mariano Vallejo) and which already advertised itself as the future metropolis of northern California. Reasonably enough, the promoters of Francesca believed that Yerba Buena had changed its name in a deliberate attempt to confuse potential settlers and investors and forthwith changed its own name to Benicia—a fact which did little to diminish San Francisco's eminently superior position as the bay region's logical port-of-call. (Benicia's only legitimate claim to glory, finally, came when it was selected as the site of a national armory in 1852, and when it was utilized briefly as the state capitol in 1853.)

Yet not even Bartlett's harmless—in fact, felicitous—name-changing escaped criticism. Sam Brannan, who, among others, already considered himself the leading citizen of the town, thoroughly resented the fact that he had not

The first residence of Sam Brannan—a veritable mansion in the San Francisco of 1847.

been consulted on the matter. His *California Star*, which had begun publication on January 7 as San Francisco's first newspaper, steadfastly refused to recognize the town's new name for more than two months. Moreover, Brannan opened the paper's columns to the charges of those opposed to Bartlett's rule, including one allegation that the *alcalde* had misappropriated no less than $747 in municipal funds (which an investigating committee later discounted). Bartlett, doubtless to his great relief, was recalled to active military service on February 22. His successor, Edwin Bryant, had a smoother administration, but Bryant's successor, George Hyde, was not so lucky—or, perhaps, not so honest. From his appointment in June 1847 to his resignation in March 1848, Hyde spent a good deal of his time denying one charge after another, ranging from the vague accusation of "culpable negligence" to the specific allegation that he had altered the town's financial records. Many of the charges were brought by members of his own municipal council, a group of six individuals whose election had been ordered by California's military governor, Colonel R. B. Mason, in July, in order to provide for "an efficient town police, proper town laws, town officials, &c., for the enforcement of the laws for the preservation of order." Most of the charges were propagandized in Brannan's *California Star*, and all were so confused and confusing that not even the meticulous Hubert Howe Bancroft attempted to unravel them in his later history of California. Bancroft did note, however, that "so much smoke is generally indicative of more or less fire, and . . . it is perhaps necessary to conclude that Hyde was not altogether a model *alcalde*."

Be that as it may, it should be emphasized that San Francisco's population of go-ahead merchants and traders had more on its mind than the knots and tangles of municipal politics, however fascinating those may have been. Its citizens were not, for example, "indifferent on the subject of town lots," as historian John S. Hittell described it in 1878. Indeed, not. One of *alcalde* Bartlett's major actions had been the appointment, in January 1847, of Jasper O'Farrell as the town's first American surveyor. His revision and extension of the Vioget Survey of 1839 not only increased the size of the town by some eight hundred acres, and gave to its streets names since become familiar—Montgomery, Kearny, Stockton, Fremont, Jones, Taylor, Sutter, Vallejo, Hyde, Market, and so on—but included hundreds of "water lots" (land ex-

Faces that come down to us as street names: Mariano de Guadalupe Vallejo, Thomas O. Larkin, W.D.M. Howard, and Joseph L. Folsom.

posed at low tide) in Yerba Buena Cove.* On March 10, 1847, Brigadier-General Stephen Watts Kearny, then military governor of the territory, with no clear legal authority, but with a sure instinct for the demands of Yankee enterprise, issued an order to "grant, convey, and release unto the town of San Francisco, the people, or corporate authorities thereof, all the right, title, and interest of the Government of the United States, and of the Territory of California, in and to the beach and water lots on the east front of said town of San Francisco . . . except such lots as may be selected for the use of the United States Government by the senior officers of the Army and Navy now there: Provided the said ground hereby ceded shall be divided into lots and sold by public auction to the highest bidder. . . ."

With this government largesse in hand, the town auctioned off some two hundred of four hundred fifty water lots on July 20—at prices ranging from $50 to $100 apiece. In August, it offered about seven hundred of the dryland lots made available by O'Farrell's survey, and disposed of four hundred fifty of them at about $16 each. In that same month, another hundred and thirty lots were presented for sale by the town, seventy of these bringing about $29 each. In these three sales, San Francisco's pioneer settlers—among them *alcalde* Hyde, Sam Brannan, William Leidesdorff, W. D. M. Howard, Edwin Bryant, and most of the town's leading lights—acquired title to lots which in a mere six years would be worth as much as two hundred times their original purchase price.

By the end of 1847, the village had grown to nearly five hundred people, three-fourths of them American, and contained a little under two hundred buildings, many of which were *not* jerry-built shacks. Yet there still was little going on to engage the interest of any self-respecting nineteenth-century hustler. True, the grog shops and gambling saloons, the restaurants (if they could be so called) and boarding-houses of the town were doing a fairly brisk business, what with the influx of San Francisco's share (perhaps two hundred) of the nine hundred fifty settler-soldiers called the New York Volunteers, an occupation army sent out to garrison the towns of California in March 1847, after the Treaty of Cahuenga Pass in January ended the "Conquest" of California, as well as vagrant sailors from the ships that put in to San Francisco Bay with increasing frequency. True, California's first newspaper, the *Californian*, had recognized the drift of the future and moved its operation from Monterey to San Francisco in May, becoming immediately the natural foe of Brannan's *California Star*. True, *alcalde* Edwin Bryant had declared in March that "The site of the town of San Francisco is known to all navigators and mercantile men acquainted with the subject, to be the most commanding commercial position on the entire eastern coast of the Pacific Ocean, and the town itself is, no doubt, destined to become the commercial Emporium of the western side of the American continent." Even so, the most sanguine of the town's residents could not reasonably have anticipated a growth rate much in excess of that quietly taking place up in Oregon, whose American population far outnumbered that of California, and whose development was moving along with a slow, steady, inexorable grace. Sooner or later, it was commonly believed, destiny would move in San Francisco's direction; no one knew when, and no one expected it to happen tomorrow. But it did.

---

*It also resulted in what came to be called the "O'Farrell Swing," a two-degree correction of the street plans laid out by Vioget in 1839. The consequent shift of street alignments left many buildings jutting out into several thoroughfares until 1906. The water lots themselves figured prominently in the Dr. Peter Smith land-sale fraud of 1851 (see Chapter III).

James W. Marshall, the man who found an empire glittering in the tailrace of Sutter's sawmill.

Tomorrow was January 24, 1848. On the morning of that day, James Marshall, a dour, moody person given to fits of passion and depression, made an inspection tour of the nearly completed tailrace of a mill he had contracted to build for John Sutter, the founder and proprietor of New Helvetia and its bastion, Sutter's Fort. The mill was located on the South Fork of the American River, about forty-five miles east-northeast of the fort, and in the lower foothills of the Sierra Nevada. Walking along the edges of the newly dug ditch, Marshall noticed something that winked and glittered in the red earth. He got to his knees and dug it out, holding it and fingering it reflectively. The next morning, he found more of the same, and three days after that he stumbled out of the rain into Sutter's office in the fort, trembling with agitation. "He drew out a rag from his pocket," Sutter remembered. "Opening it carefully, he held it before me in his hand. It contained what might have been an ounce and a half of gold-dust—dust, flakes, and grains. The biggest piece was not as large as a pea, and it varied from that down to less than a pinhead in size."

That tiny, dirty-yellow pile resting in the palm of Marshall's calloused carpenter's hand was more than gold—it was the stuff of dreams, the hope of centuries, and the history of San Francisco's next fifty years.

Sutter's mill on the South Fork of the American River, where the town of Coloma sprang up.

S UTTER, justifiably afraid that the news of gold would rob him of the labor force he needed to keep his eleven-square-league empire in the Sacramento Valley functioning, strove mightily to keep the discovery a secret. But every day Marshall and his workers found more and more gold; every day, more and more people learned of it; every day, word of it dribbled and drifted throughout northern California. By the end of March, Edward Kemble, who had been hired by Sam Brannan as editor of the *California Star*, reported that gold had become an "article of traffic" at New Helvetia. A few days later, he journeyed to the site of the discovery to see what was what. Marshall's workmen, apprised of his imminent arrival, threw away their gold-digging equipment and went back to work on the construction of the mill. Kemble returned to San Francisco and contemptuously announced that the whole business was a "sham"—as "supurb [sic] takein as was ever got up to guzzle the gullible."

San Franciscans dutifully went about their business . . . except that early in April a settler from the American River region arrived in town, ordered a burroful of provisions, and offered in payment a sack containing half a pound of gold . . . except that later that month Kemble's employer, Brannan, not so skeptical as his editor, journeyed to the gold site himself, looked around, perceived what a genuine gold excitement could do not only for the trade of his Sutterville general store but for San Francisco itself, returned to the town with a vial full of dust, and marched up and down Montgomery Street waving it over his head and shouting in his loudest Mormon-preacher voice, "Gold! Gold! Gold on the American River!" All day, he elaborated on the richness of the discovery, passed the heavy vial around to the town's citizens, let them heft it and rub its gold between their fingers.

What the presence of the stuff itself apparently could not do, publicity could. By the end of May, perhaps as many as one hundred fifty San Franciscans—out of a population that had by then grown to more than eight hundred—had gone off to what were already called the "diggins." Hundreds more followed from Monterey, Santa Barbara, San Jose, and Los Angeles as the news spread south. Soldiers stationed in garrisons from Sonoma to San Diego deserted; navy and merchant seamen jumped ship; servants disappeared, settlers left their crops, *vaqueros* left their cows, city officials abdicated, newspaper editors suspended publication, merchants and saloon-keepers locked their doors—it was a grand rout, at least temporarily, of all that had been pieced together as the new civilization in California. On May 29, the editor of the *Californian* complained that all his help had deserted him and announced the suspension of the newspaper: "The whole country, from San Francisco to Los Angeles, and from the sea shore to the base of the Sierra Nevada, resounds with the sordid cry of *gold*! GOLD! GOLD!—while the field is left half planted, the house half built, and every thing neglected but the manufacture of shovels and pick-axes, and the means of transportation to the spot where one man obtained one hundred and twenty-eight dollars' worth of the *real stuff* in one day's washing, and the average for all concerned is *twenty dollars per diem*!"

What they found was incredible, a treasure that could be picked up out of the earth by anyone, with no more expertise required than the ability to use a pick, pan, and shovel and the willingness to sweat. Eons before, mountain building and fracturing had deposited liquid gold in a great system of veins that extended some three hundred miles along the Sierra Nevada range; the deposits cooled and solidified, and during several millennia of erosion were exposed and crumbled, washed by wind and water down the slopes of the mountains, coming to rest wherever their weight overcame the ability of the elements to move them. And that was where the fortunate goldseekers of 1848—more than six thousand of them by the end of the year, including contingents from Oregon, Mexico, Peru, and Chile—found them, as dust, as flakes, as golden pebbles and fist-sized nuggets. The "real stuff" existed in such abundance that it was not so much mined as harvested, gathered with not much more effort required than if it had been sheaves of wheat.

Johann August Sutter, the Swiss grandee of the Sacramento Valley.

At one spot near the canyon of the Middle Fork of the American River that summer, men took out $800 a day. On a sand bar in the Yuba River, another group harvested $75,000 in three months. At another spot, a man rode away with thirty pounds of gold from a single four-foot square of earth. A moderately successful effort might produce as much as $600 a week, and even "poor" ground yielded as much as $15 a day—at least five times the daily salary a working man in the states could expect. It has been estimated that between $30,000 and $50,000 worth of gold a day was being taken out of the ground in the summer and fall of 1848—and by year's end it had amounted to at least $6 million and quite possibly as much as $10 million.

Ten million dollars was a great deal of money in 1848—in modern terms, the equivalent of $50 or $60 million. It was certainly enough to inspire the military commanders in California to let Washington know what was going on. In July, Commodore Thomas ap Catesby Jones dispatched Lieutenant Edward F. Beale across Mexico with descriptive, detailed reports and a small sample of California gold. In August, California's military governor, R. B. Mason, sent Lieutenant Lucien Loesser via Cape Horn with similar reports—and a tea caddy stuffed with two hundred thirty ounces of gold, worth about $3500.

Even before these military minions reached Washington, word of the gold discovery had arrived in the East. By September, interest in the subject had reached such a pitch that the dour journalistic genius James Gordon Bennett was driven to editorialize somewhat nervously in the September 29 issue of his *New York Herald:* "No doubt the golden tales of these golden streams will excite the imaginations of many ardent and sanguine minds and lead them to think of packing up and removing off to regions where they may hope to

The evacuation of San Francisco to the Sierra placers—May, 1848.

become rich thus rapidly. To all such we would say beware of the mania of hasty money making; beware of seeking to become rich by sudden and extraordinary means; be assured that all the gold in the world will not make you happy; pursue, quietly and steadily, the sober path of regular industry; be thankful, contented, and act with honor and honesty, and then you will be happier in the enjoyment of a peaceful conscience and a peaceful life than all the gold of California can make its possessors.''

Golden tales and golden streams. . . . Bennett did not realize what real excitement was. In early December, Lieutenant Beale arrived in Washington. His reports and gold samples were turned over to the War Department and from there were sent immediately to President James K. Polk. On December 5, in his last State of the Union address, Polk announced to the United States what Sam Brannan had said to San Francisco, though in this case with such authority and moderation as to drive the whole country mad with excitement: ''It was known that mines of the precious metals existed to a considerable extent in California at the time of its acquisition [well, no, it was not ''known''; Polk was understandably trying to justify his unpopular war with Mexico, a war that had dragged on for nearly two years, and had cost more than thirteen thousand American lives and $100 million]. Recent discoveries render it probable that these mines are more extensive and valuable than was anticipated. The accounts of the abundance of gold in that territory are of such an extraordinary character as would scarcely command belief were they not corroborated by the authentic reports of officers in the public service, who have visited the mineral district, and derived the facts which they detail from personal observation.'' A few days later, Lieutenant Loesser arrived in Washington with his tea caddy full of gold, which was quickly placed on public display in the War Department, and not even James Gordon Bennett could restrain himself in the *Herald*'s edition for December 6: ''The gold region in California! Startling discoveries! The El Dorado of the old Spaniards is discovered at last. We now have the highest official authority for believing in the discovery of vast gold mines in California, and that the discovery is the greatest and most startling, not to say miraculous, that the history of the last five centuries can produce.''

So stick a pin in California! Stick another pin at the Golden Gate! Stick yet another in your own back end—and *Oh, Susanna*! Everybody sang *Oh, Susanna*!; so much so that John S. Hittell, with the pious insight of an older era, thought that the song itself sent people to California: ''The song here referred to . . . gave the California fever to thousands, who without its stimulus would have remained in their native towns. Written by Jonathan Nichols, who left Salem, Massachusetts, in the ship *Eliza*, on the twenty-first of December, 1848, for the land of gold, it was sung everywhere and by

Typical scenes from the mines of the golden foothills in the spring and summer of 1848.

everybody, and at concerts, and in the theatres, even when poorly rendered, was received with more fervor by the multitude than was shown to the well executed airs from the most brilliant operas."

A confusion of cause and effect. What excited their fervor was what they read on Wednesday, December 6, about what Congress had heard from President Polk on Tuesday, December 5; and what they thought about was what E. Gould Buffum, lately an "officer in the public service," was in fact *doing* on Thursday, December 7. They didn't hear from Buffum that Thursday, but they knew it, all right: "I soon had a large rock in view. Getting down into the excavation I had made, and seating myself upon the rock, I commenced a careful search for a crevice, and at last found one extending longitudinally along the rock. It appeared to be filled with a hard, bluish clay and gravel, which I took out with my knife, and there at the bottom, strewn along the whole length of the rock, was bright, yellow gold, in little pieces about the size and shape of a grain of barley. Eureka! Oh how my heart beat! I sat still and looked at it some minutes before I touched it, greedily drinking in the pleasure of gazing upon gold that was in my very own grasp, and feeling a sort of independent bravado in allowing it to remain there. When my eyes were sufficiently feasted, I scooped it out with the point of my knife and an iron spoon, and placing it in my pan, ran home with it very much delighted. I weighed it, and found that my first day's labour in the mines had made me thirty-one dollars richer than I was in the morning."

Thirty-one dollars a day looked like good pickings to ex-Lieutenant Buffum—as it did to a hundred thousand other Americans who in the last months of 1848 and the first months of 1849 thought that they, too, might do well to risk their time, health, and small capital to reach the golden placers. And $31 had looked big to San Franciscans when they first heard, or first believed, the reports of gold. It is said that no more than seven male citizens were left in town in July of 1848 (although it is also said that the Fourth was a more-than-usually glorious two-day celebration, with grand suppers and balls). However many were gone at once, most San Franciscans had at least visited the mines at an early date. They had "seen the elephant," and, like Sam Brannan, many decided that it could be milked at the less obvious end. Buffum found it so when in October he picked up supplies in San Francisco before he left for the mines. He didn't buy much, what with dried beef at 50¢ a pound, shovels and crowbars at $10, tin pans and red flannel shirts at $5, and ordinary boots at $16. "Gold dust and coin were as plentiful as the sea-shore sands," Buffum wrote, "and seemed to be thought about as valuable." The price of goods was what the traffic would bear; the price of gold dust, though it was agreed by the merchants to be worth $16 an ounce, was what the eager seller would take—maybe $12, perhaps $10, even as little as $8. In the mines, prices were vastly higher, and gold went sometimes as cheap as $6 an ounce, yet it was quickly becoming obvious that San Francisco offered the most fertile diggings for the nimble-witted merchant and speculator. As miners straggled back to San Francisco for the winter of 1848–49, most of them well-heeled and fully prepared to indulge themselves in whatever luxuries they could find in a town that was still little more than a frontier village, businessmen, landlords, shopkeepers, gamblers, and publicans of the nascent city began to get a taste of the wildly profitable days to come.

They got a substantial bite on February 28, 1849, when the first installment of the great rush of 1849 came in the form of the steamship *California*. The *California*, pioneer vessel of the government-subsidized Pacific Mail

Rainy season in the growing town of San Francisco when the streets were "impassable, not even jackassable."

Steamship Company, had left New York on October 6 for the long voyage around South America to Panama, whence she was to inaugurate service between the isthmus and San Francisco. By the time she reached Panama, the gold excitement had been epidemic in the East for almost two months; fifteen hundred people had sailed from Atlantic and Gulf ports to Chagres, on the east coast of the isthmus, and made their way across the fever-and-cholera-ridden waist of Central America to meet the *California*. Four hundred lucky ones crowded aboard; the rest were left to make the best of it, their numbers growing from new arrivals, despite the embarkation of many aboard sailing vessels (and a few in rowboats). By the beginning of May 1849, the *California*'s four hundred had been added to by the thousands, and San Francisco was well on its way to becoming San Francisco, *chrysopolis*. In the town's first published book (printed by none other than Washington A. Bartlett, the town's first *alcalde*), *California as It Is and as It May Be: Or, A Guide to the Gold Fields*, F. P. Wierzbicki described the new city: "The town has led the van in growth; there is nothing like it on record. . . . In fact, it looks very much like one of those cities only built for a day. Its houses, built of planks and cotton sheetings, cannot last but for a day; however, whatever it may lack in quality they make up in quantity. Four months ago the town hardly counted fifty houses [not true], and now it must have upwards of five hundred, and these are daily increasing, even a theatre is spoken of as being built. From eight to ten thousand inhabitants may be afloat in the streets . . . and hundreds arrive daily; many live in shanties, many in tents, and many the best way they can. . . . The freaks of fortune are equally as remarkable in this place as everything else connected with it; some men who two years ago had not a cent in their pockets, count by thousands now; property that a year ago could have been bought for five or six thousand dollars, now pays a rent of thirty thousand dollars per annum. . . ."

Destiny had indeed touched the erstwhile village of Yerba Buena. But was the promise it brought to the town a two-headed coin? Some came to think so, among them Hubert Howe Bancroft, who described the celebration that accompanied the arrival of the *California* in February in downright cynical tones: "It was a gala-day at San Francisco. The town was alive with wintering miners. In the bay were ships at anchor, gay with bunting, and on shore nature was radiant in sunshine and bloom. The guns of the Pacific Squadron opened the welcome with a boom, which rolled over the waters, breaking in successive verberations between the circling hills. The blue line of jolly tars manning the yards followed with cheers that found their echo in the throng of spectators fringing the hills. From the crowded deck of the steamer came loud response, midst the flutter of handkerchiefs and bands of music. Boats came out, their occupants boarding, and pouring into strained ears the most glowing replies to the all-absorbing questions of the new-comers concerning the mines— assurances which put to flight many of the misgivings conjured up by leisure and reflection; yet better far for thousands had they been able to translate the invisible, arched and flaming letters across the Golden Gate, as at the portal of hell, *Lasciate ogni speranza, voi ch'entrate*—all hope abandon, ye who enter here. Well had it been were Minos there telling them to look well how they entered and in whom they trusted, if, indeed, they did not immediately flee the country for their lives."

However this may be, it would have been hard to find a group less likely to perceive invisible portents in the sky. The thirty-eight thousand who came by sea to California in 1849, and the forty-two thousand who came overland,

A second-class hotel in gold rush San Francisco.

participated in a mass excitement of unique character. They were beguiled by admitted avarice, prompted by plain fact, and sought nothing that belonged to someone else. The thoughtful historian must denigrate a movement motivated by such obvious passions and simple-minded goals, a vast outburst of energy innocent of the trumped-up justifications which conceal a lust for violence in a fog of noble abstractions. Yet the discovery of gold in California occasioned what may have been the merriest—and least depraved—mass assault in history. That many, perhaps most, of the gold-seekers who sailed through the Golden Gate or tramped across all the rocks and hard places of the West lost more than they gained, that some lost their health and some their lives (perhaps five thousand of them on the overland journey alone), could be guessed by one who has never heard the story of the Gold Rush. But one thread runs through the thousands of stories and reflections—in the form of letters, diaries, journals, articles, and books—of those who gambled with their money, time, and lives to come to California: the *excitement* of it, the *wonder* of it, the feeling that they were party to a great event in history.

They were. Of all the resources of the earth, useful or merely ornamental, none has had so much power to absolutely warp the mind of man as gold. The lust for it has haunted Western civilization since Jason trapped it out of Balkan rivers with sheepskins and Alexander looted it from the kingdoms of Persia. That lust shaped the Spanish conquest of the New World, and not even the sober Anglo-Saxon colonists of America's eastern seaboard were immune to it (among the several duties of the Jamestown settlers of 1607 was to search for gold under the direction of Captain John Smith). Finally, in California, a land as little known to most of the rest of the world as the plains of Afghanistan, all the dreaming after gold that had built empires, started wars, deposed kings, and annihilated whole peoples was distilled into one incandescent ray of hope. That hope, that dream, which would become many more things than gold, illuminated San Francisco. Touched with it, the city became fully as magical and myth-ridden as the seven golden cities of Cíbola in Spanish legend. Broadcast over the plains and deserts and mountains of America and all the oceans of the world, the call to San Francisco was a clarion of opportunity, of possibility, of new beginnings and great expectations. Not all the bald, sober facts or negative reports in the world—and there were plenty, even during the rush—could dilute the strength of that message, and those who came to San Francisco came with the light of tomorrow in their eyes. Such was the conditioning that gold inspired. Great expectations—and the inevitable corollary, great disappointment—were the warp and woof, the very fabric of San Francisco's early American life. Like some kind of hallucinogen, gold heightened, distorted, and accelerated reality, propelling it in spurts, bursts, and great, explosive movements. The chronicle of the years that accompanied and followed the Gold Rush is not so much a history as the record of a seismograph.

"Oh, Susanna!
Don't you cry for me,
For I'm off to California,
With a washbowl on my knee."

"Seeing the Elephant"——*a popular lettersheet of the gold rush years.*

Chapter II

THE ACTUAL METROPOLIS

SAN FRANCISCO in the fall of 1849 saw the constant arrival of ships loaded with immigrants from the East. When Bayard Taylor returned from a tour of the mining districts in December, in preparation for his departure to the Atlantic, he was astonished at the growth of the city: "Of all the marvellous phases of the history of the Present, the growth of San Francisco is the one which will most tax the belief of the Future. Its parallel was never known, and shall never be beheld again. I speak only of what I saw with my own eyes. When I landed there, a little more than four months before, I found a scattering of tents and canvas houses, with a show of frame buildings on one or two streets, and a population of about six thousand. Now, on my last visit, I saw around me an actual metropolis, displaying street after street of well-built edifices, filled with an active and enterprising people and exhibiting every mark of permanent commercial prosperity."

Though it would seem that four months in the mines may have dimmed Taylor's recollection of the amenities provided by the most ordinary sort of established town, he must readily be forgiven his astonishment at the progress of San Francisco. He noted that the prices of almost everything were still outlandish—and erroneously predicted that they were likely to stay at a high level. Gambling and drinking were the principal sports of the city, the company of ladies being priced too high to be very time-consuming. The fancy dress of businessmen and ladies of the night was complemented by knee-high boots, and pneumonia was all the rage—for the unusually heavy rains of San Francisco's first season as a city turned the streets into bogs. Altogether, the fledgling city was a wonderfully astonishing mess.

Business ruled supreme. The hundreds of men who owned and dealt in real estate and goods applied themselves no less frantically and single-mindedly to the pursuit of fortune than a gang of placer-miners uncovering a rich gravel-bar. No labor was too great, so long as it offered a large short-term profit; and no investment was worthwhile which did not suggest a quick return. The improvements in building methods which Taylor noted were no

"Everything can be had cheap at San Francisco."

*Dennison's Exchange and the
Parker House, facing the plaza
before the fire of December, 1849.*

*David Broderick, whose
uncommon grasp of the San
Francisco scene in the 1850s made
him the leading politico of the city
and the state.*

more than what was necessary to insure the bare habitability and utility of a structure, no more than what was required to guarantee a high rental and quick return of investment in competition with inferior buildings. The streets, which had not previously been seen as valuable assets, became worthy of any effort and expenditure as soon as they became impassable in the rainy season. The merchandise must go through! Characteristic of the times was one method of filling the boggy sinks in the streets: it cost money to send a horse and wagon and men out to cut brush and haul it back; so when the streets got so bad that the Street Commissioner's budget could not handle the job, the merchants heaved boxes and bales of merchandise in momentary oversupply (and, hence, worthless) into the pot-holes. A cartload of tobacco or stoves or anything else that would not sell *right now* was worth less than a cartload of brush.

On Christmas Eve, 1849, the rains let up long enough for the principal business section of the city to burn down. The catastrophe had been long expected, but of course no preparations had been made to meet it. And if the men of substance and property were indifferent to the threat of a general conflagration, the thousands of casual residents of the city could not have cared less, even when the town was burning. Bayard Taylor, who saw the outbreak of the fire just as he was preparing to leave San Francisco, commented that ''At the time of the most extreme danger, hundreds of idle spectators refused to lend a hand, unless they were paid enormous wages. One of the principal merchants, I was told, offered a dollar a bucket for water, and made use of several thousand buckets in saving his property. All the owners of property worked incessantly, and were aided by their friends, but at least five thousand spectators stood idly in the plaza. . . . It is not to be disputed . . . that constant familiarity with the shifting of Fortune between her farthest extremes, blunts very much the sympathies of the popular heart.''

That the popular heart was not bleeding as the gambling hells facing Portsmouth Plaza went up in smoke seems quite likely, and had there been any popular manifestation of sorrow it would certainly have been misplaced. Within a few days the ground of the burnt district was cleared, and new and more substantial buildings were going up—though the new buildings were not yet so substantial as to offer any resistance to the next fire.

On Christmas Day, 1849, some leading citizens who had been volunteer firemen back in the states gathered in sight of the ruins to organize a fire brigade. Among these men was David C. Broderick, one of San Francisco's most illustrious—and illustrative—citizens of the Golden Era. Broderick had cut for himself a modest notoriety in New York, where he was foreman of a fire company (even as William Tweed), a saloon keeper, and an officer of public trust. Such broad-spectrum service in the general welfare was typical in an age respectful of the plainer virtues, and in San Francisco Broderick found conditions so favorable to open-handed, simple-minded chicanery that greatness would have been thrust upon him had he not sought it. Consider how the Honorable David C. Broderick improved the summer of 1849: requiring modest wealth to free his heart and mind for full-time public service, Broderick associated himself with Fred Kohler (another New York fireman) in a scheme well calculated to lay a nest egg. While fools dug up the hills for gold and wise men traded shirts and shovels to fools for gold, Broderick and Kohler, with a simplicity of reason which staggers the imagination, manufactured money. Gold was everywhere, but coin was in short supply. So the two of them melted up gold dust and cast it in $5.00 and $10.00 slugs. They put four dollars' worth of gold into a five-dollar piece, eight dollars' worth into a ten-dollar piece. Lest one imagine that the labor of it absorbed an undue share of the profit, they were also making money on the gold itself; as there was no mint or government assay office in California to buy raw gold, it could often be bought at a discount—particularly in the mining regions. Thus, a ten-dollar slug might have in it gold that cost Broderick only six dollars (and we can presume that fresh raw materials were purchased with Broderick & Kohler slugs). Altogether, it was a handsome little business, and it appears to have netted Broderick enough in a few months to permanently remove him from the degrading necessities of commerce.

Fires, firemen, politics, venal politicians, crackpot commerce, and distracted speculators characterized the turmoil of San Francisco in the early 1850s. And these phenomena were often connected, sometimes in such seemingly devious patterns, that the contemporary observer could only surmise the sense of the whole, and the historian is at a loss to rearrange all of the details into a picture that is either entirely lucid or logical. Consider Broderick again: A well-to-do retired businessman within six months of his arrival in San Francisco, he was elected state senator in January 1850. Shortly before his election, he participated in the formation of a fire department, and shortly after that he organized and became the foreman of the first properly equipped volunteer fire company. He "read the law" (presumably sometime in the latter part of 1850), was elevated to the presidency of the second legislature (where he managed to prevent the election of any U.S. senator for the term commencing that year), resigned from the legislature to serve as clerk of the State Supreme Court, and in the meantime gained complete control of the Democratic party in San Francisco. In 1852, he campaigned to be elected by the legislature as U.S. senator; he failed, but tried in January 1854 to get the legislature to elect him to fill the other, vacant, seat a full year before an election would normally have been held. He failed also in this astonishing coup, but used his followers to block the election of a senator in 1855, and to prevent the vacant seat from being filled in 1856. In January 1857, having a majority of the legislature at last firmly in his pocket, he got himself elected to the full term which that year became vacant and summarily dictated the terms under which the other senator, William Gwin, might have back the seat he had been unable to occupy for the last two years because of Broderick's maneuvering. (This last bit of chicanery put a finish to Broderick's otherwise brilliantly single-minded career, for in 1859, David S. Terry, justice of the Supreme Court of the State of California and a political ally of Gwin's, shot Broderick to death in a duel).

We may safely assume that Broderick's interest in the fire department was also so wonderfully direct as to be almost elusive. It was only natural that there was immediate interest in the formation of a fire department after the serious conflagration of Christmas Eve, 1849. It was equally natural that David Broderick and others, who had been firemen "back in the states," should take the lead in organizing this vital civic service. What must strike us as a bit strange is not that something was done, but that so little was done: there was almost no fire-fighting equipment in the city, and it would have taken time to procure it from the East—but no city appropriation was made to get it; scarcity of water was certain to hamper efforts to control any future fire—but no concerted effort was made to dig cisterns. The merchants and the people had other things on their minds—and so, one may suspect, did San Francisco's first firemen.

In the 1850s, all major cities in the United States had volunteer fire departments. A chief engineer and several assistants and watchmen would be

Senator William M. Gwin, Broderick's rival—and his executioner by proxy.

on the city payroll; but manning the pumps of one powerful fire engine required anywhere from fifty to sixty men for effective and continuous work, and hardy volunteers were the economically feasible answer. Though all kinds of citizens might belong to volunteer companies, it is not surprising that a job which called for intermittent bursts of the most man-killing labor, a job where the rewards of glory went to the companies that turned out fastest, dragged their two-ton engines through the streets at the quickest run, and pumped the longest and most furiously, should tend to become dominated by men whose most notable characteristics were their handiness in a street brawl and their indifference to the modest pleasures of the mechanic's or clerk's life. The support of these street-corner athletes was apt to involve the fire companies in broad public activities, ranging from theatrical "benefits" to naked graft. Merchants publicized donations of equipment to fire companies (W. D. M. Howard, for instance, gave the company organized on June 14, 1850, a $4,000 pumper, for which generosity the company was named the "Howard") and we may surmise that tribute in cash must also have been solicited of merchants and more or less cheerfully paid over in the interests of protection. To what extent some volunteer companies engaged in the equivalent of the "protection racket" is a matter of conjecture, but it is certain that many of the firehouse loungers were not morally above such a scheme. It was a simple enough idea, and no other forthright swindle seems to have been overlooked in the San Francisco of the early 1850s.

Well-organized groups of toughs with no visible means of support and plenty of spare time made valuable political shock troops, particularly in a town as disorganized and devil-may-care as San Francisco. A fire company that owed its material and spiritual well-being to a politician was an instrument perfectly suited to roust out the vote in its ward, intimidate the opposition, protect or break up (as the circumstances warranted) political rallies or conventions, and generally serve as a visible symbol of political authority and energy.

Some of the "bully b'hoys" of San Francisco's volunteer fire department in the early 1850s.

IF AT THE VERY APOGEE of the Gold Rush the fire departments of San Francisco looked like a "good thing" to some fellows who knocked about a bit, then what can we imagine was the state of more obviously lucrative public and private endeavors? Perhaps one can say that conditions in San Francisco tended to solidify, and finally institutionalize, practices that elsewhere would have been seen as falling somewhere between "sharp" and downright crooked. Schemes that would appear desperate or unlikely in New England, say, became run-of-the-mill business in San Francisco. Observers "fresh from the States" boggled at their first sight of San Francisco commercial activity—and generally speculated as to how soon the bubble was going to burst. The bubble stayed aloft for a long time because there was an essential difference between the California boom and the other harebrained mass speculations that Americans have wallowed in from time to time: the gold was *there*—in unprecedented quantity—and gold was the one and only commodity that was, as a practical matter, almost insensitive to the normal fluctuations of supply and demand. It is true that in 1848 and early 1849 gold itself frequently sold at a substantial discount locally, and was cheap in terms of commodity prices (if fresh eggs sold at a dollar each, with many other prices in proportion, one may say that gold had declined in value). But this situation did not obtain for long in San Francisco, though the absolute production of gold increased each year until 1853. By 1850, shipments of goods and materials came in such abundance and with such regularity that commodity prices were within reason, often not much higher than New York prices. "Everything can be had cheap at San Francisco," was a sentiment expressed by people in the mining camps.

Labor, on the other hand, was a commodity that came high in California throughout the 1850s, for the price of labor tended toward the average that a man thought he might make if he went off to dig in the mines. An "ounce"— $16—was the standard daily wage of the early 1850s. The cost of money itself remained high, two or three percent a month being a quite ordinary rate. Capital came so dear because speculation could be so profitable. Which brings us full circle—back to the fact that tens of thousands of miners were producing a commodity—gold—of durable market value, and that the wealth started at the bottom, at the base of society, thus creating a previously undreamed-of demand for every type of goods and service. A "boom" in any given area, then or now, is apt to be mostly a state of mind reinforced by some significant influx of money from "outside." But in gold rush California the state of mind was reinforced from within by unheard of quantities of new money.

An intellect—or instinct—that could divine the real nature of the gold rush economy and exploit its unlikely possibilities was the most valuable thing a man might possess. Broderick had it; so did Sam Brannan. H. H. Bancroft has given us an account of one of Brannan's business brainstorms, which sheds quite a bit of light on the nature of the sharp operator in the early 1850s: "One day, persuant to notice, Gillispie [an auctioneer] put up a cargoe of tea to sell. At the hour, there upon his box sat Sam, smoking, and spitting, and whittling, thinking perhaps of the extravagant price of wives in the market, and how much it would cost to people Zion at current rates; thinking of the temple to the living God which he was to rear in the wilderness; thinking of anything except lucre, and the price of tea. 'Ten chests with the privilege,' began Gilles-pie. 'I will sell not less than ten chests, the purchaser to have the privilege of taking as much more at the price sold as he pleases.' Around the open boxes merchants were blowing and crushing, and smelling and tasting; Sam sat serene. 'And how much am I offered?' Gillespie went on. 'Thirty-five cents, thirty-five; forty; and five; fifty; fifty-five cents I am offered; sixty. Are you all done gentlemen? Sixty cents, going; sixty cents, once; sixty cents, twice; third and last time—' 'Sixty-one!' came from the top of the box. 'Sixty-one, sixty-one cents, and sold. How much will you take, Mr. Brannan?'

A banking house in the more settled days of 1853.

"Now, there was tea enough in that ship to give every grocer in town a good stock, and the bidders present had all so reckoned, and had deemed it folly running it up to a high price when they could just as well buy it low. The tea was then worth in the market one dollar and a quarter, or two dollars and a half, or five dollars, according as it was held and controlled. Brannan was the heaviest buyer there; he might take fifty chests out of the five hundred. So they reasoned, and were content that Sam, the ravenous, should first satisfy himself. Imagine, therefore, their chagrin as in answer to the auctioneer's question, 'How much will you take, Mr. Brannan?' they heard come from the top of the box, where the eyes were still bent on the continual whittling, in notes like the snarl of a coyote, 'The whole damned concern!'"

Certainly, cornering the market was not a new idea, and the men bidding against Brannan in this case were no fools. What Sam saw better than they was that his customers would as soon pay one price as another, so long as it was a choice of obtaining what they wanted or going without. *They* perhaps had lingering traces of reason: a man could go without tea if the price were unrea-sonable. But Sam knew that in California anything a man wanted became a

A Pacific Mail steamer on its way to the Isthmus of Panama—the city's main connection to the news and goods of the rest of the world.

necessity. Gold rush California was America's first experience with madcap consumption and the compulsive consumer. In a conditioning process that would earn the admiration of a modern consumer-motivation research team, thousands of men whose personal habits had once been those of the young Abe Lincoln suddenly became addicted to champagne, gambling, and high-priced women. Homelier wants, such as tea, they would *not* do without.

A little speculation as to what Brannan may have anticipated in this particular dealing with tea may suggest the nature of commercial enterprise in San Francisco. It would seem unlikely that Sam imagined that he could make a killing on all that tea himself at retail; what if another shipment of tea should arrive within a month or two? And then another within weeks of that? Chests of tea could be used to fill pot-holes in the streets. No, Sam would share his tea, at a handsome mark-up, with a favored colleague or two. The whole deal would be particularly sure-fire if Sam had certain knowledge that another shipment were indeed on its way. He might make a killing at retail for a few weeks, then, when the avarice of his fellow merchants was at a fever pitch, unload his excessive stock at wholesale. When his ship came in, the market for tea would collapse and Sam would be bidding last at the auction again. The big loser would be the Eastern merchant who owned that next shipment of tea.

One would think that the normal system of commerce would imply the placement of orders with Eastern wholesalers by San Francisco merchants; the agent of the San Francisco house would order so many chests of tea, or so many woolen shirts, or so many hundred pounds of beans, and the San Francisco merchant would be obligated to pay for them. But the news of the gold discoveries and the departure of tens of thousands of gold-seekers occurred before there was any certain and speedy means of communication with California. Eastern merchants, knowing that there would be a large demand for all kinds of necessities, loaded ships for the four- to six-month voyage to San Francisco, trusting to the Yankee enterprise of the shipmasters or supercargos to dispose of the cargoes profitably. Disposal of the goods by auction soon appeared the swiftest and surest way of getting the best possible return.

During 1849, the Pacific Mail Steamship Company's run to Panama, overland transport across the isthmus, and hook-up with Atlantic steamers on the other side began to shake down into a really dependable fortnightly service that could be counted upon to provide a thirty-day communication with New York. But the steamship rates were far too expensive for shipping bulk cargo, so by the early 1850s shippers relied upon the great clipper ships, which usually consumed four months in the voyage from New York to San Francisco by way of the Horn. Add a few weeks lost in office work and loading, and one finds a five- to six-month delay between the time that a merchant in San Francisco placed an order and the date that it would arrive at the Golden Gate. Under such circumstances, it is hardly surprising that San Francisco merchants were only too glad to institutionalize the system that had been necessary in the early days of 1849; hence, auctioneering became one of the most notable mercantile pursuits in San Francisco, and the inevitable losses resulting from periodic glutting of the market with goods that had been in demand six months earlier were borne by the consigners, rather than the San Francisco consignees.

Thus, there was money in retail merchandising whether the prices were as low as in New York or not. There was even more money in real estate. Shop space, warehouse space, and dock space brought such high returns that it seemed that no new building, no sheet-iron shed, no pier for the discharge of cargo could earn less than ten percent per month. Land itself was, of course, a prime object of speculation. Buying and selling, building and speculating and profiteering, "solid" San Franciscans differed in no way from the "looser" elements except in their superior skill and judgment in utilizing the more generally accepted *modus operandi*. Everybody gambled, in the precise as well as the general sense. And fortune was accepted as the common denominator in spectacular success and catastrophic failure. The idea that luck ruled destiny was nothing new; but in gold rush San Francisco this was no mere philosophical saw—it was bought entire and acted out. Note, too, that the proposition was acted out by a populace that viewed itself as a collection of *winners*. Fatalism is the disease of losers; winners are afflicted by *hubris*, that insolent self-confidence that offends the laws of man and nature and invites the retribution of the jealous gods.

Was the fire department organized mainly for political gain? Then quite logically San Francisco was visited by the most disastrous series of fires ever experienced by an American city. Five times between May of 1850 and June of 1851, much or most of the most heavily built-up part of the growing city was leveled by fire. The fires of May and June 1850 swept away all of the hastily built business district thrown up between the shores of the cove and Portsmouth Plaza. The loss in these two fires alone was estimated at about $6 million, a huge figure for the time, more than many respectable cities in the country were worth entire, a sum equivalent to about twenty percent of the total gold production for the year 1850. A third fire in September, though not so great, should have served as a reminder that the one-two punch of May and June was not the result of any special or unlikely circumstances, and indeed, brick and iron buildings, equipped with heavy iron fire-shutters, became the popular type of new construction in the winter of 1850–51. Montgomery Street was swiftly lined with three- and four-story brick buildings as San Francisco began to look like a real city—not just the *only* city west of St. Louis.

Wharves pushed out from the ends of the principal streets that ran down to the cove—Market Street, California, Sacramento, Clay, Washington, Jackson, Pacific, and Broadway. No longer did steamer passengers alight from small boats at Clark's Point; now, sailing ships discharged alongside piers rather than into lighters. Hundreds of ships abandoned by their crews lay anchored in the cove, though conditions had by now settled enough so that first-class packets and clipper ships could get crews. Ships departed almost as often as they arrived. In July of 1850 it was reported that 526 vessels lay in the harbor, most of which were at least temporarily laid up. Some were abandoned, some remained in the care of their masters, some were used as floating warehouses. A few, such as the *Apollo* and the *Niantic*, drawn well inshore, were being surrounded by the advancing wharves and had been roofed over for use as warehouses, lodging-houses, or other business premises. Many lay farther out in the stream, ready to sail at an early date.

Work on the hopeless streets began in earnest in the summer of 1850. Grading for sewers required a great amount of cutting and filling, but by the end of the year most of the business district had graded and planked streets. The lesson of the previous rainy season had not been lost—and political organization had progressed to the point that half a million dollars' worth of work must have made good sense to quite a few people. It was just a start; cutting down the sand hills and filling in the cove went on throughout the 1850s. The grades established in 1850 proved insufficient as the waterfront was pushed a thousand feet into the bay, and new grades had to be adopted within four years. That the engineering ideal of 1853 called for cutting Telegraph Hill down a

The great fire of May 4, 1850, which wiped out nearly all traces of colonial San Francisco.

A representation of the splendid gold medals which the city's incautious aldermen voted themselves to memorialize their incumbency when California joined the Union.

couple of hundred feet argues excessive enthusiasm on the part of the street contractors and the aldermen; the engineers were pliable enough, but fortunately Telegraph Hill was not.

The Mexican-village government of San Francisco was finally scrapped in 1850, a charter issued by the provisional state government, and the proper American offices of mayor and aldermen instituted. The mayor that year was the last *alcalde*, John Geary; the aldermen were all new, but they learned fast, as the number of "indignation meetings" by the citizenry illustrated. Not satisfied with the opportunities that their individual enterprise might develop, the aldermen voted themselves salaries of $6,000 (more than their counterparts a hundred years later would be paid). Even at this early date, San Franciscans expected more imaginative swindles of their elected officials than that, and Mayor Geary may have saved his board from public violence by vetoing their salary vote. But the high point in the brief career of the first board of aldermen coincided with the high point in the political year for California. On September 9, California was admitted into the union; the glorious news reached San Francisco on October 18, and was the occasion of the greatest civic celebration to date. San Francisco's contemporary annalists drew a scene which expressed the life and spirit of the city: "Flags of every nation were run up on a thousand masts and peaks and staffs, and a couple of large guns placed upon the Plaza were constantly discharged. At night every public thoroughfare was crowded with the rejoicing populace. Almost every large building, all the public saloons and places of amusement were brilliantly illuminated; music from a hundred bands assisted the excitement; numerous balls and parties were hastily got up; bonfires blazed upon the hills, and rockets were incessantly thrown into the air, until the dawn of the following day."

Comic relief to the grand celebration was provided by the distinguished board of aldermen, who, it was found, had voted themselves expensive gold medals commemorating their incumbency at the time the great news arrived. Suspected municipal corruption the citizenry would endure in near silence; the attempted salary grab was the occasion of popular indignation; but this *insolence* completely discredited the council. Though no action was taken at the time (hanging being considered perhaps an excessive punishment for the crime), the offending board was swept out of office at the next election.

This, then, was Bayard Taylor's "actual metropolis," burning down and building up, fomenting constant mercantile schemes, chasing the illusion of the main chance, almost blindly seeking the outlines of the city it was meant to be.

Letters of Gold . . .

Among the unusual institutions of the California Gold Rush, one that has languished in anti-quarian obscurity has been the popular lettersheet. Printed in the millions and preserved in the dozens, the lettersheets met two important personal needs of the times: they were a lively visual keepsake for the folks "back in the States" and they were a quick means of cutting short what should have been, from a dutiful son, a much longer letter.

The typical lettersheet was of thin blue paper folded once, with the illustration on the front, leaving the two inner pages for the letter and the back free for the address if the sheet were folded in half again and then into thirds as a self-mailer. Yankee printers with the gold rush spirit never missed a chance to turn a fast buck in getting out new lettersheets, and we have seen sheets depicting current catastrophes in the Golden State with letters on them dated the day after the event. The most successful single sheet published was J. M. Hutchings's "Miner's Ten Commandments" of 1853. It sold 300,000 copies, enough to give one to every resident of the state in those years.

Surprisingly few remaining lettersheets in the great American libraries, east or west, have *letters* on them; the sheets that got saved tended to be mint-condition souvenirs that never saw the mails. More surprising, historians have tended to publish as illustrations only those virgin sheets. We like the ones with letters on them and all of our sheets and notes come from well-used goods.

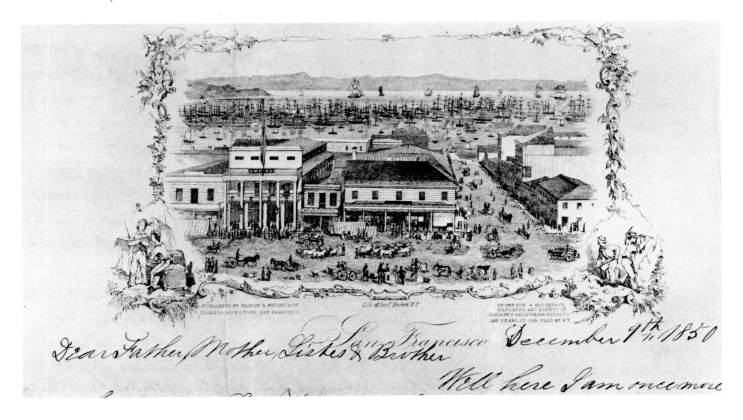

Dear Father, Mother, Sisters & Brother   San Francisco December 9th 1850

Well here I am once more

San Francisco   December 9, 1850
Dear Father, Mother, Sisters, & Brother
        Well here I am once more in the city of San
Francisco having lost my all on the Stanislaus river which
so discouraged me that I have left the mines, to which I
shall never return. I have worked like a cart horse all the
time from sun rise until sun set with the exception of a
couple of hours during the heat of the day. As yet we have
had but very little rain & the Indians prophesy a dry winter
as this is the seventh year. There will be a great deal of
suffering in this country during the winter as the mines are
rapidly becoming exhausted but there will be a few lucky
ones who will strike a pile while thousands scarcely earn
their board although they work very hard. It is impossible
for any person to imagine this country in its true light
unless he has been here to see that monstrous Elephant.
As Anthony has said the miner gains nothing but the
speculator all.   I have learnt much of mankind since I left
home, having had a better opportunity to study them in this
far off country than I had at home. I left Charlie Pierce in
the mines, he was enjoying perfect health. John & Herrick
are both well. The Albany boys in town, Dennis Mahoney,
James Pangburn, Samuel Rosenkrans, Issac Wilson,
William Nugent, Jacob Ten Eyck, Wm. McCoy, Danl.
Crudden, Mortimer J. Smith, Wm. Hosford, Robt. Harris,
Geo. Porter, Wm. Welch, Geo. Y. Houshonse, Geo.
Bement, W. Kearney together with many others whose
names I cannot think of at the present are all in the enjoy-
ment of excellent health. Poor Johnny Noyes, son of Peleg
Noyes who keeps the helfway house died last Friday

morning the 6th at 5 minutes past 3.   I sat up with him the
night on which he died together with Wm. Welch. If you see
his father inform him that he expired without a struggle &
the Albany boys gave him a Christian burial. The funeral
service was read by the Rev. Mr. Wheeler & I took note of
the number of the board which was placed at the head of his
grave, so that his folks can have his body brought home if
they wish at some future day. The number is 827. His
disease was cholera & many are daily dying. . . .
        Tell Billy on my return to the mines I met C. Pearce & he
informed me that he (Wm.) had left Stephen's bar, so I did
not know where to find him or I should have joined him
again. I came within 4 miles of him once when he was at
Columbia on the American diggins as many call them. He
has suffered greatly they inform me with dysenterry and if
I had seen him I could have cured him by giving him only
10 drops of Dr. Wings Kill Devil which kills the disease. . . .
        San Francisco is a different place altogether from what it
was last year (1849) this time, as the houses are built of
wood and brick while the streets are well planked, that it is
bound to be a great city, there is not the least doubt.   Long
wharf is gradually extending itself into the bay & is at the
present about one mile long, many other wharves are in a
fair way to catch up with it.   The city is also extending itself
over the bay and a great many pile drivers are engaged in
driving the piles to errect buildings upon. While I am
writing the funeral procession of Jack Smith, a sporting man
is passing. First in the procession is a band of music followed
by about 80 men, then the hearse & 3 carriages, lastly 18
horsemen. His death was caused by being shot about 3

weeks ago by Judge Jones of Stockton, a man who has murdered 10 or 12 others but who is always found guiltless, as his pocket is long. I saw a specimen of the Missouri giant this morning. He is 19 years old & 7 feet, 4 inches in height. I send this by Mr. Saml. Strong together with a specimen which is the wreck of all I once possessed. Its weight is ½ an ounce. Do with it as you please for I don't want it only to keep it in the family. . . .

As yet there is not a bindery in the country but whoever establishes one first will reap a golden harvest as he could command any price for statework & blank-books for the merchants. I also send a few engravings of this place, they are very correct. The Empire House on this sheet is kept by Mr. John W. Bucklin of New York. He is doing well. You must not have any apprehensions about me for I have so many friends here they would not see me in want. I have now only $1.50 in my pocket but I do not care for before many days are over it will be without the dot in the center, such is California. I am not perfectly satisfied with the mines having given them a good trial for 8 or 9 months. I saw Hazelton the 3rd Sunday in July at Jacksonville on the Tuolumne. I rode my mule in the morning and arrived at my camp in evening. I am well.

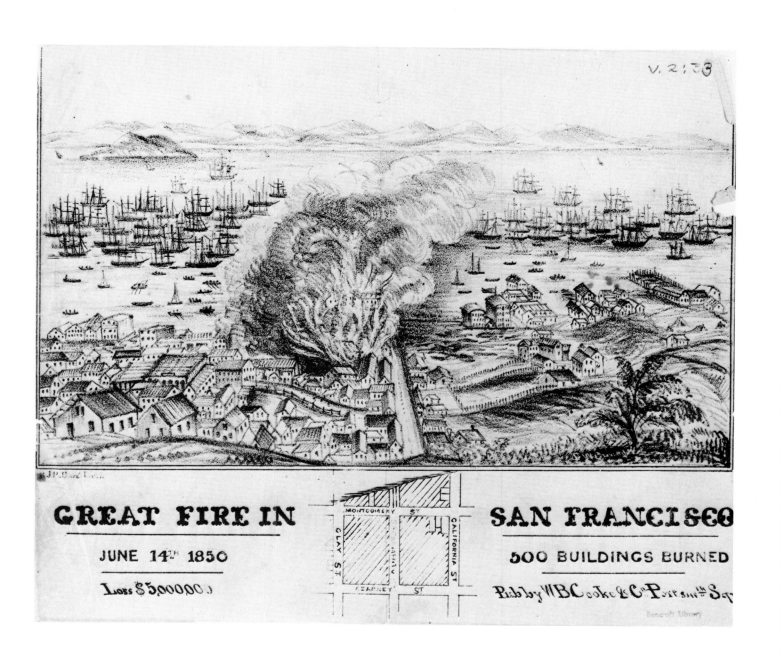

GREAT FIRE IN SAN FRANCISCO

JUNE 14ᵗʰ 1850   500 BUILDINGS BURNED

Loss $5,000,000   Pub by WBCooke & Cᵒ Portsmᵗʰ Sqᵉ

A PROSPECTING PARTY.

STARTING.

NOT EVEN THE COLOUR

THE END OF THE MULE

RETURNING.

Lith. & Pub.d by Britton & Rey San Francisco.

Forbs town calafornia   Aprel 1855
*Dear brother   i rite to inform you that i am well at present
and hope you and the folks ar the sam paper must bee
very Dear in the plase ware you all are   i think you Neglect
to rite to me or my leters do not come to you. . . i have been
well since I rote with the exception of about thre weeks   i
was taken with the Disentory and rather neglected it and it
got the short of me as i think would not hav been sick   i
had to hire a hand in my plase at four dolars per day but i
got the same pay   had to pay the doctor ten dolars a visite
he come seven times   had to pay 8 dolars a week for board
witch cost me some money but i hapened to have it and
some left   so it want so bad as it might   I se plenty of men
dead broak but i have not yet in that fix   i have plenty of
money to fetch me home if i wanted to come but i would not
come home if i had a pasage in the cabin for nothing   i like
this cuntrey so well on acount of the weather   it is so
pleasant here   so cool in the night that you can sleep so nise
but i dont sleep but half the night and work half the day   i
think this is as healthy a plase to com as ever. . . i have got
aquainted with a grait many miners   they are very joly
felows and have good times and very fond of duling. . . they
tell hard story about California and it may bee treu but if*

*a [man] will not gamble and do as he should he can do beter
here than he can in the states but i would not advise any
one to come for it is very hard geting here with good health
i dred the trip going home more than any thing else   it is so
bad on them darnd old steamers and crosing the istmus. . . i
am working down on the claim ware i was when i rote last
the claim paid two thousand dolars the two last weks thare
is 12 hand on the claims ware i work   i have two claims
on the same flat in a company of seven   we are going
to prospect it soon   a man can hold two claims   one by
preemption and one by purchas but you have to represent
them by hiering a man to work on them   it was the law
here that a man could hold to many as he could represent
but they had a miners meeting last fall an altered the
law. . . i had a pain in my guts to speek polite but they
would not let me walk so they took two poles and tacked
one of the blankets on it and i got on it and they carried me
to the house about ¾ of mile   i got thare   the doctor put
a musterd plaster on me witch was bout as bad to the diseas
and give me calimal and quinine and god knows wat els
i dont   i was fraid he would ill avail me so i hid the powders
and pretended it was lost to the man that the doc left the
medicine to give me. . . so good by and the best to all*

THE MINERS. . . .
The letter from
Forbes Town (above
and at left) shows
scant familiarity with
the rules of punctua-
tion and spelling—
but it tells the story.
At right another
popular lettersheet.

LIFE IN THE MINES

Slap Jacks

Rush for new Diggings

Treed

Nooning

To John Titcomb, Waterford,   *By A. H. T. San Fran Cal*

DOWNIEVILLE AT THE FORKS OF THE NORTH YUBA RIVER.

300 miles above San Francisco

Published by S.W. Langton.   Sketched by A.W. Grippen.   Justh & Quirot Lithographer

Nov. 1st 1850   *Sold by Cooke & Le Count Montgomery St.*

FOOTNOTES TO HISTORY. . . . These two letters from the gold region are masterpieces of economy. The view above is a missive from A. H. Titcomb of San Francisco to John Titcomb of Waterford. Near the top, "A. H. T." has lettered "dam," and below it, on the bank of the stream (above the area where all the miners are digging), "Titcomb & Co." Thus John, back in Massachusetts, learns what it would indeed take a few thousand words to convey.

At the right is an expressive description of the entertainments sought by the generality of gold seekers. Girls like "big mary" were in truth scarce.

"Gambling in the Mines," no place, no date, but sent "back to the States" to some old friend. . . . *This you see is a spesaman of gambling in the mines their is a dam cite of it going on here and i have had my share of it smith and i are just sharp enough for the best of them i wonder how big mary gets along i think she would do well to com here such girls as she are scers here smith carreys the mark yet she gave him nothing more*

Jefferson H Jepson

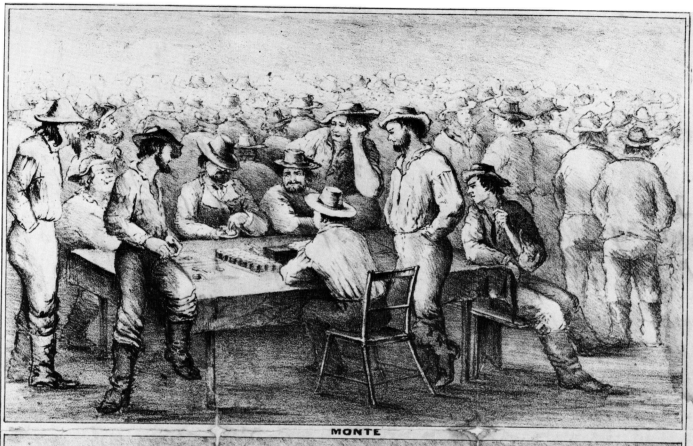

MONTE

Lith.& Published by **BRITTON & REY.**   **FARO**   San Francisco California

TREMENDOUS EXCITEMENT !

Samuel Whittaker and Robert McKenzie rescued from the authorities, and hung by the Vigilance Committee, on Sunday August 24th at 3 o'clock P.M. in the presence of Fifteen thousand People. —

Lith. & Publ. by Justh. Quirot & Co Calif. corner Montg. Sth S.F.

Sept 1st 1851

Mr Wm Hewitt
    Dear Friend
       I send you the drawings of the execution of several of the blackest villains that ever scourged the world as disgraced humanity—I would send you papers if they would ever reach you.

    My health is good and has been since I saw you.

    My success has far surpassed my expectations in business. I have cleared over $10,000 00/100 in the lumber business since the first of May and my prospects are good for as much more before the first of December.

    I have an interest in a mining operation which brings in the cash in great shape—we are taking out from 100 to 189 ounces a day. We are running a steam engine—I employ a man to represent my interest for $5 00/100 a day. We have ground or claim sufficient to last fifty men through years.

    I would write more but time forbids.

    Please remember my sincere regards to Miss Wheeler daughter of Mr Wm. Wheeler.

    She was at Suffield School several terms while I was there and has but few equals in modesty, amiability & talent.

    Please say to Mr. Wm. Randall that I disown him as a father, and at the same time heartily dispise him.

    I think of returning home this fall or summer on a short visit. Shall have my Mother's Aunt's & Grandmother's remains reburied and a fine monument erected to their memory. I design to have engraved on my Mother's side of the monument
    "Vengence is mine and I will repay saith the Lord"—
    Remember me to all inquiring friends
       Yours most respectfully
       Wm. [?] Randall

Write Soon—

Both the first and the second vigilance committees of San Francisco produced a spate of timely lettersheets. The one at the left ("Tremendous Excitement") has written around the edges of the picture three legends:

> *I would tell you all about this affair if I had time. The vigilance committee are doing up the work brown. Sam Brannan is president.*
>
> *Three were hung at Sac. City Aug. 22, 1851, two by the Authorities and one by the people.*
>
> *You will perhaps ask which I favor, the Authorities or people. I answer that 'I am some people.'*

The lettersheet on the following pages (overleaf) is a document of remarkable interest, for it memorializes the first *legal* execution in San Francisco. According to the perhaps overwrought historians of the times, as many as a thousand citizens had been murdered before the unfortunate José Forner was apprehended and executed for a crime that probably would have gone unnoticed had he come from Pike County rather than Valencia in old Spain.

The gallows was erected near the peak of Russian Hill, some ten thousand spectators turned out for the unprecedented event, and afterwards the complacent citizenry suffered murder to continue unabated.

JAMES STUART HUNG BY THE VIGILANCE COMMITTEE ON MARKET ST: WHARF, ON THE 11ᵗʰ OF JULY 1851 .— IMMENSE MULTITUDE PRESENT .— 500 OF THE VIGILANCE COMMITTEE ON DUTY AT THE EXECUTION .— *His confession & evidence proved him guilty of the murder of Chas. Moore, Sheriff of Yuba County, — of the murderous assault & robbery of Mr. Jansen in this city, & of the Captain of the brig Jas. Caskie in this harbor — of the robbery of the Custom house at Monterey — besides numerous other robberies & murders. No criminal was ever more daring or successful — more reckless or cold blooded. He was a Sydney convict, transported for life for forgery. His last words were "I die resigned — my sentence is just."*

VIEW TAKEN FROM THE STORESHIP BYRON.
Foot of Market S⁻ Wharf San-Francisco.

Publ. & Lith. by **Justh Quirot** & Cᵒ Calif. Corn. Montᵍ Sᵗ· S.F.

CONFESSION OF JOSÉ FORNER y BRUGADA.

On the day that the killing was done, to wit : On the evening of the 8th of October, about the hour of 4 o'clock, company with two young friends, talking of going to dine, they did not wish to go so early. I said, well, I would take a wa and see the Steam Paddy work. I then parted from my friends and walked towards Happy Valley ; and while I was looki at the machine at work, one Jose Roderiguez (the deceased) came up to me and slapping me familiarly on the shoulder, sa "Hallo, José, what are you doing here?" I returned for answer, that I had come out for a walk, I at the same time notic that the deceased looked strangely at me. After a few moments he asked me to come and take a drink with him, I said n thank you, that I must away and obey a call of nature, I then left him and went on a sand hill, took off of my body my mon belt, which contained some four hundred dollars, I laid the belt on the ground, at the same time I took off my knife, that al I laid on the ground: whilst I was in the act of dressing myself, deceased came running up to me, and saw my knife laying the ground, which he instantly seized, and said, "I want your money," I said that I had but two or three dollars, which y can have if you wish it. He answered, "No, you have more and I will have it," at that moment he jumped towards me, I ste ped back to avoid him, when he struck me a blow with the knife, which took effect in the calf of my leg, I exclaimed that was a d——d scoundrel, what did he mean. He ran down the hill, I after him, he dropped the knife, I picked it up wh running after him, he made an effort to get the knife away from me, what I done afterwards, God only knows, I was fran with rage. I confess that *I did* intend to kill him, believing, at the time, that it was his intention to rob me and perhaps kill me if necessary in its accomplishment. The money which I had when arrested, was my own, I had worked hard for a p tion of it, th other portion won at cards. I was cook and confectioner at the Jackson House where I received $125. I a worked at the Nueva Mondo and at the Laguna: from these two places I received between $50 and 60, the balance of the m ney I won at cards at the El Dorado, Polka and Arcade: in all about $400

SKETCH OF THE LIFE OF JOSÉ FORNER.

I was born in Valencia, (Spain) in the month of May, 1820, of highly respectable parents. My uncle is Alcalde of Va lencia, and all of my family, with but few exceptions, hold office under the Spanish government. I am worth in Valencia fro $4000 to $5000 in real estate. At the age of 16 years I went to learn the trade of confectioner with my uncle; served wit him 5 years; from there I went to Barcelona, was three years in the service of Don Jina Costa; from thence I went with le ters of introduction to the brother of my last employer Don Juan Costa, at Havana, Cuba, worked there two years; then we to my native place Valencia; from there to Madrid; from thence to Barcelona; then again to Havana, was there three or fo months in the house of Dominicas; from thence to Vera Cruz, Mexico; thence to Puebla; thence to the city of Mexico; thenc to Acapulco, from there to the city of San Francisco, where I have been working five or six months. I had about $75 whe I arrived here. I worked for the proprietors of the Jackson House, the hotel Nueva Mondo and the Laguna.This is the first tim that I ever was in prison, and never wronged any man of one dime. The money found on me was my own.

Signed,

Jose Forner y Brugada

JOSÉ FORNER,

Aged 32 Years, a Native of Valencia, Spain. Executed in San Francisco the 10th of Dec. 1852, for the Murder of José Rodriguez.

[Published at the WIDE WEST OFFICE, 181 Clay Street, San Francisco.]

THE GRIZZLY AND HIS CAPTORS.

To Willey & May I send this picture showing how the Spaniards catch the Bears in Cal., you must be good children and I will send you some gold in all my letters to show you the way it grows here. The gold here is mostly fine but we found one piece last week worth $2.50. I would like to send that but it is in bad shape to do up, I think our sister Charlotte has done the clean thing by writing me. I am very much obliged to her and will write her an answer in about 2 weeks from this date. I will try and see her Brother as Grass Valley is only 8 or 10 miles from me I have been there. I should like to get acquainted with him very well. It is a hard place to find a person except you know the name of the place. My paper is very dirty & pen bad so will excuse the bad way it is written. Kiss the Babies & tell them I would like them very well. Write often & tell all the news give my respects to all Yours Truly N. A. Chandler [Michigan Hill, May 6th, 1853]

THE REVOLUTION OF THE PEOPLE,

THE COUNTY JAIL IN SAN FRANCISCO BESEIGED BY THREE THOUSAND CITIZEN SOLDIERS, ARMED AND EQUIPPED.

☞ SURRENDER OF JAMES P. CASEY & CHARLES CORA, ☜

To the Vigilance Committee, on Sunday, May 18th, 1856.

THE FOLLOWING ACCOUNT MAY BE RELIED ON AS CORRECT, BEING COMPILED FROM THE MOST AUTHENTIC REPORTS OF THE CITY PAPERS.

Early in the morning a movement was visible in the concentration of a large body of men at the two meeting places of the Vigilance Committee on Sacramento street. The night previous, all who had been mustered into companies and provided with arms, were thoroughly drilled, and up to the time the papers of yesterday went to press, nothing was known of the course of action to be pursued. The Executive Committee held a late session, and previous to its close, all members of the armed corps were notified to be on the ground early in the morning. At 10 o'clock orders were given to prepare for a demonstration on the jail, the Committee having resolved to obtain possession of the persons of Casey and Cora.

The first movement on the part of the Vigilance Committee was the dispatching of an advance company of one hundred men, armed with pistols and knives, who approached the jail in small squads from every direction. This was successfully carried out without creating any attention from the populace. This company acted as scouts, and on the concentration of the armed body they marched up to the hill on the east of the jail. About 11 o'clock, a brass six-pounder, escorted by a company of citizens armed with flint-lock muskets, was conveyed from Captain Macondray's store, on Sansome street, and planted on Broadway, directly in front of the entrance to the jail. The passage of this troop through the streets created intense excitement, and in a brief space of time the hills and streets and house-tops in the vicinity of the jail were covered with anxious spectators, to whom nothing was definitely known as what was about to follow; this was premonitory of a decisive s and and peremptory action. From half past eleven to a quarter past twelve, the companies of the Vigilance Committee, to the number of near fifteen hundred, armed _____ ___ l___ quietly marched through various streets to the scene of ___ ___ ___ ___ Kearny, Dupont and Stockton streets, in _____ ___ ___ giving way with alacrity, the ___ ___ ___ of being ___

been on duty having been dismissed on the formation of the line of troops on the exterior. Previous to this demand, the knife and fork were removed from Casey's cell. The President of the Committee made a formal demand for the possession of Casey. The Sheriff promptly acceded, stating that he was in his cell. The President entered it, and in the presence of those surrounding him, informed him of the purpose of his visit. Casey expressed his willingness to go, and requested that he might have a fair trial, and not be dragged through the streets, which were assured him. He was then hand-cuffed by Marshal North, and in company with two of the Committee and the Marshal, the latter at Casey's request, he was conveyed to a carriage placed in front of the jail door. Before leaving the jail, a letter was handed to the Sheriff, informing him that the Committee would return in an hour for Cora. The carriage was then surrounded by a heavy detachment of troops, and proceeded to and through Kearny street to Pacific, and through to Montgomery, up to Sacramento to the Committee rooms, the old Appraisers' store, where they arrived twenty minutes past one. Casey was immediately taken up stairs and confronted with the Judges who were to determine the issue of life or death. The escort remained at the Committee rooms as a guard.

THE EXCITEMENT.

On Casey's being taken into the Committee room, the attention of the community was divided between the jail and the Committee's head quarters; the greater portion of whom, however returned to the scene of action, where the larger portion of the armed force still ___ this time ___ ge accession was made to th ___ ranks of persons ___ th ___ ___ lances ___ ___ ___

San Francisco May 20th 1856

a few more words. today the streets are thronged with people anxiously awaiting to see Casey and Cora Hung. everything is done with perfect order, but we think tomorrow will be the day, all business is suspended and pleasures laid aside. This morning their was great hopes of Mr Kings recovery half past 1 o'clock this afternoon he expired he has lived 6 days since he was shot through the Breast. just as it was known he was dead, every store, and place of Business was Closed, and all draped in Mourning. Hotells dwellings Houses etc. Flags all bordered with black everything is draped with Black and white aboth here. I never saw only Black in any other place. Wilsons Xchange looks Beautifully the whole Front is Festooned with both Colors, and so is the whole street the front of Charleys Store is covered and even the Cobblers little shantys on the side walk is trimed, king was the poor mans friend its now most 12 o'clock the streets are crowded with people and very quiet perfect order prevails. The steamer has not arrived yet out 30 days today at 12 o'clock for 6 days we have not done one stich of work only look out of the windows be sure and get the package of papers this time I dont know as you can read this for I cant write goodnight

Mary

MORE SHEET THAN LETTER . . .
Just as the peak of the real
Gold Rush was in early '52
rather than just before the
bust of '54, there was a commercial "overshoot" in
lettersheet development
culminating in the San Francisco vigilance excitement of
1856. The sheet on this
spread had both front and
back printed, with the space
in which this note appears
devoted to a six-point-type
description of four scenes
most publicly obvious in
the vigilante seizure of
power.

But the tide had run its
course. With the triumph of
the middle-class San Francisco Committee of Vigilance
over the free-wheeling political and social adventurers
(and criminals), one line of
legitimate succession from
1849 came to an end. And by
1856, the lettersheet itself
had gone somewhat stodgy.
They were printed in ever-
diminishing quantities for
another fifteen years, but
they were less and less in
step with the needs and
tastes of the new times.

ASSASSINATION

Pub. by Britton & Rey.   FUNERAL OF J⁹ KING.

h, 1856.

a great state of
sination of Mr.

y weapon, but
treet by Casey,
—to which Mr.
d at Casey.—
resented a large
aw and defend
king deliberate
h a well direct-
nown.
ain, but seeing
Pacific Express
d shot; some
d told him to
ased, and show-
of two or three
would go, but
as he was not

ng occurrence,
g in broad day-
justly aroused
mmunity.
L, MAY 18TH.
were formed in-
deep, directly
tizen's Guard"
them, and all
a deputation of
l to call at the
place them in
sey. Without
ired to the cell
him that the
ing at the door
d that he was

22ND.
r the ceremon-
et was literally
hildren, almost
Washington to

SURRENDER OF THE JAIL

hurch services,
we have ever
rmed, and fol-
ntain Cemetry.
Stockton street
Montgomery,
to the Lone
he occupied in
tgomery street,
en the last por-
orner of Stock-
ront had reach-
Bush, a distance

ND CORA.*
ect were being
g, at the church,
as going on at
ommittee.
athering at the
nittee were sur-
e, who had got
execution, and

was arranged,
f the Commit-
and of muskets
ets in the imme-
cleared by the
onets that were
ade the scene
of the field pei-
mmand Davis
and the other

ock every thing
signs of the ex-
n and the cord
the scoffolds, or
of of the build-
both launched
emn and awful
nd silence was
ho were specta-

EXECUTION

The Sydney Duck John Jenkins, hanged from the beam of the old adobe Customs House at 2:00 A.M., June 11, 1851. This lettersheet view was published on June 12, as shown by the date of a letter on the back to "Dear Mother and Sister," which reads, in part: "They did right in hanging. There is more rascals & murders in this city than any other in the world of the same size. A man steps out of his office a few minutes and returns and finds himself robbed. . . . A few hanging matches will bring them to."

Chapter III

LET EACH MAN BE HIS OWN EXECUTIONER

WHILE THE PROBABLE, possible, or simply apocryphal antics of a handful of stiff-legged gunfighters have provided the script for a full-blown mythology on the theme of law and order in the West, by far the most impressive struggle between organized villains, crooked sheriffs, grafting politicians, and alarmed citizens was acted out not in six-gun and saddle-leather country, but in the streets and counting houses of San Francisco. This is not surprising, given the nature of the town. It was conjured into existence by a dream called gold, propelled by fearsome and only barely controlled energies, and populated by as loose an amalgam of people as might be found in any one place at any one time anywhere in the world. In short, the question was never *if* such a conflict would arise, but merely when. And the answer was "almost immediately."

The emigrants to California during the great rush of 1849 had included all of the disparate types of humanity, save, perhaps, any large numbers of the infirm or indecisive, the great or the ladies of the great (or "ladies" of any sort, for that matter). Doctors by the hundreds left their patients to recover as they might from the Draconian specifics fashionable to medical science, such as it was; lawyers by the cartload departed for the predictably more lucrative tumults of a golden land; ribbon clerks and yard-goods merchants, editors and parsons, fugitives and jurymen packed up and went to California.

Among the first to get to San Francisco had been those who had the most mercurial temperaments, the least to pack, and a certain flexibility in their attitudes toward the whole idea of law, order, and—most definitely—justice. New Orleans, the lusty, brawling metropolis at the mouth of the Mississippi River, had been the first "eastern" town to hear of the discovery and extent of the gold mines from an official messenger, and New Orleans was the port in the United States most convenient to Panama. One may meditate with profit upon the varieties of colorful citizens *that* town belched forth when tickled with

"Are we to be robbed and assassinated in our domiciles?"

55

A fancy ball at the California Exchange, complete with a few ladies who might have been described by J. S. Hitell as "neither maidens, wives, nor widows."

The City Hotel, one of San Francisco's grander establishments and a resort popular with the Hounds.

the news of what California held. The sweepings of the Ohio and Mississippi followed swift upon their heels, and with the same promptness came the *crème de la crème* of Sydney, Australia's nocturnal element, those undesirables—convicts, indigent poor, and political dissidents—whom the British government had dumped in Australia on the theory that out of sight was indeed out of mind. They were called "Sydney Ducks," among other things, and slipped quite naturally into the underground milieu of San Francisco. At about the same time Callao, Peru, and Valparaiso, Chile, contributed their own contingent of those who would just as soon leave in a hurry. This latter group included entrepreneurs almost as intrepid as one Eliza Farnham, who, in February 1849, had advertised in New York for a hundred intelligent, virtuous, and efficient females to accompany her to San Francisco, to the end of improving the moral tone of what she quite rightly felt must be rapidly becoming a thoroughly depraved situation (she ended up with three women, all of them middle-aged and two of them married). The South American exporters were at once more practical and more sensitive to the social yearnings of the community. They shipped up the kind of women a shrewd, gold-laden miner, just down from six months in the wilderness, could deal with on a solid business basis.

Thus, San Francisco became in the summer of 1849 a wild, wide-open town, a town in which gambling, whoring, drinking, mayhem, robbery, murder, and other exhibitions of high-spirited revelry were commonplace from the beginning. For the most part, the "solid" citizens of the city—those, for example, who intended to remain for at least six months and perhaps longer in the pursuit of more or less legitimate enterprise—were willing to look the other way. They had business, lots of it, to transact, and so long as their manipulations were not seriously threatened by social disorder they were generally indifferent. They would acquiesce in cases of the most flagrant miscarriage of justice, would suffer an active criminal element to operate almost unchecked, would ignore jobbery, bribery, and all kinds of civic chicanery, so long as the merchandise kept moving, so long as the paper and the gold dust kept changing hands. But they would not tolerate outright insolence forever. And they would not be *run over*.

The first significant expression of this took place in the middle of that summer of 1849. At that time, the most consequential civic organization was a group of roving thugs who styled themselves the "Regulators"—or sometimes the "Hounds," as the spirit moved them. A forthright gang, the Hounds set up headquarters near the City Hotel, which they called Tammany Hall, from whence they issued at night-time intervals to eat, drink, and make merry (without paying), and to assault the South Americans encamped in "Little Chile" on the slopes of Telegraph Hill. The extortions they practiced upon the *chilenos* made good San Franciscans shake their heads and sigh in regret and disapproval. Less acceptable was their habit of marching through the streets on Sundays with drum and fife, club and revolver; such displays amounted to a flaunting of the outrages they perpetuated while the better burghers were abed.

The origin of the Hounds was left in decent obscurity by the early historians of the city, very possibly because what John Henry Brown (keeper of the City Hotel and partner in the Parker House) said was all too true. Brown had it that the Hounds arose out of the desire of the leading merchants to protect ship captains landing cargoes at the port from the desertion of their crews: "The merchants raised a company of ten persons, and signed a paper, in which they promised to pay them twenty-five dollars for every runaway sailor they brought back. These men were called the Regulators. This paper was signed by Edward Harrison, W. D. M. Howard, James Layton, Captain Folsom, Robert A. Parker, and many others. The only purpose for which the company was formed was for the protection of captains of vessels, as the sailors would run away every chance they got, and the Regulators were found to be of great service, both by the shipping and the city. They were not called Regulators very long, however, as they took a new name, and were known as 'The Hounds.' Some very desperate characters joined the company, most of whom have been hung in this country for murder and other depredations, which they have committed [Brown was writing in 1886]. I will mention some of the leading characters: Captain Roberts, Jacob Powers, Tom Edward (who to my certain knowledge has murdered three men in this city), a man named Curley and four others from Sydney, named Red Davis, Curley Bill, Sam Terry and Barney Ray. Soon after these men joined the company, I would see them pass the hotel very often with a quantity of clothing. In conversation with one of them, he said they had taken the clothing as confiscated goods, as the Mexicans would not pay them their share for keeping the town in good order."

The act of keeping the town in good order, of course, had not been in their original charter, and as the Hounds grew more and more impartial in their extortions and assaults (and perhaps as the town and the shipping grew so large that their actual services were no longer effective or needed), the business community that had hired them in the first place became more and more alarmed. Finally, on Sunday, July 15, 1849, the Hounds went too far. That day, after their usual parade, they stormed Little Chile in broad daylight, shooting up the "greasers" good this time. Monday, the suddenly aroused citizenry formed itself into a body of constables, with the consent and blessing of *alcalde* Leavenworth. W. D. M. Howard was chosen president of the meeting that organized the citizens, and Sam Brannan took up a collection for the relief of the maltreated *chilenos*. Armed with muskets and revolvers, the two hundred thirty special officers made short work of rounding up the Hounds. Judges, prosecutors, and defense counsel were produced, the villains expeditiously convicted, and sentence pronounced. Even though one of the prosecution witnesses was a *chileno* dying of gunshot wounds, the court was satisfied with moderate punishment. The leaders of the Hounds were sentenced to long terms at hard labor, the rank and file to briefer imprisonment "in whatever penitentiary the governor of California might direct." As there was no penitentiary—not even a county jail—the men were soon at liberty. But their organization was smashed, and most of them did not show their faces around town for some time.

The Hounds attack Little Chile at the foot of Telegraph Hill.

Duty done, the special officers disbanded and went back to business as usual. Yet a little less than a year and a half later foul insolence once again reared its head and the citizens were inspired to take action. The occasion was the robbery of Mr. Jansen, of C. J. Jansen & Co., on the evening of February 19, 1851. Jansen was alone in his store when two men, posing as customers, struck him with a "slung shot" (blackjack), beat him senseless, and fled with $2,000 from the till. As robbery and even murder were common enough crimes, as the assault on Jansen was by no means the culmination of any unusual activity among the hoodlums of the town, and as Jansen was not killed and the amount stolen not very large, it is not easy to see what all the subsequent fuss was about. The explanation probably lies in the fact that Jansen was a merchant and that he had been struck down in his *own store*. The arrogance of the attack made it an assault on all of the "best people" in town.

William T. Coleman lectures at City Hall, February 22, 1851.

Of course, there could have been no popular uprising without an identified criminal. He was provided the next day by the arrest of the notorious Sydney Duck, one James Stuart, who had been sought on a number of charges, the most serious of them being the murder of the sheriff of Auburn. The insolence of the assault was compounded by the insolence of the criminal, who not only denied the attack on Jansen, but claimed his name was Thomas Burdue, not Stuart. Jansen could identify him as Stuart, though, and could also identify another man the police had picked up. The courtroom was packed at the arraignment, and more than five thousand men gathered about the building. The second criminal, Windred, drove the populace to fury when he produced an alibi—the classic defense of every thug brought to trial in that era—in the form of a friend who claimed that he had been playing cards with Windred at the time of the assault. Only the intervention of the militia saved the prisoners from immediate execution.

The mob at the city hall was no mob at all, contemporary observers assure us. It was the *people*, many of the best people. They were prepared to act in an orderly fashion, but they were not going to suffer another outrage against justice, another mockery of the judicial process, complete with false swearing, bought juries, and obscure motions by the defense. A handbill, perhaps the work of Sam Brannan, the apostate Mormon turned merchant prince, expressed the more extreme view of how the matter might be handled: "CITIZENS OF SAN FRANCISCO: The series of murders and robberies that have been committed in this city, seems to leave us entirely in a state of anarchy. 'When thieves are left without control to rob and kill, then doth the honest traveller fear each bush a thief.' Law, it appears, is but a nonentity to be scoffed at; redress can be had for aggression but through the never failing remedy so admirably laid down in the code of Judge Lynch. Not that we should admire this process for redress, but that it seems to be inevitably necessary.

"Are we to be robbed and assassinated in our domiciles, and the law to let our aggressors perambulate the streets merely because they have furnished straw bail? If so, 'let each man be his own executioner.' 'Fie upon your laws!' They have no force.

"All those who would rid our city of its robbers and murderers, will assemble on Sunday at two o'clock on the plaza."

Some of the thoughts expressed were so much nonsense. For one thing, the plight of the "honest traveller" was at best a peripheral issue: honest travelers might be assaulted, robbed, or even killed in San Francisco without benefit of influential public sympathy. For another thing, every man *was* his own executioner, and if a citizen of good character found cause to take a pot-shot at a suspicious-looking individual, he was not apt to be subjected to any rigorous official inquiry.

But, "to be robbed and assassinated in our domiciles": this was close to the heart of the matter, "our domiciles" meaning "our stores." The merchants were the leaders of the people that gathered to see justice done to Stuart and Windred. The violence suffered by one of their number was the overt cause of their action; the long-standing inadequacy of legal redress was what kept up their enthusiasm and finally led to their taking over the legal machinery themselves. "We are the mayor and the recorder, the hangman and the laws," said Brannan. "The law and the courts never yet hung a man in California; and every morning we are reading fresh accounts of murders and robberies. I want no technicalities."

The inability of the courts to convict known criminals was not entirely the result of corruption in the judges themselves. A central defect in the system lay in the means of selecting juries: the twelve men good and true were not rigorously screened as they are today, but were the first twelve men the bailiff encountered outside the courtroom who were not obviously in a hurry to do something else. Hence, in any ordinary case, it was a sure bet that one or more of the jurors had been either bribed before his selection, or intended to sell his vote as soon as the defense attorney made an offer. Mayor John Geary tacitly recognized this situation when on Sunday, with some eight thousand citizens gathered around the courthouse, he suggested to the leading merchants that they appoint twelve of their number to sit as jury in the Stuart-Windred case.

Geary's compromise was entirely unsatisfactory, not only because the temper of the people was up, but because it left open the second monstrous loophole in San Francisco justice. Geary may have promised that the trial would take place the following day—but once it was in the hands of the court, who could tell what might happen? Even as today, it was then a fairly easy matter for attorneys to show cause for delay in legal proceedings. In gold rush San Francisco, this practice time and again permitted criminals to go free. The population was young, and on the move; two weeks' delay, and chances were that most of the witnesses for the prosecution would be scattered from Weaverville to Panama. In the case at hand, the chief witness—Jansen—was in some danger of immediate death from his wounds, and might easily succumb to secondary infection or disease if the trial could be strung along by legal hanky-panky.

But if the merchants were out for blood, it was only for a little blood. If they feared personal violence more than citizens in most other occupations, they also feared general violence more than did the average man. The uncouth Brannan might despise niceties and formalities, but most of his colleagues seem to have sensed that they could very easily jeopardize their own best interests by openly scoffing at the laws. They found their logic and their spokesman in a young merchant named William T. Coleman, who addressed the mob, at once exciting their fervor for swift and impartial justice, and at the same time calling upon them to appoint a committee to organize a "people's court," complete with judge, jury, prosecutor, defense counsel, sheriff, and clerk, and to abide faithfully by its considered judgment.

Although at one extreme the mayor raised a small armed force and declared that he would attempt to secure the prisoners in the event of a "guilty" verdict, and at the other a rude band organized with the intention of hanging the prisoners without benefit of any fol-de-rol, the middle ground of the ad hoc committee prevailed. The trial proved fair enough, for the jury disagreed, to the chagrin of the "public prosecutor," William T. Coleman, and most of the populace. The thoroughly frightened civil authorities made good their previous dereliction by swiftly trying and condemning the prisoners to long sentences. The alleged Stuart was shipped off to Marysville to stand trial for the murder of Sheriff Moore of Auburn. Windred illustrated the final defect in the local judicial system by escaping from prison.

Those who wanted to "clean up" the city were left completely dissatisfied by the procedings of late February. The object of the popular uprising having been so limited, the organization that it created—the trial committee—was useless once the case of Stuart and Windred was disposed. Suspected undesirables still arrived on ships from Sydney and South America, and the "honest traveller" who ventured into "Sydneytown" (as Clark's Point, near the base of Telegraph Hill) still had reason to fear every bush—or doorway.

John W. Geary, last alcalde and first mayor of San Francisco.

Moreover, there had been reason to believe, or at least suspect, that arsonists had kindled one or more of the great fires of 1850. Unsuccessful arson attempts had been detected, and one good-sized conflagration—the destruction of the City Hospital, operated by Dr. Peter Smith—was generally acknowledged to have been deliberately set. As the anniversary of the fire of May 4, 1850, approached, it was rumored about that the town was to be burned again in commemoration of that spectacular event. Just before midnight on May 3, a fire broke out in a paint shop bordering the plaza. Within minutes the fire was raging out of control.

The sturdy brick buildings with iron "fire shutters" that the prosperous merchants had built after their previous sad experiences with fires proved death-traps to those few so foolish as to close themselves inside. The fire department could do nothing to contain the blaze, spread by embers whirled through the air and by tongues of flames that pumped through the spaces underneath the newly planked streets and sidewalks. Before noon of May 4, all of the business section of the city was reduced to ashes and rubble. Literate San Franciscans could find a worthy parallel to their calamity only in the destruction of Moscow during Napoleon's invasion. The aggressive citizenry at once set to work rebuilding the city—for there were still miners in the interior with gold in their fists, and ships still sailed through the Golden Gate every day with shirts and shoes and sealing-wax. The energetic pursuit of business interests was uppermost in the minds of the very best speculators and merchants. But just below the surface of their frantic daily routine, there must also have been seething the conviction that something must be done, that someone must be punished, that there was *some* spark in the activities of the committee of the preceding February that should be rekindled. On June third, a suspected incendiary was hauled into court. A crowd formed, crying for blood and Brannan. The prisoner was spirited away by the police before Sam could take charge of the proceedings, and the populace dispersed. The incendiary was indicted—twice; both times his counsel found judicial flaws in the indictment. The anniversary of the disastrous fire of June 14, 1850—the second of the city's great fires—drew near, and again, rumors of an incendiary attempt upon the city sped about the town.

The anniversary fire of May 3 and 4, 1851, burned the city to the water's edge and beyond. The editor of the Alta California *was disgusted with the fire fighters: "We look with apparent satisfaction upon the sprightly attempts of the recruits of penaldom to illuminate our city free gratis."*

On Sunday, June 8, a couple of citizens decided that something more substantial than the volunteer night patrol of merchants (established after the Jansen mugging) was needed in San Francisco. Confident of a favorable reception, they went to see Sam Brannan, who immediately fell in with their plans, and lent his prestige as an amateur law-enforcer to an invitation to other reliable persons to meet the following day. By Monday night the general scheme of a "Committee of Vigilance" was determined; by Tuesday night it was an organization with constitution, by-laws, headquarters, and some two hundred members. The by-laws made the purpose of the committee explicit: the deportation of scoundrels. The initial resolutions of the committee notified undesirables to "leave this *port*": they were not to "get out of town by sunset" in the supposed tradition of the Old West; rather, they were to take sail from the shores of California. Almost from the moment of its inception the San Francisco vigilance committee was in communication with similar committees that sprang up in all of the major towns in the state, and this league of vigilantes was not in business for the purpose of shunting criminals from one town to another.

When the committee assumed the power to deport persons (and to restrain others from landing), it had taken upon itself perhaps a little more than some of the Tuesday signers had realized. Physical seizure and confinement of persons was implied in the assumption of this duty—though undoubtedly many people who joined the committee did not think much beyond the probable efficacy of threat. It is apparent that such a committee, having no means of jailing malefactors for any extended period, would have to back up its threats with the ultimate threat—death. Perhaps even the majority of the original vigilantes were prepared to hang a Sydney Duck who failed to obey their order of banishment, but under normal circumstances the decision would not have been an easy one. Circumstances, as it turned out, were not normal, and the committee had committed itself to a hanging before midnight of the very day on which it was organized.

Unfortunate John Jenkins, a husky Sydney convict, chose Tuesday evening to run afoul of the fresh-born committee, and thereby unwittingly made certain that the Committee of Vigilance became the *whole* law of San Francisco for so long as it chose to be that law. Poor Jenkins committed an offense so unlikely and outrageous, so perfectly calculated to sear the souls and inflame the brain tissues of the worthy merchants who composed the committee, that it must be accounted a work of art rather than a fluke of fortune. He stole a safe full of money from an office on Long Wharf and tried to row off with it in a skiff. Pursued, he threw the safe into the Bay; captured, he maintained a surly defiance; brought before the hastily reassembled committee, he insulted the accusers; condemned to hang, he replied, "Bosh!" anticipating speedy delivery from this kangaroo tribunal. The nature of the affair, and the nature of the criminal, combined to strengthen the resolve of the committee, and by the time the trial was over, the only question was whether to hang him immediately or to wait until morning, as William T. Coleman—always a stickler for ceremony—suggested.

It is more than likely that the hang-him-now advocates sensed that the future of the committee would be best served by committing the entire membership to a bold act before any second thoughts or quibbles arose to divide the organization. Sam Brannan, never one to quibble when there was hanging to be done, stepped outside, harangued the crowd that had assembled by the committee rooms, and offered the committee's judgment to be ratified by the mob. The majority approved; Jenkins was dragged through the streets to a hanging in the plaza. Officers of the law made a token effort to rescue the prisoner; they were told to mind their manners. Organized scoundreldom made a bolder attempt; they were driven back by a show of arms. By this time the vigilantes were so feverish that some of them thought to hang Jenkins from the liberty pole in the plaza. "Don't desecrate the flag!" howled others, propelling the victim toward the adobe customhouse at the end of the plaza. The rope was cast over the projecting roof-beam. "Every lover of liberty and good order lay hold," spake Brannan; and it was done.

Thus was the committee committed. A coroner's jury could hardly overlook the incident, and enemies of the committee attempted the obvious tactic of singling out vigilantes for possible individual prosecution. The committee responded with a statement, signed by one hundred eighty members, insisting that all of them were equally implicated. And there the matter stood—forever.

New members joined the vigilantes daily, until by September there were over six hundred enrolled. Its major work of deportation proceeded quietly, and with enough success that by September 9 it could call itself "adjourned," thereafter for some months maintaining only the nucleus of an executive committee—and the implied threat of instant reorganization.

In the ruins of the city, agitation to root out thugs and incendiaries pressed forward in earnest.

The hanging of the real James Stuart at the Market Street wharf. "This was a sorry spectacle—a human being dying like a dog, while thousands of erring mortals looked on and applauded!"

THE HANGINGS by the committee of 1851 have always excited a lively interest, and with good reason, for each of four executions conducted by this first vigilance committee in San Francisco exposed an important part of the nature of the organization. In the first case, Jenkins's crime aggravated the passions of the vigilantes and his execution committed them to strong and fearless action. Yet in Jenkins's case, the punishment was somewhat excessive for the crime; he was of known "bad character," but he was not tried for any murders he may have committed.

The second trial and hanging showed a considerable development in decorum and sensitivity to the possibility of wronging an individual. This case concerned the well-known James Stuart, and also concerned the wisdom of popular justice. The James Stuart in this case was not the same James Stuart who had been accused of mugging Jansen, and had claimed he was Thomas Burdue, and had almost been hanged by a "people's court" in February. No, this was the *real* James Stuart! To its credit, the committee was just as quick about sending a representative up to Marysville, where Burdue was about to be executed by the legal authorities for Stuart's crimes, as it was about trying and hanging the real Stuart. Burdue, by now reduced to a pitiful state as the result of his unfortunate resemblance to Stuart, was rescued in the nick of time, and the San Francisco vigilantes made what financial amends they could to pay him for his trouble.

The third and fourth hangings were accompanied by open and armed collision with the law in August, when two of Stuart's associates, Sam Whittaker and Robert McKenzie, were seized from the committee rooms by Sheriff Jack Hays, the famous Texas Ranger, who was busily developing the potential of San Francisco's most lucrative political post. The loss of the prisoners was a startling blow to the prestige of the committee, first, because the vigilantes had previously refused to deliver up these men (although they had turned many other minor criminals over to the authorities), and second, because the sheriff had been ordered to seize the men by Governor McDougal and the mayor, and third, because it seemed unlikely that the sheriff could have managed his grab without the collusion of some members of the committee itself. The flawed organization of the committee, which for once provided the legal authorities better intelligence than that ordinarily enjoyed by the vigilantes, gave its leaders cause for alarm; the open defiance of its authority by the previously wishy-washy forces of the city, county, and state required that the committee either take some swift, bold action or get out of business. The leaders chose to move with secrecy and strength. On Sunday, August 24, thirty-six vigilantes seized the county jail in a clockwork maneuver, bundled the prisoners into a coach, and to the prearranged tolling of the Monumental Engine Company bell raced them to the gallows on Battery Street and hanged them.

Thus was the Committee of Vigilance master of San Francisco when it retired from active prosecution of criminals. Yet at its moment of greatest strength—when it seized Whittaker and McKenzie from the jail and hanged them—it showed its weakness by acting in feverish haste. The character of the committee was akin to that of its chief instigator and first president, Sam Brannan. All of the hangings had for one reason or another been carried out in unseemly haste; only Stuart, among the executed, was certain to have been a murderer—and he had been convicted of a capital offense not by the committee, but by the trial of his unwilling proxy, Burdue, in Marysville. All of the hanged were Sydney Ducks; neither they, nor the criminals turned over to the civil authorities, nor those run out of town, had much of anything to do with the civic corruption that permitted or encouraged their depredations. It was probably the incendiary attempts, more than any other criminal action, which prompted the formation of the committee; ironically, on June 22, two weeks after the formation of the vigilantes, just about all of the city that had not been burned on May 4 was destroyed in a conflagration that was almost certainly set by arsonists bent on plunder.

What the San Francisco vigilance committee, and its associate committees in the provinces, had done was to kick out of California what San Francisco's annalists called "the sweepings from the prisons and the thieves'-alleys of other lands." The popular conviction that the vigilantes had "cleaned up" San Francisco was wildly optimistic. The Committee of Vigilance, in deporting hoodlums without quibbling over the rules of evidence, and in preventing suspicious characters from landing, performed a service beyond the competence of even the most honest civil authorities; yet it failed to insure that honest government would succeed the committee's own honest efforts. The reason for this failure is at once simple and obscure: this collection of civic leaders, successful men who dominated a large part of San Francisco's business and real estate, had a larger stake than anyone else in the developing "system." That the system was hopelessly corrupt was probably not much to the taste of most of them, but it was much easier to take arms against a loosly organized gang of outsiders—all of them born losers—than it was to reconstruct a society within which they, after all, were getting on very well.

Inevitably, then, the Committee of Vigilance had not even adjourned before the tastiest political coup heretofore attempted was pulled off. In April 1851, there had been a new election of city officers under a new city charter. The government of the salary swindles and gold medals had been turned out. The new charter provided for the April election and stated that subsequent elections were to be held "thereafter annually at the general election for State officers" (i.e., in September). Common understanding therefore had it that since the April election took care of 1851, the next election for city officers would take place in September of *1852*. And it was probably David C. Broderick's *uncommon* understanding which prompted the Broderick Democrats to print ballots for the statewide election of September 3, 1851—which ballots included a complete slate of city offices. By the time the April incumbents and their supporters developed second thoughts about the meaning of the charter provision, it was too late to print up their own ballots—the election was over. (Perhaps it should be explained here that the official—or "Australian"—ballot with which we are familiar is a comparatively recent innovation. Middle-nineteenth-century American elections were free of such creeping bureaucracy. A voter could draw up his own ballot if he pleased, though as a practical matter it was the politicians who made up the tickets and handed them out at the polls. A regular Democrat, then, would accept the ballot handed to him by one of Broderick's boys, step into the polling place, fold his ballot, and drop it into the box. No sticky ink pads, no little X's to make, no confusion over a multitude of names—no need to read the ballot, or to be *able* to read, for that matter.)

The Democratic sweep in September 1851—by a small but unanimous vote—was contested by the incumbent officers, who refused for a time to deliver up their seats. A suit brought by Stephen R. Harris, elected mayor in September, was fought through to the State Supreme Court, which, by a vote of 2-to-1, declared his election valid. The other old city officers finally gave up without fighting their cases through the courts individually. So it was that

The temper of the times: a frolic in the Green Devil saloon.

Broderick sneaked in a whole slate without really winning an election.

This electoral swindle that accompanied the culmination of vigilance action was trifling by comparison to the land fraud that got into full swing a few days after the committee had been organized. Starting on June 14 there was sold at public auction, over a period of more than six months, the most valuable part of the public lands held by the City of San Francisco. Because of the peculiar circumstances surrounding the sales, the property sold for a small fraction of its value at that time, and an even smaller fraction of the price it should have fetched in the succeeding years during which it would have been placed on sale as the development of the city and its commerce suggested or required. Even while poor Jenkins was swinging from the roofbeam of the customhouse for swiping an inadequate lock-box, some of the officials who could not save him for the legal courts—and probably some of the executioners themselves—were already plotting a steal beyond the comprehension or capabilities of a regiment of Sydney Ducks.

Who was criminal, who was culpable, and who was duped was not clear then or now. But that *some* foul conspiracy was afoot was certain. What happened was that early in 1851 Dr. Peter Smith, administrator of the City Hospital, demanded that the promissory notes—or scrip—with which the city had paid him for his services the previous year (as it did with all its creditors) be converted to coin of the realm. The amount was $64,000. The city government (that government of the $6,000 salaries and gold medals) did not have the money, or claimed it did not, so Smith took the city to court, receiving a favorable judgment early in April. On April 21, a new city charter was passed by the voters. Among other things, it provided for the creation of a Funded Debt Commission to take possession of the real property of the city and with that as collateral to convert the municipal scrip to proper bonds. In May, the state legislature passed a funding bill, the enabling legislation for the whole procedure. Even so, Smith, unlike the rest of the city's creditors, refused to accept bonds in payment. He insisted on cash, and had his court order to back him up.

Consequently, on June 14 (just a week after the formation of the vigilance committee and the hanging of Jenkins), Sheriff Jack Hays advertised 103 water-lots, seven blocks of beachfront property, and seven additional lots belonging to the city for public auction in order to satisfy Smith's claim. As the property was now in the possession of the Funded Debt Commission, and in a sense was not any longer "city property," there was some question in the popular understanding as to the legality of the sale. That doubt was reinforced by a statement issued on the day of the auction by the Funded Debt Commissioners: "A sale of a large number of city lots is advertised to take place this day, by virtue of an execution in the hands of the Sheriff, in favor of Peter Smith against the city of San Francisco. The public are hereby notified, that the city has no legal title to the said lots. . . . The public are therefore cautioned to disregard the sale to be made by the Sheriff to-day, and the undersigned have given this notice so that no one can complain hereafter that they were purchasers without actual notice of the title held by the undersigned." This was an admirably forthright statement, and the public took in the sense of it.

As a result, there were few and small bids for the property. The first sale came nowhere close to satisfying the Smith claim, bringing in only a little over $19,000. The second big auction—of the city's wharves, the old city hall lot, and the lot on which the City Hospital had stood before being burned—came on July 8. It was no better attended than the first, requiring a third and a fourth

The temper of the times: dinner at Delmonico's in the early 1850s was a dainty treat for well-heeled gourmands.

sale, until at the final sale, on January 30, 1852, some two thousand acres of city lands were disposed of to foolish buyers and the Smith claim was finally taken care of—at enormous cost to the citizens of San Francisco, for the California Supreme Court subsequently found that the sales had indeed been quite legal.

Some questions about the whole business presented themselves at the time and still do. Did the Funded Debt Commissioners issue their statement in a deliberate attempt to keep down the number of bidders and drive down the prices of individual bids? We do not know; what we do know is that the commission's chief counsel, who had written the statement, was shortly afterward appointed to the bench of the State Supreme Court and was one with the unanimous judgment that declared the sales legal. Was the fine Irish hand of David Broderick somehow behind the whole scheme? We do not know; what we do know is that his name appears as the purchaser on more than thirty of the lots sold. Was Peter Smith himself in collusion with some of the most prominent citizens in town, acting as a kind of "front man" so that they might obtain the best of the city's lands at cut-rate prices? We do not know; what we do know is that Smith's name appears as the purchaser of nearly seventy-five percent of all the lots sold at auction, that shortly after the last sale he disappeared, and that his name is never again encountered in the history of San Francisco.

"Let everyone therefore keep his own thoughts on the matter," the annalists of San Francisco cautioned in 1854. Indeed. Quite likely, the fraud was not so great when first planned. Quite likely, it "just grew." Quite likely, no single agent or agency was responsible—for none was ever clearly exposed. And quite likely, a good-sized quorum of the "best citizens" were more or less implicated. One thing is certain: the citizens of San Francisco were cheated out of the most valuable part of their common patrimony under the eyes of a vigilance committee that looked the other way, chased some foreign scoundrels out of the state, hanged a few, and fatuously advertised itself as the savior of the community.

The Great Seal of the city of San Francisco fittingly memorialized the six great fires of 1849–1851.

The Perfect Likeness of a Legend . . .

The first truly momentous event in the history of the world to be covered extensively by photography was the Gold Rush. Daguerre's stunning process was introduced in France in 1839 and news of it brought to America in the same year by Samuel F. B. Morse. It became a familiar technique during the 1840s and by 1851 stood ready to record the faces and the scenes of the new El Dorado. Indeed, San Francisco and the mining regions soon became more thoroughly daguerreotyped than any other place in the United States. For a few cents, a gold rush adventurer could send home a pictorial lettersheet; for a few dollars, a living portrait of himself. At the same time daguerreotypists often went outdoors to make pictures on their own account, sometimes with the idea of sale to an eastern gallery, sometimes because they were photographers and they wanted to practice their art.

A special interest attaches to daguerreian views in that they are unique, in the same sense that a manuscript is unique. There was no negative from which to make multiple copies. The polished silvered plate in its ornamental guttapercha box was the entire product. Some of the gold rush daguerreotypes were copied photographically in the late nineteenth and twentieth centuries, and a few were published or widely circulated. But only in the last few years have photographic researchers taken much trouble to look for original daguerreotypes and procure good photographic copies from them.

It is *then* that one sees really clearly such images as the face of the San Francisco banker and newspaper publisher whose assassination led to the astonishing revolution of the Second Committee of Vigilance. That face on the right is the *real* James King of William, not the murky or imaginary character who has appeared as "illustration" in numerous places.

A portrait of a daguerreian artist himself—at his most flamboyant—appears below, somewhere in the gold fields with his studio-van set up for business.

NEWS AND NEWSMAKERS. . . . The daguerreotype could record only scenes that would stay put for a minute—or at least twenty seconds or so. Yet the period finally produced at least one actual news-event photograph, the view above, which was made the day of James King of William's funeral, just after the mile-long procession had passed down Montgomery Street on May 22, 1856. The shadows suggest the picture was taken around one o'clock, about the time that King's assassin, James P. Casey, was hanged by the vigilantes.

The banner was put up that morning by fire company Number 3, "The Howards." Of the brawling fireman hero-bums that made up the live-in volunteer companies of the period, the outfit named for W. D. M. Howard reflected the decent sense of propriety (and conservative business subsidy) that made them not only the "Social Three," but positive civic political leaders as compared to the hoodlums of David Broderick's Number 1 and Casey's awful Number 10.

What a document this "news first" happens to be!—a connection among revolution and political gangsterism and sound money power caught just past high noon on the fateful day of irrevocable vigilante decision. And where? The building dominating the scene is the celebrated Montgomery Block, greatest thing west of the Hudson in 1853, survivor of the 1906 fire, and only in our times stupidly destroyed. At the right of the alley is the barely discernible sign of the *Daily Evening Bulletin,* King's savage and effective voice.

Details: sharp at the right is the meticulously dentilled fringe of the awning of the Pacific Express Company (always shown in "artist's conceptions" of the scene), beneath which King was shot down as he turned the corner from his office into the mainstream of San Francisco's great street of purposeful business. And note that the varied figures on the Montgomery Block balcony and street corner have held quite still, no doubt entirely conscious that an historic view is being fixed in silver.

POWER IN A PORTRAIT. . . . We think that the occasion of this group portrait of four of the merchant princes of gold rush San Francisco was a coincidence of their joint presence in New York during travels in the early 1850s and their joint consciousness of their distant and pioneer importance. How the original portrait ever got back to San Francisco we cannot say. Nor do we know what has become of the perfect original plate that holds the image of these archetypes who Americanized a province of Mexico, a province that could only have been seized and used by some grabbers with real grip.

At right is W. D. M. Howard, rich and getting richer. Center, old Thomas O. Larkin, first American Consul, richer than Croesus in land grants. Front, left, Jacob P. Leese, first American merchant of San Francisco and doing well. Top right is Sam Brannan, a newcomer of '46, so shrewd and bold that he'd buy out the bunch for cash by midnight if they showed signs of panic. The face with the affable smile (top left) is not positively identified, but obviously belongs to someone of much comprehension but perhaps a lesser grip.

THE CITY! RISING FROM THE WATERS, RISING FROM THE FIRES. . . . This frontier village scene is San Francisco's Montgomery Street just before it was wiped out by the fire—in this case the fire of May 4, 1851. The west side of the street was the more substantial, with many brick buildings comparable to the Merchant's Exchange building (at the center). The buildings seen here were built out on the old shoreline of Yerba Buena Cove—and the construction already extended much further seaward. Two years later the massive Montgomery Block stood on the site of these auctioneers' quarters.

The scope and the spirit of the city's successive metamorphoses was summed up by Bayard Taylor when he revisited San Francisco early in 1850 after a sojourn in the mining country: *Of all the marvellous phases of the history of the Present, the growth of San Francisco is the one which will most tax belief of the Future. Its parallel was never known, and shall never be beheld again. . . . When I landed there, a little more than four months before, I found a scattering town of tents and canvas houses, with a show of frame buildings on one or two streets. . . . Now, I saw around me an actual metropolis, displaying street after street of well-built edifices, filled with an active and enterprising people and exhibiting every mark of permanent commercial prosperity. . . .*

Bayard Taylor again: *The great want of San Francisco was society. Think of a city of thirty thousand inhabitants peopled by men alone! The like of this was never seen before. He who cannot make a bed, cook a beefsteak, or sew up his own rips and rents is unfit to be a citizen of California.*

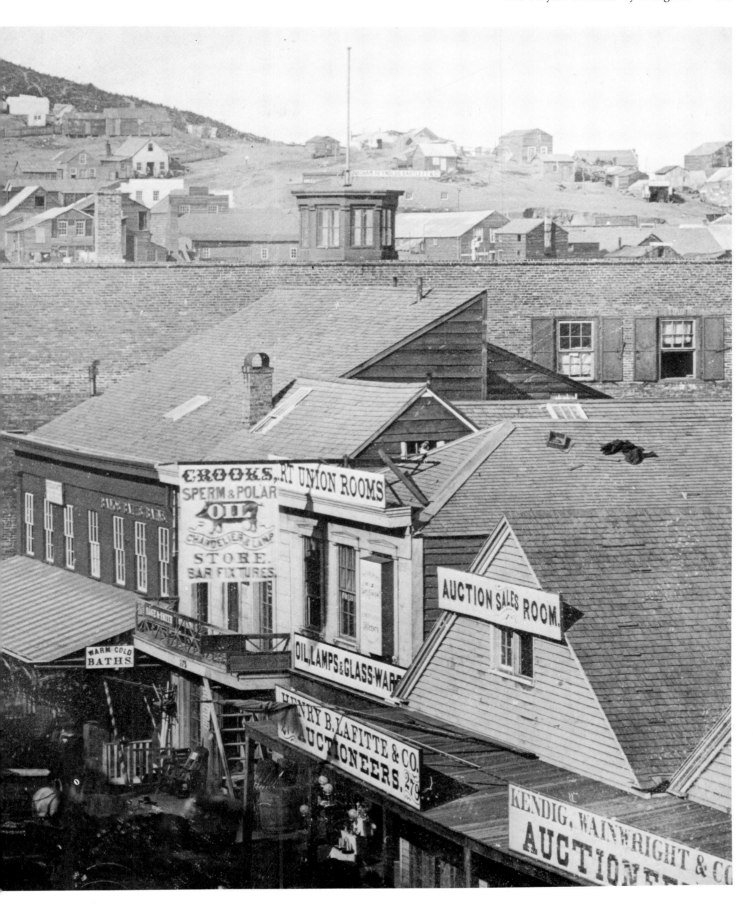

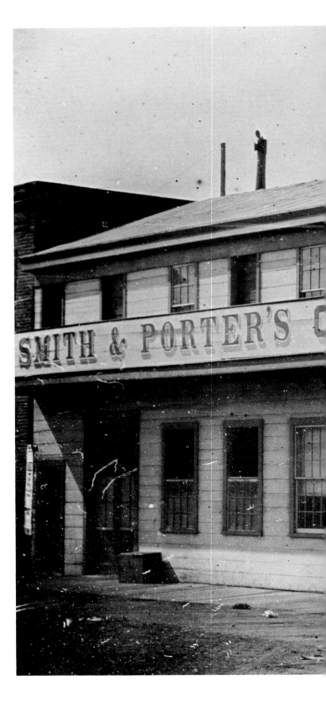

IN THE PACIFIC METROPOLIS. . . . It is not hard to imagine why a daguerreotypist would photograph the new quarters of such a distinguished personage as S. Brannan, but why Smith & Porter's Coffee Saloon? One theory is that the second floor briefly provided the "cheaper rooms" sought by the executive committee of the vigilantes after the hanging work and deportations of the summer of 1851. Certainly such a tenant would have added greatly to the celebrity of what otherwise appears to be an undistinguished restaurant at the corner of Sansome and Sacramento streets. The same date would apply to the Brannan quarters, which would appear to be a post-fire makeshift, even though the building is brand new. Sam may be one of the men in the doorway—they all look mean enough.

EVERYBODY'S GOLD. . . . The view above is probably one of the earliest daguerreotypes made in the placers. It took rich diggings to make a little fortune by such primitive means, but rich diggings there were. Of life in the mines, one goldseeker of 1850 wrote home, *You can scarcely form any conception of what a dirty business this gold digging is. . . . A little fat pork, a cup of tea or coffee, and a slice or two of miserable bread form the repast of the miner; a pair of coarse boots, a hickory shirt, wool hat, pants, and a coat of a peculiar dirt-colored material form his raiment.* At left we have a genuine prospector with equipment and raiment fresh from the hardware and drygoods store. At right are a pair who undoubtedly have "seen the elephant" and admire to give the hometown folks a less conventional glimpse of life in El Dorado.

OLD PROS. . . . Digging gold never was perfected into easy work—with more elaborate means you just moved more dirt and bigger rocks. In the two portraits (left and right), we have young men who have seen all sorts of rare sights and are very deliberately trying to convey just that impression. The portrait artist may have been the miner-turned-daguerreotypist who penned the following doggerel: *There's Golden Lake and Nelson's Creek and diggins dry and wet,/ And dams and claims and ten pound lumps to coax the green 'uns yet;/ There's little hills to mount besides—they're not all dug away!/ The Elephant is yet alive in Californi-a.*

A REAL METROPOLIS OF THE PACIFIC. . . . By 1854, San Francisco was more than that remarkable town whose swift growth had so impressed visitors of the "early days" two or three years before. There really *were* scores of substantial business blocks that would have done credit to thriving eastern cities of the second rank. The abandoned ships of the first rush had long since been refitted or broken up, and well-built piers and warehouses served a flourishing and regular commerce with the whole world. At the time this view was made, the gold rush boom had peaked; prices would break and banks would fail before long. But it was still a brawling gold rush city, where the vigilantes had not yet finished their work.

San Francisco had everything. A genuine silversmith, with plenty of buyers for his wares. A black "mammy" for the Selim Woodworths, as befitting a leading merchant and "Number 1" of the first vigilance committee. Even a Lola Montez to excite the roving eye of Sam Brannan and everybody else—with the exception of the stuffier dramatic critics.

HERE'S LOOKING AT YOU! . . . Faces of all sorts peer back from the mirror-like daguerreotypes of gold rush days. Sometimes you find a face you know. At left is Captain Edgar Wakeman, hero, hangman, humorist, and hijacker. He "stole" the fine riverboat *New World* from the U. S. Marshal in New York and brought it out to the Sacramento River to cash in on the biggest money route in the history of navigation. He put the rope around Jenkins's neck when the vigilantes of 1851 moved at midnight, and he directed the execution of Stuart. He saved a steamer foundering in a gale off the Carolinas. He relaxed in later years and filled Mark Twain's head with tales. Altogether, a man of parts.

OF 1851. . . . "In business and pleasure the San Franciscans were *fast* folk; none were faster in the world. A month with them was considered equal to a year with other people."

One said of the great adventure: *I would not for ten thousand dollars have stayed at Madison and lost what I have seen, and although the trip and my life here is not calculated to polish my manners or improve my morals, still I shall take care not to run down hill too far. . . .*

ALL GOLD RUSH CONNECTIONS TURN COLORFUL. . . . Little Reginaldo del Valle may be unnerved by the daguerreian equippage—or by the prospect of Don Luis del Valle winding up in prison. It seems that in early 1854 the Mexican consul of that name in San Francisco had been mixed up in outfitting one of the frequent, illegal southward-bound filibustering expeditions exported by gold rush California, this time one supporting the legitimate government of Mexico. After much ado, nothing came of it all.

The official membership certificate of the great *Committee of Vigilance, the committee of 1856.*

Chapter IV

THE DICTATORSHIP OF THE BOURGEOISIE

IT HAS FREQUENTLY been observed that complete disregard of civic responsibility (not to mention rather faint standards of personal ethics) was part of the glorious outburst of human energy that peopled the American West and developed its resources, built its cities, and established its commerce. It was indeed. Though it is patently absurd to insist that economic development must be a function of moral turpitude, there is no doubt that careless enthusiasm does get things built up, torn down, dug, filled, bought, sold, traded, and pushed around.

The reckless irresponsibility of the characteristic San Franciscan of the early 1850s brought law and government to ruin, but it seemed to be great for business and building. Land prices, rents, and profits advanced to levels that would have been accounted ridiculous anywhere else in the country, and continued to advance through the end of 1852. In that year, some sixty-seven thousand immigrants landed in San Francisco, and another thirty thousand came overland to California; toward the end of the year, gold production hit perhaps its highest rate. But in 1853 the tide of immigration began to ebb; the export of gold reached its peak but production was imperceptibly on the wane. The momentum of entrepreneurial enterprise released in gold rush San Francisco carried the business of city-building through 1854 and beyond. But commodity prices slipped in 1853; rents and real estate started a downward trend in 1854; gold production was visibly off in 1854—though it was still widely believed that the decline was temporary. Yet it was in these years, from the end of 1852 through 1855, that the city took on a look of permanency. Stone paving appeared in some of the principal streets, as did street lamps (first oil, then gas). Pretentious commercial buildings, hotels, and theaters, built of granite from China or the Sierra Nevada, or of brick faced with stone or stucco, sprang up all over the downtown district. "Fireproof" warehouses lined the streets close to the waterfront. Plank roads led to favorite resorts near Mission Dolores. The comfortable homes of the well-to-do and rich dotted the slopes of Rincon Hill, and an astute promoter had gone so far as to lay out an imitation

"Absolute obedience, absolute secrecy. . . ."

of a fashionable London residential square on the sunny southern slope of the hill, calling it South Park.

The historian J. S. Hittell, in 1878, quite rightly marked 1853 as a turning point in the fortunes of San Francisco: he called the rest of the decade "the Golden Era in Decline." But Hittell had the benefit of hindsight. Such otherwise astute observers as the authors of *The Annals of San Francisco*, writing in the early part of 1854, saw no impending decline. Their description of the state of the citizenry in 1853 expands on the evils of prostitution and divorce, the popularity of dueling, and the wretched prospects of anyone so unfortunate as to lose his health and livelihood. As for the healthy male, with gold in his pocket, it was still the same old San Francisco: "As we have said, during 1853 most of the moral, intellectual, and social characteristics of the inhabitants of San Francisco were nearly as already described in the reviews of previous years. There was still the old reckless energy, the old love of pleasure, the fast making and fast spending of money, the old hard labor and wild delights, jobberies, and official and political corruption, thefts, robberies, and violent assaults, murders, duels, and suicides, gambling, drinking, and general extravagance and dissipation. The material city was immensely improved in magnificence, and its people generally had an unswerving faith in its glorious future. Most of them were removed from social trammels, and all from the salutary checks of a high moral public opinion. They had wealth at command, and all the passions of youth were burning within them. They often, therefore, outraged public decency; yet somehow the oldest residents and the very family men loved the place, with all its brave wickedness and splendid folly. . . . Though there be much vice in San Francisco, one virtue—though perhaps a negative one—the citizens at least have. They are not hypocrites, who pretend to high qualities which they do not possess."

If San Franciscans did not affect the holier-than-thou attitude we identify with hypocrisy, they did pretend to many homely virtues they often did not have. A certain frankness, honesty, and generosity which had characterized at least a large enough part of the population during the early days of the Gold Rush to impress visitors and newcomers (the bag of gold dust left unattended and undisturbed, the complicated business deal consummated by a handshake and a gulp of raw whiskey)—this rugged, virtuous simplicity of spirit passed quickly into contemporary folklore; it became an accepted "fact," unquestioned and untrue. In an age when the *code duello* furnished the occasion for popular Sunday outings, even newspaper editors were apt to be shy about challenging the bluff and assumed virtues of their fellow citizens. Indeed, the knowledgeable authors of San Francisco's *Annals* showed an almost total restraint when it came to specifically identifying prominent persons whose frauds

Aces up and on the ascendency in a town dedicated to the pursuit of the main chance.

A daguerrean panorama of 1853, looking northeast from Nob Hill and showing, left to right, Russian Hill, Telegraph Hill, the business district and the forest of masts in Yerba Buena Cove—by then the greatest port west of New Orleans.

and vices "were well known to everyone." The only important citizen of the period who was publicly convicted as a swindler was, of all people, "Honest Harry" Meiggs, and at that it was only by fleeing the country and confessing his sins that he was exposed.

Harry Meiggs was the first celebrated victim of the business depression that began in 1854. A successful lumber dealer with a wharf and a mill at North Beach, just north of Telegraph Hill, Meiggs early on had convinced himself that expanding commercial and industrial San Francisco must logically come his way, that he should therefore buy as much North Beach property as he could lay hands on, and that large investments in street improvements and the construction of a great wharf would precipitate the inevitable boom. His confidence spurred him to financial outlays far beyond even his own considerable means, but his high reputation for judgment and honesty made it possible for him to borrow large sums, and his general popularity earned him a seat on the board of aldermen. Apparently, however, "Honest Harry" was as badly fooled as his creditors by the ill-secured prosperity of 1853, with the result that he was just one step behind the economic cycle. In the spring of 1854, he found himself caught in a fast-declining real estate market. Paying, say, three or four percent per month—in advance—on his borrowed and invested capital, he had little choice but to scratch up new loans to pay the interest on the old ones. Soon, he was borrowing at ten percent per month, and it is said that he paid interest as high as one percent *per day* on occasion.

Though by all accounts a most impressive man, Harry Meiggs could not have raised the new funds he constantly needed to manage his pyramiding debts solely by a winning smile and a hearty grip. Those who were beginning to question his methods found them out after October 6, 1854, the day Meiggs bundled his family aboard a chartered barque and disappeared over the western horizon. A vast amount of the paper he had offered his usurers as security was worthless—some of it consisting of imaginative forgeries, some of it an immense over-issue of stock in his lumber company, and a dismaying amount of it in a heap of fraudulent "city warrants." The illegal warrants quite rightly aroused the liveliest distress, and Meiggs's success in offering them as collateral exposed glaring vices in the city management. The warrants, paid out in lieu of cash by the supposedly penniless government, were non-interest-bearing notes which creditors were confident would be redeemed in cash or bonds at some indefinite future date. The city paid its contractors perhaps four times the cash value of their services in warrants; the warrants themselves circulated at close to half their par value. In the case of the warrants, as in that of scrip, gold went into the city treasury and paper came out, a device which permitted city officials and their associates limitless opportunities for jobbery, and at the same

time provided the wherewithal for streets and sewers and other desirable civic improvements.

The irresponsible fashion in which the civic authorities issued these warrants became all too clear when Meiggs's dealings were exposed. It appeared that the mayor and controller would sign a few books of blank warrants at a time, so that a clerk might just fill out the notes as needed. Alderman Meiggs, who held many legitimate warrants in connection with his North Beach improvement activities, simply walked off with a full book of signed blanks (which was never missed) and filled them out as he needed, offering them to businessmen and bankers at the usual discount.

Never has the departure of a leading citizen of San Francisco been accompanied by as much general and genuine manifestation of grief as the day after Honest Harry left for Chile. It seemed that the whole public suffered—from public officials to public women. Even Harry's laundress was said to hold some worthless paper. It was claimed that some $800,000 in unredeemable paper had been left in the hands of Meiggs's creditors, and while this figure no doubt included a goodly percentage that quick-witted creditors found it convenient to add to their real losses, there can be no doubt that Meiggs's failure as well as his frauds had an unsettling effect on the business community. Young William T. Sherman, cashier of the San Francisco branch bank of Lucas, Turner & Company, called the whole business "the great Meiggs failure, swindle, forgery and flight forming in all its details a perfect epic of crime . . . by far the most serious disaster that has befallen a community like ours. When confidence in men at best was small, now we suspect everybody for Meiggs was deemed incorruptible." Meiggs's failure was precipitated by the decline in real property values, and this, along with the exposure of the city warrant fraud, cast suspicion not only on men, as Sherman suggested, but on the whole credit structure, and implied that *any* paper based on local values might be questionable.

At the beginning of 1855, the position of the banks in San Francisco was precarious, as the decline in the value of real estate and merchandise, in rents and in profits, made it increasingly difficult to convert substantial assets, however real or great, into ready cash. The biggest and most profitable banks were perhaps in the most precarious position; they were the biggest because they had pursued the most liberal policies. And the biggest of them all, Page, Bacon & Company, was the first to fall. In February of 1855, news reached San Francisco that the parent and associated house in St. Louis was going under. Although the resident partners in San Francisco insisted that the local branch was a separate institution and thus in no danger, they could not stave off a run. When the mighty Page, Bacon & Company had to suspend payments, depositors of other banks thought it might be best to pull out their money and sleep with it under their mattresses for a night or two. William T. Sherman, whose Lucas, Turner operation was one of the few that did not have to suspend payment even temporarily, said that it was at his counter that a Frenchman, half dead in the screaming crush of people, gasped, "If you got the money, I no want him; but if you no got him, I want it like the devil!"

The failure of Page, Bacon was immediately followed by the collapse of Adams & Company, the proprietors of the huge express and banking business that Wells Fargo later fell heir to, and certainly the largest business institution in the state. The blow of this failure, which injured thousands of citizens, was compounded by suspicions of deliberate fraud, for Adams & Company closed its doors long before it had paid out its available reserves of cash and gold. The assets of the company were turned over to a receiver selected by the partners,

James King of William, in this somewhat stilted version of the affair that appeared in Frank Leslie's Illustrated Magazine, *awaits the arrival of James P. Casey's bullet before staggering over to the express office.*

and wound up in the hands of Palmer, Cook & Company, a banking house involved in various irregular dealings with the state treasury, and which (there was reason to believe) had been wont to exchange favors with the ubiquitous political boss, David C. Broderick.

THE BANK PANIC and general business depression of 1855 were more than mere incidents in the economic history of San Francisco, for they caused a large part of the citizenry to reappraise its true conditions and long-term interests—with results that were dramatic in the extreme. So long as speculation was the chief business of the merchant class, so long as a seemingly permanent boom endorsed any man's greediest fantasies, the private citizen had good reason to leave public affairs to those who chose to speculate in that business. Where "everyone" is getting rich, municipal corruption often is an object of a kind of rueful civic pride. Such was the general attitude of the citizens of San Francisco until the bubble burst in 1855. Then, suddenly, the unmerited affluence of fraudulently elected officials became an affront increasingly hard to put up with.

The case of one prominent person—admittedly an extreme case, a case that in its untimely conclusion led directly to armed revolution in San Francisco—illustrates the connection between financial disaster and civic reform. James King of William had been one of the first bankers in San Francisco, among the first in importance and reputation as well as in point of time. Financially embarrassed (i.e., potentially bankrupt) as the result of unsuccessful land deals in the interior of the state, he had retired from proprietorship of his own bank in 1854, taking his accounts, good will, good name, and liabilities to Adams & Company, where he was installed as cashier (roughly equivalent to manager). The failure of Adams & Company in 1855 thus robbed King of his new income and prospects, while leaving him with some of the insider's knowledge of the dubious maneuverings that had brought him, probably through no fault of his own, to such a low estate. As energetic as he was vindictive, he scraped up the capital to start a newspaper, the *Daily Evening Bulletin*, and proceeded to assault the obscure but nonetheless real alliance in corruption that extended from Palmer, Cook through the lowliest ballot-box-stuffer in the volunteer fire department.

King's *Evening Bulletin* was an immediate success. The unrestrained editorial attacks by the knowledgeable, respected, and bitter young publisher at once fed and followed the growing popular discontent with the prevailing system. If his charges were often vague, or did not admit of proof, that was the approved journalistic style of the day; if his life were threatened, that was the approved *anti*-journalistic style, and he could carry a gun (and did). Inevitably, he was shot; and at last the fates conspired to see that James King of William's final tribulation was not overlooked.

James P. Casey, editor of the obscure *Sunday Times*, foreman of the Crescent Engine Company #10, an inspector of elections who had recently turned up winner of the board of supervisor's seat for his ward (when no one had known he was even running), was the man who shot King. The afternoon *Bulletin* of Tuesday, May 14, 1856, had published the fairly well-known truth that Casey had served a term at Sing Sing before repairing to San Francisco. A couple of hours later, when King left his office in Merchant Street, Casey, who we assume was less enraged by the Sing Sing article than by King's incessant harassment of current political institutions, stepped out of that favorite

*William Tell Coleman, who
demanded nothing less than
"absolute obedience, absolute
secrecy" before taking over the
reins and ropes of the second
Committee of Vigilance.*

watering-place in the Montgomery Block, the Bank Exchange, called to his enemy, and, when King turned, dropped him at fifteen paces with a ball from a Navy Colt. King staggered into the express office at the corner of Montgomery and Washington and collapsed to the floor. Casey hastened to the protective jail-house, while those of his partisans who were witness to the event recounted that Casey had called to King, "Draw and defend youself!" before he shot down his armed opponent. Such niceties of detail, so they thought, would be of great moment in the distant day of Casey's fair and formal trial before a body of his peers. But Casey had shot the Archduke, and the details now at issue had nothing to do with courts and cops and cross-examination.

The first detail to be decided was whether or not Casey was to be hanged by the mob that night. If good, simple-minded Sam Brannan had been in town to harangue the populace—Sam who as recently as the previous November had been arrested and restrained for imploring the people to promptly hang the gambler Charles Cora (killer of U.S. Marshal Richardson and a crony of sundry politicos)—there might have been vengeance before dawn, and an end of it. But Sam was out of town, and the man whose sleeve was finally plucked by those who sought action was Brannan's cold-blooded rival in extra-legal citizenship, William Tell Coleman. It will be recalled that Coleman was the instigator of the popular tribunal of February 1851, that formal but still illegal court that fortunately failed to convict the false Stuart. Coleman had come to the fore in Brannan's vigilance committee after the initial excitement; and when the "committee of the whole" adjourned, his more patient determination was among the qualities that had placed him in the "Committee of Thirteen" that had continued—though informally—the purely vigilant function of the organization.

When, during the excursions and alarums of the evening following King's shooting, Coleman was first asked by various of the aroused citizens to take charge of a popular movement, to personally lead a reconstructed vigilance, he approved the idea, but declined the leadership. Being pressed again, as groups met in several places to agitate for the reorganization, he agreed to issue the call, as one of the Committee of Thirteen. The subsequent notice to the members of the old vigilance committee to meet the evening of May 15, 1856, appeared in the morning newspapers. When they met, and Coleman was for the third time offered the crown, his reply was ready: "On two conditions I will accept the responsibility: absolute obedience, absolute secrecy." The acceptability of the conditions being agreed, an organization quite different from the vigilance committee of 1851 sprang into being—and in so few minutes that one might imagine that William T. Coleman had spent more than a little time daydreaming about the ideal structure of vigilance.

The vigilance committee of 1856—the *great* vigilance committee—was very much an extension of the personality of William T. Coleman. It was his to a vastly greater extent than the committee of 1851 had been Brannan's. In 1851 Brannan happened to be at the center of the organization. (Even then, Coleman could have been the first leader.) The nature of the first committee, its institutional personality, was more akin to Brannan's behavior than to Coleman's; it was an organization of conflicting interests, of blunt confrontations (in one of which Sam was worsted and retired, temporarily, in a grand huff), an organization of the sort that could lend itself to the plot of a classic western epic. In 1856, Coleman built an organization that represented the distilled experience of an intelligent and single-minded revolutionary.

Revolutionary? Yes: for what else is armed seizure of power? An accident of circumstance? This was the man who on February 22, 1851, talked to his fellows in the street, observed the mob about the city hall clamoring for "Stuart's" neck, went home to change from his Sunday best to his daily wear (don't scuff the velvet in a common riot), and returned to push his way through the multitude, mount the balcony in the face of a dozen shrieking demagogues, and outline the details by which the popular will was to be done—and *was* done. It had been a blow to Coleman that the administrative goals of his popular tribunal were not achieved; also a stroke of luck, as it turned out, that an innocent man was not solemnly hanged; a lesson in ends and means, finally, that his dramatic seizure of power that day had ultimately been limited to a goal so trifling as the potential execution of a single misidentified scoundrel.

Not again. A committee of two hundred was Brannan's style: say your piece and vote your choice; hear me out and hang him if you've guts enough! Old style, true style; right is right and *damnation*! Brannan's style, not Coleman's. Brannan reacted, Coleman organized, and "Dictatorship of the Bourgeoisie" is perhaps the most appropriate definition of the constitution that Coleman handed down to his colleagues on the night of May 15, 1856. To form the initial executive committee, Coleman chose five trustworthy associates, and these chose some others, with his approval. All power was in the hands of the executive committee, including the power to accept or reject applicants for general membership and to cast out any member who did not behave himself. The general membership was formed into military companies, and while the rank and file had no control over the organization, there was provision for some participation in that the executive committee would submit decisions for which it did not want to be solely responsible (such as a sentence of death) to a board of delegates for ratification.

The practiced Coleman thus produced an organization that was nearly perfect, after its fashion. Any discussion or controversy as to proposed action was held in the secrecy of the executive committee room; any decision was unanimous and final; any action was implemented instantly by an armed force sworn to obey. Dissension was thereby eliminated, and opponents of the committee were confronted not by a body of ordinary men, with their disparate personal interests, their various private weaknesses, and their individual emotions or sympathies, but by a terrible machine—or so it seemed to those who tried to buck it.

William T. Coleman and his like-minded associates had not created this formidable and frightening organization merely to hang Casey, though this notion was current at the time and persisted through many subsequent accounts and recollections. That this was not the basic purpose of the committee was officially demonstrated on Friday, May 16, when Governor J. Neely Johnson and banker William T. Sherman, now also general of the almost nonexistent state militia (a curious foreshadowing of his distinguished Civil War record), called on the committee and attempted to persuade Coleman to desist in his preparations in exchange for the promise of a swift and impartial trial of Casey. These "Law and Order" men seem to have heard in some polite evasions what they hoped to hear, but Coleman went right ahead nevertheless, in a few days gathering a force powerful enough to overawe any possible combination that could have been brought against it within the space of months. By Saturday, May 17, the committee had *five thousand* citizens organized into companies and was busy fortifying its headquarters on Portsmouth Square with cannons and sacks full of sand—giving it the name of "Fort Gunnybags." Against the size, speed, single-mindedness, and sheer effi-

The offices of the ancestral Call, *one of the few gold rush newspapers to survive into the twentieth century.*

Daguerreotypist as advertising genius. This newspaper bill of 1856 is less startling when one reads the finer print: "Mr. Shew is prepared to take either 'Improved' or 'Patent Ambrotypes' of BABIES or children of any age, no matter how restless or frolicsome, or cross and contrary; no matter how many attempts have been MADE by other artists without success, only come to Shew's Daguerrean Gallery between the hours of nine, a.m., and two, p.m., and you can get good pictures FOR THREE DOLLARS warranted equal to any that can be obtained at other establishments at any price."

ciency of Coleman's operation, the opposition of the Law and Order people, including the state government, stood baffled and disorganized, and never recovered. Even William T. Sherman, later to distinguish himself as one of history's most masterful quellers of civil disturbance, gave up in disgust; after two fruitless weeks of trying to secure federal assistance for his militia from Admiral Farragut at Mare Island and arms from General Wool at Benicia Arsenal, he resigned from his state commission. The probable fate of less formal opponents had been demonstrated within a day of the committee's organization. The *Herald*, alone among the daily newspapers, made the error of editorializing against a revival of vigilance. The merchants of the committee forthwith merely suggested that all merchants might do well to advertise elsewhere—and the *Herald*, the wealthiest and most respected journal in town, was ruined. The committee, from its inception, acquired both muscle and the freedom to exercise it.

And so it did, with dispatch. On Sunday, May 18, two thousand vigilance infantry marched silently to the county jail, placed cannons opposite the entrance, and demanded the surrender of Casey. Sheriff Scannel (who, it was popularly believed, had paid $100,000 for his post) looked over the assorted street-brawlers that made up his command, sighed, wept a bit, and gave up his fellow volunteer fireman to all-too-certain justice. While they were at it, the vigilantes took Charles Cora, the still-unconvicted murderer of Marshal Richardson. The only hope left the civil authorities (as well as Casey and Cora) was that James King of William, still lingering near death, might survive. That was a slim hope indeed, for although his wound was not of a necessarily fatal variety, he had a score of the city's best physicians attending him—a circumstance which, given the state of the medical arts, was, as H. H. Bancroft put it, "surely enough to kill any man though he had not first been shot." King did die, on Tuesday, May 20. Casey and Cora got a prompt and secret trial, and on Thursday, May 22, as the funeral cortège of the martyred editor wound toward the cemetery at Lone Mountain, the ballot-box-stuffer and the gambler were hanged outside Fort Gunnybags.

THE SHOWMANSHIP with which the seizure and execution of Casey and Cora was conducted was of more importance to the guiding spirits of the vigilance committee than was the disposal of two killers. No one could have known better than Coleman that hanging a couple of thugs and perhaps running some others out of the country was not going to clean out a system of entrenched political corruption to which acts of violence were inevitably, but only casually, associated. It was important that Casey was a political crook; it was important that Cora was a gambler with political connections; above all, it was important that the committee make its awesome show of power, and to show this power (as it did) in a manner so measured and restrained as to suggest that vigilance had hardly flexed its muscle.

It is entirely probable that Coleman realized from the first that the deep-rooted corruption of San Francisco politics was more a function of popular psychology than of individual depravity. In this sense, exposure of the evils under which the community labored was more important than the summary punishment of ballot-box-stuffers. The committee had both the staff to investigate and the might to punish those who fell afoul of its investigations. Operating as both grand jury and criminal court, its pronouncements and actions were undiluted by the piecemeal pace and attendant arguments of the usual legal process. As the committee had unlimited jurisdiction and powers, when it spoke, the populace listened and learned. This, and not mere vengeance, was its purpose and its function.

The major portion of the "work" of the vigilance committee—the pursuit, arrest, interrogation, trial, and deportation of a score of the most notorious political scoundrels, the "encouraged" departure of as many as a hundred more, and the thorough revelation to the public of the details of political corruption and skulduggery—took about a month. Later historians have suggested that the committee might logically have adjourned at about this time, since it had accomplished a good deal more than even the committee of 1851. Such would not have been likely, for this committee was not merely dedicated to the temporary eradication of malefactors; it was out to change the very system under which they had been allowed to operate. With this determination in mind, its massive military organization, though it theoretically might be adjourned *sine die* (as had the committee of 1851), had to be maintained so long as there was the slightest possibility that the deported criminals (and those who had fled on their own account) might flaunt the authority of an unarmed vigilance by returning to the city immediately and going back to their old ways. Moreover, it could not abdicate the power it had seized so long as there was even a hint of organized opposition—even that of the confused and nearly helpless "Law and Order" organization—for any such show of weakness would have diluted the fear it had struck in the hearts and minds of those city officials not actually run out of town, and would thus defeat its purposes.

Exactly how long the committee might have chosen to remain in control of the city was rendered a matter of conjecture during the last week in June, when it acquired a prisoner it could neither convict nor release. This was David S. Terry, formerly of Texas, one of that class of roving Southern politicos who had found in California opportunities that had been denied them at the crowded statehouses, customhouses, and other public hog-troughs of their native states. Terry, associate justice of the Supreme Court of the State of California, was one of those to whom the organization, the objectives, and the very composition of the vigilance committee were anathema. (In the presence of Sherman, Terry once put his feet up on a stool, leaned back grandly, and denounced the vigilantes as a bunch of "damned pork merchants.") Surrounded by advisors such as Terry, Governor Johnson led the Law and Order party to an unrealistic stand against vigilance. Abandoned by supporters such as Sherman, the Law and Order people had been left free to indulge themselves in feeble raging and inconsequential counterrevolutionary plots. The culmination of one of these pointless conspiracies resulted in an altercation between Judge Terry and a vigilance patrol. A shot was fired, probably accidentally and certainly harmlessly, but the fearless Terry, no doubt believing his time had come, was determined to take at least one of the scoundrels with him. Drawing his favorite Bowie knife from his vest, he spitted Vigilance Officer S. A. Hopkins through the neck.

Associate Justice Terry's moment of truth, June 21, 1856.

So, on the evening of June 21, 1856, the committee found itself with a prisoner that it could punish only at deadly peril to itself. It had been the committee's strategy to assault criminal politics by sweeping out from under the machine the lowliest and dirtiest mechanics, to expose the nature of the mechanism, and to frighten the leaders and office-holders into at least temporary honesty. It hedged against any possible reaction to its own "lawlessness" by avoiding direct action against any but the most obvious felons. Now, however, it had no simple-minded crimp or arm-twister on its hands, but a justice

J. M. Hutchings, a transplanted Englishman, not only gave us the classic "Miner's Ten Commandments" and Hutchings California Magazine, *but provided Charles Nahl with a medium through which the artist could express himself and illuminate his times. One of Nahl's efforts was a series called "California Types." Above is "The Englishman," and we may safely assume it is not a version of Hutchings himself; the surly wretch on the opposite page was called "The Hybrid."*

of the Supreme Court of the State of California, who might reasonably say that he had only defended himself against a gang of thugs, a representative of the highest system of law in the state who had done no more than defy a manifestly illegal body. Yet for the committee to meekly release Terry would be to display precisely that weakness in its structure which it could not afford to show. An awesome front of power, purpose, and integrity was essential to its effectiveness.

In this spectacular dilemma, the vigilantes followed a course both bold and cool: they instantly seized every cache of arms known to belong to the Law and Order forces in San Francisco, and quietly held Judge Terry pending the recovery or death of the wounded Officer Hopkins. To be sure, Terry was brought to trial promptly, for it was a part of vigilante law that any assault upon one of its officers was a grave and serious offense; but the trial was spun out over a month. By the time the final judgment was rendered, two more murderers had been hanged, and nearly every sign of resistance to the committee had been stamped out. By then, too, Hopkins had recovered, and Coleman apparently decided that vigilance might safely adjourn. Terry was convicted by the executive committee, and after a week of wrangling with the board of delegates (which was all for vengeance, and if possible, blood) was simply released. Both the release of Terry and the decision for adjournment suggest that the one force that the committee might fear—federal intervention—loomed as an increasingly likely possibility.

The committee went out with as much showmanship as it had come in. On August 18 its four regiments of infantry, two squadrons of cavalry, its battalion of artillery, battalion of riflemen, battalion of pistolmen, and battalion of police paraded before the citizenry of San Francisco. The military organization then disbanded, although the executive committee remained in indefinite session, holding meetings until November of 1859.

THE ORGANIZATION and conduct of the vigilance committee of 1856 stamped it as one of the most remarkable *ad hoc* popular institutions the United States has ever seen; certainly, no other organ of popular justice ever conducted its affairs with such impressive probity and ended its efforts amid such general applause. If some observers (for the most part in places far removed from San Francisco) condemned the theory under which the committee operated, deploring the very notion of the citizenry taking the law into its own hands, there was almost no respectable or informed opinion at the time which could find serious fault in the actual *deeds* of the committee. But far more remarkable than the conduct of the committee of 1856 was the successful achievement of its long-range goal. For ten years after the committee's adjournment San Francisco was known as one of the best-governed cities in the United States.

The astonishing feat of "permanently" cleaning up San Francisco politics was accomplished by a joint effort of the committee and a group of prominent citizens who had supported, but not joined, the committee. Though the vigilantes publicly denied any intention to meddle in politics, it would appear that there was a very close relationship between the end of the committee and the appearance of a political party agreeable to the goals of vigilance: on August 8, the executive committee had privately decided to adjourn the military organization soon; on August 11, a mass meeting of citizens organized what was later known as the "People's Party"; on August 13, the vigilance board of delegates was notified by the executive committee of the decision to disband. What is more, the People's Party, which controlled San Francisco politics until after the end of the Civil War, was organized along lines every bit as peculiar (one might say un-American) as the vigilance committee itself. At the public meeting of August 11, twenty-one citizens were appointed to a nominating committee, and this nominating committee held permanent and almost absolute power in the party. The nominating committee perpetuated itself by appointing its successors before each election. It worked up its slate of candidates for each election in secret, choosing nominees from both the regular parties and among independents. It submitted its ticket without discussion to a popular meeting, which had the limited option of accepting or rejecting the whole slate of candidates. It is difficult to believe that this somewhat autocratic political organization was not the product of the calculating imagination of William T. Coleman.

The new city administration, elected in the fall of 1856, immediately introduced reforms most pleasing to the "pork-merchant" mentality. The cost of operating the entire city government in 1856–57 was only thirty percent more than the cost of supporting the volunteer fire department *alone* in 1854–55. Funds for street improvements, heretofore a lucrative source of civic jobbery, were doled out at the rate of about one dollar for every $1,000 that had been squandered two years before. Even the school budget was satisfactorily pruned. Taxes were reduced. City officials, released from the time-consuming demands of imaginative corruption, were so attentive to public affairs that not so many were required. The police force, now headed by the former chief of the vigilante police, made the streets for the first time really safe for the nocturnal wayfarer—even though these streets were no longer lighted by the merry glow from dance halls and gambling palaces, or by street lamps, for that matter. For, in the words of H. H. Bancroft, "The gas company ran up enormous bills against the city, and, as usual in such cases, protested they could take no less. Thereupon, the new officials turned off the gas, and each supervisor, judge, or other public night-worker brought his tallow-dip, whose dim but honest flicker argued a brighter, purer light than any hitherto flashed by brazen iniquity."

Thus flickered the dawn of a new era.

Between April 20 and August 9, 1858, more than 23,000 semi-hysterical goldseekers deserted San Francisco for the gold placers of the Fraser River in British Columbia. Those who were able returned in a matter of weeks, no richer than they had been when they left; only a few could have served as the inspiration for the storekeeper who displayed a human skeleton in his shop window labeled "A Returned Frazer River Miner."

Chapter V

THIRTY DAYS FROM WALL STREET

NOTES ON THE LAST spring of a decade: By May of 1859, thirty-two-year-old William Chapman Ralston, cashier in the banking firm of Fretz & Ralston with offices on the southwest corner of Clay and Montgomery streets, had already made his name in a career that had been as successful as it had been complex. At sixteen, after a childhood spent on a farm on the banks of the Ohio River, he had become a shipping and passenger clerk on the great packets that steamed down the Ohio and Mississippi rivers from Cincinnati to New Orleans. At twenty-three, he abandoned a position as chief clerk of the steamer *Convoy* and set off for California via the Isthmus of Panama in 1849; he got as far as Panama City, where he went to work for two old friends, Cornelius Kingsland Garrison and Ralph Stover Fretz, former riverboat pilots who were then operating a banking and shipping trade. At twenty-five, he captained the 1,100-ton steamer *New Orleans* from Panama City to San Francisco, and for the next three years made steady runs between those two cities and New York as general agent for the Independent Opposition Line (later the Nicaragua Transit Company), a venture organized by Cornelius Vanderbilt to undercut the virtual monopoly of the Pacific Mail Line. At twenty-eight, he settled permanently in San Francisco as the line's representative, and at twenty-nine oversaw the organization of the banking firm of Garrison, Morgan, Fretz & Ralston, later reorganized as Fretz & Ralston. And now in 1859, with his remaining partner old, ailing, and more than willing to let him run the bank, Ralston's position seemed as solid as any man's could in the curious world of San Francisco finance. Hard work, a brilliant attention to detail, and a usefully fertile imagination had brought him far, and tomorrow glittered with possibilities.

Adolph Heinrich Joseph Sutro, twenty-nine years old in the spring of 1859, had his own possibilities—though not so immediate nor so sure as those of Ralston. He had just returned to his tobacconist's shop on Montgomery Street (one of three in which he had an interest) from the Fraser River of

> **"Everyone will have a chance for a gold ring or a broken leg."**

William C. Ralston at the height of his power in 1873.

Adolph Sutro in the comfort of his San Francisco study, perhaps 1885.

British Columbia, where, in the summer of 1858, he had joined twenty-three thousand other Californians in a scramble after gold, an abortive little rush that for a time had enlivened a San Francisco still suffering the effects of the panic of '55. ("The Coroner of this city," a San Francisco reporter had written in 1858, "complains that the new diggings have put an end to the suicides.")

For Sutro, as for most of the goldseekers, the Fraser River adventure had been one more entry in the old story of too many people after too little gold. Not that it was going to get him down. Little ever had; little ever would. Born in Prussia in 1830, he fled a Europe gone mad with turmoil and undirected revolution in 1850—but not before he had displayed a remarkable instinct for the intricacies of machinery, had built and operated a textile plant, and had gained such proficiency on the piano that Felix Mendelssohn had recommended him for the music conservatory in Brussels. The young Sutro landed in New York in the fall of 1850 and immediately was stricken with the California fever. Gathering a few bolts of German cloth and a trunkful of notions, he booked passage via Panama in October on the steamer *Cherokee* (among whose passengers were John C. Frémont and family). He arrived in San Francisco in November, sold out his little stock of goods, became a commission salesman, founded a small clothing store in Stockton, returned to San Francisco, ran a store on Long Wharf, another on Clay Street, a third on Sacramento, and finally settled down to the operation of the three tobacconist shops. By 1859, he had established a solid, if by no means spectacular, reputation as a tradesman. But his genius for machinery lay as yet untapped, and his eye for the main chance never lost its gleam.

Henry George, who was not yet twenty in the spring of 1859, had so recently arrived in San Francisco, and with so few resources, as to have almost no visible prospects at all. However, as he noted in a self-inflicted phrenological analysis shortly before his arrival in the summer of 1858, his bump of hope was of "generous proportions." Doubtless, it was that bump that led him, like Sutro, to the goldfields of the Fraser River that summer, from which he returned quite as empty-handed but with his swelling anticipation undiminished. He had some reason for confidence, for he had been making his way in the world since his early teens. After five months of high school in Philadelphia, he had left to become an apprentice seaman on the East-Indiaman *Hindoo*. After this, he became a typesetter in a print shop, then a steward on the lighthouse steamer *Shubrick*, and now a typesetter in a small printing plant in San Francisco. Between shifts, he stayed at the What Cheer House, a temperance hotel for men; its small library included a battered copy of Adam Smith's *Wealth of Nations*. Tough-minded and inquisitive, for all his lack of formal schooling, George was fascinated by the book, and when not seeking extra work or looking for an outlet for the energies expressed by his "larger than normal" bump of amativeness, he bored through the maze of Smith's economic theorizing.

This disparate trio, similar mainly in their lack of formal schooling and in the strength of their hopes for themselves, stood at the bridge between an era whose awesome energies were swiftly guttering out and one whose own peculiar energies would shape their lives and the life of the city. Two of them, Ralston and Sutro, would in large degree share in the making of the new era. George, the seaman-printer, would struggle desperately through most of its first ten years and emerge as the only one of the three to clearly understand how profoundly the new era had crippled the hopes of all those who had found in San Francisco a mirror of the dream.

IN THAT SAME SPRING of 1859, on a sere desert ridge in Utah Territory—present-day Nevada—one hundred eighty miles from San Francisco, a reasonably grubby collection of placer miners was blindly scuffing the new era into existence. "Old Californians," they liked to call themselves, part of that scattered and obsessed contingent of frustrated refugees from the disappointments of the Gold Rush who, over the next twenty years, would open up nearly every major mining camp in the intermontaine West. These particular men, according to one who remembered them from the time, were unlikely architects for destiny: "Of the miners, these I particularly remember: Henry P. Comstock, an industrious visionary prospector, though little more than half-witted. James Finney, 'Old Virginia,' frontier hunter and miner, a man of more than ordinary ability in his class, a buffoon and practical joker, a hard drinker when he could get the liquor, and an indifferent worker at anything. Peter Riley, half-witted and half-cracked, lazy and stupid. Joseph Kirby, sober and honest, but indolent. Wm. Sides, who . . . afterward stabbed to death one John Jessup. . . . John Berry, 'Uncle Jack Berry,' a great lover of the 'ardent.' Captain Chapman, who was with the troops at Santa Fe during the Mexican War, a large man deficient in courage and in much that goes to make up a man. 'Dutch Baker,' no other name known, a hard drinker and of little force. Wm. Williams, 'Cherokee Bill,' a dangerous man without one spark of honesty or real manhood." Such are the materials of history.

Since 1851, these men and a few dozen like them had been scratching at thin traces of color in Gold Canyon, a cleft that cut far up the southern side of Sun Mountain north of the Carson River. By the spring of 1859, several of them had staked out claims near the head of the canyon, on a ridge that bordered the southern end of a shallow, narrow valley. At about the same time, another group, having abandoned Gold Canyon, had reached the head of Six-Mile Canyon on the northern ridge of the valley. Within days of each other, the two groups found gold outcroppings so rich that they glittered with the stuff, and soon Gold Hill and the Ophir Diggings, as the two sites were respectively named, were crawling with miners. The only difficulty these "autochthons of the placer-camp age," as historian Charles H. Shinn called them, found in working the new diggings was the heavy, dark, almost claylike soil in which the gold was found. This "damned blue stuff" clogged their mining equipment and was altogether troublesome. They cursed it enthusiastically.

Henry George just before he departed San Francisco in 1880, never to return.

In the last week of June, two interested observers, a Truckee River Meadows rancher by the name of B.A. Harrison and a local trader, J. F. Stone, followed up a hunch and sent two sacks of the miners' throwaway dirt across the mountains for analysis by J. J. Ott in Nevada City and by Melville Atwood in Grass Valley. Both assays showed the "damned blue stuff" to be tremendously rich in silver as well as gold—Atwood later claimed that his sample revealed a value per ton of $3,000 in silver and $876 in gold. A handful of people were in on the assays in Nevada City and Grass Valley, and before the end of the month several had sped across the mountains and offered fistfuls of money to the astonished and delighted discoverers of what would become known as the Comstock Lode. All of them sold out their claims in a matter of weeks. Among the buyers was George Hearst, a California mine developer and speculator, who promptly dug some thirty-eight tons of ore out of his new Ophir holdings, packed it on mules, and hauled it over the mountains that winter for smelting in San Francisco. The net profit on the venture was $91,000.

Even in a city accustomed to thinking in terms of millions, that was an impressive figure, and by the spring of 1860 the news of silver whistled through San Francisco, "borne on the wings of the wind from the Sierra Nevada," J. Ross Browne wrote, "wafted through every street, lane, and alley . . . whirling around the drinking saloons, eddying over the counters of the banking offices, scattering up the dust among the Front Street merchants, arousing the slumbering inmates of the Custom-House. . . ." Thousands of listeners, infected by the disappointments of the rush to Gold Bluff in 1851, the rush to southern Oregon in the same year, the rush to New South Wales, Australia, in 1852, the rush to the Kern River in 1855, and the rush to the Fraser River in 1858, firmly steeled themselves against hope. Another ten thousand succumbed with enthusiasm, packing up their picks, pans, and shovels, all the paraphernalia of the long-gone placer-camp age, and footing it across the summer mountains to the "Washoe Diggings," as they nicknamed the place. There, they threw away their picks and pans and shovels, for this was no treasure to be scooped out of the ground, but a highly complex ore that had to be blasted out of the earth, crushed, and subjected to the spectral workings of chemistry before it could be realized. All this required men, machinery, and money, items which the Everyman of this new excitement had in short supply. So they built a shack-and-shanty-town, christened it Virginia City, and proceeded to stake claims, hundreds of claims, thousands of claims (before the final demise of the Comstock Lode, there would be seventeen thousand of them). "Nobody had any money," wrote J. Ross Browne, "yet everybody was a millionaire in silver claims. Nobody had any credit, yet everybody bought thousands of feet of glittering ore. . . . All was silver underground, and deeds and mortgages on top; silver, silver everywhere, but scarce a dollar in coin."

Among those who did have money—not much, but enough—was Adoph Sutro, who had joined that summer rush to see what he could see. He indulged the speculator's itch long enough to take a flyer on a small quitclaim deed, but for the most part simply looked around and considered the possibilities. On his return to California, the seed of an idea had been planted, as he noted in a report to the *Daily Alta*: "The mine-working is done without any system as yet. Most of the companies commence without an eye to future success; instead of running a tunnel low down on the bed, and thus sinking a shaft to meet it, which at once insures drainage, ventilation, and facilitates the work, by going upwards, the claims are mostly entered from above, large openings made which require considerable timbering, and which expose the mine to wind and weather." Other things were on his mind as well, including the development of an improved reduction process for working the ores of the Comstock. By the

From the Golden Gate to Mission Dolores. Done from the vantage point of Russian Hill, this remarkably intricate woodcut panorama of 1863 faithfully rendered the myriad details of the "commercial emporium of the Pacific." For reference, Telegraph Hill and Yerba Buena (Goat) Island appear at the center.

summer of 1861, Sutro and a young chemist by the name of John Randohr had devised the Randohr-Sutro process, an uncommonly sophisticated method that was especially successful in working the refuse, or tailings, left over from less refined methods. Sutro then returned to the Comstock, bought a mill site in the town of Dayton at the foot of Gold Canyon, and by 1863 had an establishment of eight stamps, twenty amalgamating pans, and two furnaces, which brought him a monthly profit of nearly $10,000. The mill burned to the ground at the end of that same year, but by then Sutro was thoroughly entranced by the vision of an enterprise that would indeed ensure the drainage, improve the ventilation, and facilitate the work of the Comstock mines—and, not incidentally, give its proprietor thousands of dollars a day in royalties: the Tunnel, the Sutro Tunnel.

The death of David C. Broderick at the hands of the mercurial David S. Terry in 1859 was legitimate news, but we wonder if the story wasn't just a bit heavy to be included in the casual pages of the short-lived Illustrated Varieties *of September 18.*

T HE LARGENESS of Sutro's vision matched the style of a city that danced to the tune of silver, a tune whose rattling chorus all but obliterated the sounds of Civil War rumbling on the other side of the continent. While San Francisco contributed its share of the sixteen thousand men drafted or who enlisted in California (most of whom served out their time in various western garrisons) and more than its share of contributions (more than one-fourth of the total) to the Sanitary Commission (the "Red Cross of the Civil War"), the city's general attitude mirrored that expressed by California Governor John B. Weller, when in 1860 he predicted that California would not "go with the South or the North, but here on the shores of the Pacific . . . found a mighty republic which may in the end prove the greatest of all." An actual movement for the establishment of a Pacific Republic, largely a matter of perfervid newspaper editorials, had sputtered and died soon enough, but its spirit was acquiring a kind of reality. After all, even with the remarkable speed of the overland stages and the steamship lines, San Francisco remained thirty days removed from Wall Street, an isolation as psychological as it was physical. In that isolation, San Franciscans proceeded on the assumption that they had risen above the sordid concerns of the American East, much as Americans as a whole had risen above the ancient travails of degenerate old Europe. Out here on a spit of land at the edge of the continent—indeed, at the very end of the only world any of them considered worth thinking about—San Franciscans went about the business of creating a citadel of power. San Francisco money spread out over the West like ripples in a pond, financing timber interests in the Northwest, agricultural ventures in the Great Valley, land speculations in

Southern California, and mining enterprises scattered in a great fan from southern Idaho through Montana, Colorado, Utah, Nevada, New Mexico, and Arizona.

About the only enterprise of major significance that did not receive the balm of San Francisco money in these years was that of a cabal of four Sacramento storekeepers: Collis P. Huntington, Leland Stanford, Charles Crocker, and Mark Hopkins. This group, which David Terry would doubtless have characterized as a bunch of "pork merchants," had in 1861 bought in on the dream of a San Francisco engineer by the name of Theodore Judah and had organized themselves into the Central Pacific Railroad of California. The dream was nothing less than a transcontinental railroad, and by dint of Judah's studious lobbying, it was given the imprimatur of Congress with the passage of the Pacific Railroad Act in 1862, a stupendous subsidy program involving huge land grants and federal loans in the form of 6-percent thirty-year bonds. Seed money to begin construction was still necessary, but when the group approached the San Francisco money men their petition was rejected coldly and their attempts to gain any California financing at all were steadfastly thwarted. At the heart of the rejection were those interests already enjoying a fat monopoly of transportation in the state, all of them headquartered in San Francisco —the Pacific Mail Steamship Company, the California Steam Navigation Company, Wells, Fargo & Company, the California Stage Company, and the Sacramento Valley Railroad Company. These firms regarded the plans of the Central Pacific without enthusiasm, and it would have taken a foolhardy banker indeed to challenge their interests. Undeterred, the railroad group found enough financing in the East to begin construction in January 1863, and stubbornly the roadbed began to creep up the foothills of the Sierra Nevada from Sacramento.

If the Central Pacific's refusal to lie down and die troubled the city's kingpins, it did not show. They were too busy raking in the treasures from the Comstock Lode. Between 1860 and the end of 1864, that storehouse had produced nearly $38 million in ore. It had also produced a condition which up to that time had been a minor and very intermittent part of the city's life: rampant stock speculation. For if the search for California gold had been a chase after the metal itself—the very *stuff* of treasure—the Comstock excitement was in large part a chase after paper. If California gold had been something any determined man could dig right out of the ground, Comstock silver was something any man (or woman) with $20, $50, or $100 in cash could share in. One did not even have to sweat in the process. And there were those more than willing to handle the messy details of paper-exchanging. In 1862, the San Francisco Stock and Exchange Board was organized with forty members (and inevitably dubbed the "Den of the Forty Thieves"), and was soon joined by two others, the San Francisco Board of Brokers and the Pacific Board of Brokers. Every day, paper representing thousands of "feet" of Comstock claims and the hopes of widows, merchants, clerks, and former miners passed from hand to hand and the halls of Montgomery Street rang with magical names: Ophir, Yellow Jacket, Crown Point, Chollar-Potosi, Savage. . . . Even in this first phase of the mania, lives were ruined quite as frequently as they were made— probably more frequently—but for every story of miserable failure there was one of stupendous success. Why, one month a struggling corner grocer had accepted a handful of Ophir stock in payment for a long-overdue bill; the next month he found himself driving around in as handsome a brougham as existed in the city, wearing a silk hat and considering the advantages of country living. Not even the young Henry George, having soothed his bump of amativeness by marriage and increased his lot in the world by becoming foreman of a printing shop at $30 a week, could resist the siren song of Comstock silver. "If Washoe only equals the expectations entertained of it by sober, sensible men, times will be brisk . . . and everyone will have a chance for 'a gold ring or a broken leg,' " he had written to his parents. He was soon carving enough off his meager salary to dabble in a small way in the grand lottery.

Dabbling in more than a small way was William C. Ralston. In the latter part of 1860, he had dissolved his partnership with Ralph Fretz and formed another with Joseph Donohoe. As cashier of Donohoe & Ralston, the former steamboat clerk patiently collected as many Comstock accounts as he could lay hands on. This was by no means simply an example of the acquisitive instinct got out of hand, for in Ralston's view money was a tool, not an ornament of greed. By then, he also had been stricken by his own vision, a vision quite as important to him as Sutro's Tunnel was to Sutro: his desire was to make San Francisco the greatest city in the world, a veritable Xanadu of industry, commerce, beauty, and culture, and at the center of this jewel of civilization he, William Chapman Ralston, would sit as the Prince of Benevolence.

If this grandiose conception was a madness, it was a splendid madness, and Ralston pursued it with a zealot's determination, loaning his new bank's money with enthusiasm to projects great and small. When Donohoe began to mutter darkly about his partner's liberality, Ralston dissolved this latest union and in 1864 formed the Bank of California, taking all of his Comstock accounts with him. With a board of directors—headed up by local financier Darius Ogden Mills—willing to give him greater latitude than Donohoe had extended, Ralston sped after his dream. San Francisco needed a first-class theater? Very well, then, let us have a first-class theater—and the California Theatre was built. San Francisco should have a mill to make cloth from California's own wool crop? Very well, then, the San Francisco Woolen Mills were built, furnished, and staffed. And so it went—agricultural developments, township speculations, sugar refineries, foundries, San Francisco real estate, railroads, a silkworm farm, a carriage factory, a watch factory, a rolling-stock factory, a furniture factory . . . the list expanded with every twist of the man's remarkable imagination, and Bank of California money either created, controlled, or supported a startling variety of enterprises.

The great money-box from which such ventures were financed was the Comstock Lode, which Ralston characterized as "a hole in the ground with silver and gold in it." To further the bank's interest in this treasure-stuffed hole, in 1864 Ralston established a branch bank in Virginia City under the management of William Sharon. The choice of manager could not have been better for Ralston's immediate purposes. Not only did Sharon have a sure instinct for the jugular in business affairs, he was also driven by a taste for vengeance. In his own view, he had been swindled out of more than $100,000 the year before in a Comstock-controlled stock manipulation. Moreover, the timing was perfect, for most of the mines in the district—as well as the mills which depended on their production of ore—were floundering badly. The problem was water, underground water, scalding water that stank of the ages and seeped, spurted, and gushed into the mines at about the 500-foot level, terrifying miners and drowning immense ore bodies in a steaming sea. Standard pumps could not handle the flow, and production faltered, fell off, or even stopped all together. In mill after mill, the great stamps stood silent.

Into the emergency stepped William Sharon and the Bank of California.

Not only was the bank willing to loan money to mines and mills to stave off bankruptcy, it did so at incredibly low interest rates for the time—often as low as 1½ percent per month—and it soon became the largest mortgage-holder on the Comstock. When loans fell due, or when interest payments could not be maintained, Sharon was not brutal about it; he would not cruelly foreclose—provided, of course, that the company was willing to satisfy its debt by the payment of stock, which frequently "just happened" to be sufficient to give the bank controlling interest. By such coldly efficient means, Sharon shoved under the wings of the Bank of California nearly every mill in the Comstock district, giving the bank an effective stranglehold over even those mines which had escaped its actual control. If a mine wanted its ores processed, it did not go out of its way to contradict the desires of the bank.

None of which, of course, solved the physical problem of water, as the hitherto sanguine Bank of California directors nervously pointed out to Ralston. What good was control of the Comstock if it did not produce any ore? The cashier assured them that huge pumps he was commissioning from the Vulcan Iron Works in San Francisco would be able to handle the flow—and if they could not, he would simply have even bigger pumps constructed. Still, water was clearly on Ralston's mind, and when Adolph Sutro walked into his office in February 1865 to discuss his tunnel project, Ralston gave him his interested attention.

Sutro had been busy. By then, his proposed four-mile tunnel had not only been surveyed and rendered in detailed engineer's drawings but it had also been given a right-of-way franchise by the Nevada state legislature. And it was endorsed by the eminent German geologist Baron Ferdinand Richthofen, who flatly stated that "the future of Washoe, indeed, depends upon the execution of this magnificent enterprise." Sutro outlined to Ralston the tunnel's indisputable utility as a drainage system, surely more efficient and dependable than the largest conceivable pumps. What Sutro needed from Ralston was the moral support of the bank so that he could go back to the Comstock and begin negotiating with individual mines for royalty arrangements. Ralston assured

Shaft landing of the Savage Mine, Virginia City, Nevada—a scene given glass-plate immortality by photographer Timothy O'Sullivan in 1867.

him that was easily enough taken care of, for even by then the bank's power was such that a suggestion from its officers carried more than a little weight with Comstock mine superintendents. Happily assured of Ralston's support, Sutro hustled back to the mines.

By the end of the year, he was back again with twenty-three signed contracts with mining companies representing some 95 percent of the market value of all the mines on the lode. In these contracts, the mines agreed to pay the Sutro Tunnel Company the sum of two dollars a ton for every ton of ore extracted when the tunnel and its lateral drifts reached them, in exchange for the ventilation and drainage the tunnel provided. Separate clauses also set up fee schedules for the removal of ore through the tunnel, for bringing materials up to the mines (twenty-five cents per mile per ton), and for the transportation of workers (twenty-five cents each), though the contracts did not obligate the mines to use the tunnel for anything but ventilation and drainage. What Sutro needed from Ralston this time was a letter of endorsement he could use to pry eastern and European financial interests loose from the $3 million it would take to build the tunnel. (Interest rates on the West Coast, Sutro had noted, were depressingly high.) Again, Ralston complied, penning a letter under the bank's name to the Oriental Bank Corporation of London. "Too much cannot be said of the great importance of this work, if practicable upon any remunerative basis," Ralston wrote, hedging only a little. "We learn that the scheme has been very carefully examined by scientific men, and that they unhesitatingly pronounced in its favor on all points—practicability, profit, and great public utility." So armed, Sutro sailed for New York in May 1866.

Before going to the money men in New York, Sutro journeyed to Washington for yet another legislative endorsement, this one in the form of the Sutro Tunnel Act, passed by Congress and signed by President Andrew Johnson in July. The act stipulated that to "A. Sutro, his heirs and assigns," would be granted a tunnel right-of-way (superseding that of the Nevada legislature), the privilege of buying up to two sections of public land at the mouth of the tunnel for $1.25 an acre, and the further privilege of buying any mineral lands within two thousand feet of the tunnel on either side at $5.00 an acre (not including any mining claims already filed and occupied by others). With that, Sutro returned to New York, had a snappy brochure printed up, and began making the rounds.

New York money was interested, right enough, but a little curious as to one point: if the tunnel's benefits would accrue mainly to the West Coast, why should not West Coast interests put up a fair share of the construction costs? The New Yorkers demanded a "home indorsement" to the tune of $500,000 or $600,000 before committing themselves to the project. Sutro persuaded forty of them to sign a letter to that effect and doggedly made his way back to San Francisco, confronting Ralston with this latest development. Once again, Ralston obliged by supporting Sutro's petitions to mining companies for financing, and by June 1867, more than $600,000 in stock subscriptions had been negotiated, subject to ratification at annual stockholders' meetings.

The question arises of why Ralston, no stranger to the appeal of grand schemes, did not in this venture attempt to gain, if not absolute control, at least a major hold on Sutro and his project, bending them to the bank's interest— just as he and Sharon had done to the mines and mills. One consideration was certainly money; more than $2 million of the bank's assets had been expended already in loans and stock purchases in the district, often in the face of opposition from the bank's directors, often only because Ralston himself had person-

"It is as if a wondrous battle raged, in which the combatants were men and earth," J. Ross Browne wrote of the Comstock in A Peep at Washoe in 1863. A typical assortment of combatants is shown above sometime in the late 1860s or early 1870s.

Until Andrew S. Hallidie contrived the cable car (see page 121), the horse car was the principal rolling stock of San Francisco's streets, and its most charming representative was the balloon car, as shown at the top of the page. Directly above, a cartoonist caught a rush-hour scene of the 1860s. Some things never change.

ally guaranteed the directors against any loss. Neither the bank nor Ralston personally was in a position to commit the additional $2 or $3 million that would doubtless have been necessary to exercise control over the tunnel project. A second consideration may well have been the project's long-term nature; Ralston was probably not too excited—and the bank's directors would have been most unenthusiastic—about the idea of pouring millions into an investment on which a return could not be expected for years (the tunnel, in fact, took nearly ten years to complete). Better to aid Sutro in a relatively modest way, enjoy the tunnel's benefits when they materialized, and when the time came, pay out the insignificant royalty of $2.00 a ton.

That attitude, whatever its motivation, did not survive the summer of 1867. It did not, in fact, survive the first week of June. We do not know, but we can reasonably assume, that a copy of Sutro's splendid New York brochure had wandered into the hands of either Ralston or Sharon. If so, neither the brochure's language nor its stated goals, both the responsibility of Sutro, were calculated to entrance the Bank of California. Among other things, the brochure announced that the towns of Virginia City and Gold Hill would be, sadly but inevitably, ruined by a bustling young metropolis that would sprout, blossom-like, on land at the mouth of the tunnel just above the Carson River. The new town's name, not surprisingly, would be Sutro, and revenue from town lot sales was estimated at more than $3 million—presumably payable to "A. Sutro, his heirs and assigns." For another thing, the brochure exclaimed, inescapable logic dictated that miners would go to work through the tunnel, ore and waste rock would be removed through the tunnel, all supplies would be furnished through the tunnel, and—most particularly—all milling would be done on Sutro property and would utilize cheap water power from the Carson River. All those bank-controlled mills now situated at Virginia City and Gold Hill, Sutro had written, were faced with a single choice: "The only course left to them is to remove to the tunnel company land."

Of Sutro, by Sutro, and for Sutro . . . this was altogether too much. On June 7, the stockholders of the Crown Point Mining Company summarily rejected their $75,000 subscription to tunnel stock, and inexorably other companies followed suit, until by the end of the summer Sutro's $600,000 commitment had dissipated like the wisps of dream. Nor did Ralston and Sharon stop there. When Sutro returned to New York he found that letters from Ralston and Sharon had preceded him; when he petitioned Congress for federal aid, he found Nevada's two senators and its congressman instructed by William Sharon to oppose most vigorously anything of the sort. When Sutro fled to Europe for money, Ralston's close relationship with the Oriental Bank of London ensured a lukewarm reception. Blocked at every turn, in spite of his maddening persistence, Sutro reeled about like a drunken man for more than a year, from Virginia City to San Francisco to New York to Washington to Europe to New York to Washington to San Francisco to Virginia City.

Sure that he now controlled the tobacconist who had wanted to be king, Ralston turned Sharon's peculiar genius loose on the Comstock in earnest. It was not enough, Sharon had decided, merely to exercise power; that power had to be broadened and fortified until it could rule the Comstock like a sledge, ensuring a one-way flow of treasure into the coffers of the Bank of California. Methodically, he went about his business, gaining control over the lumber companies that sent a snakeline of timber down from the slopes of the Sierra Nevada, over the water company that serviced the town, over teamster operations, over provisioning—over everything, in fact, but the bars, restaurants, hotels, theaters, brothels, and medical facilities of Virginia City (though he doubtless would have snapped up what he could along those lines). He consolidated the bank's mill properties into the Union Mill & Mining Company and laid plans for their removal to the Carson River (not, however, to Sutro property), and, by January of 1869, had begun construction of the Virginia & Truckee Railroad for the transportation of ores (as well as other materials and passengers) from the Comstock mines to the reconstructed mills.

In ten years, Ralston's dream had come a long way toward fruition. His control over the money-hole of the Comstock was close to absolute, and it was finally beginning to pay off in a pleasing manner. The monstrous pumps he had installed and would continue to install had indeed enabled mine after mine to function below the old water-line of five hundred feet, some of them carving their way down to nearly a thousand feet. In two of the bank's own mines alone, the Kentuck and the Yellow Jacket, the value of ore extracted in 1867 and 1868 exceeded $6 million, and the bank's mills had siphoned off the lion's share of the whole district's production of more than twenty-five million. In San Francisco, Ralston was still spreading the bank's money around like a fool at a fire, most of it in local real estate and much of it in a single speculation, the Montgomery Street Real Estate Company, a scheme engineered with young Asbury Harpending to control property rights along a proposed extension of Montgomery Street from Market Street southeast to San Francisco Bay.

Down in the bucolic surroundings of Belmont, Ralston's estate spread like a summer villa of one of the doges, and on the corner of California and Sansome streets in San Francisco, the blue-stone walls of the new Bank of California building—patterned after the library of Saint Mark in the Piazza di San Marco in Venice—had risen elegantly in the summer of 1867. From the balcony outside his expansive second-floor office, Ralston could have watched, in the beginning of 1869, the purposeful bustling of the streets below and congratulated himself that his personal energies had helped to create it. It was, he would have reminded himself, only the beginning, for the Central Pacific Railroad, once the goat of San Francisco finance, had by then conquered the summit of the Sierra Nevada and was now racing across the desert for a spring or summer meeting with its eastern counterpart, the Union Pacific. Ralston (and nearly everyone else in San Francisco) firmly believed that the completion of the transcontinental railroad would send real-estate values whirling to new heights, would inspire an influx of experienced tradesmen, skilled workers, and eastern investment capital, and would create a market for vigorous young San Francisco industries—including those which Ralston had built himself. 1849, 1859, 1869 . . . for the third successive time in San Francisco's history, a new age would dawn with a new decade, and once again William Chapman Ralston would be there to harvest the seeds of destiny.

Sacramento steamer ticket, ca. 1865.

The City of the Sixties . . .

The cityscape of the late 1860s and early '70s is nowhere more thoroughly documented as in the views made by Eadweard Muybridge for sale to a public always eager to see what the storied metropolis of the Pacific was *really* like. Muybridge achieved lasting fame as the pioneer of motion photography with his stop-action sequences of Leland Stanford's trotting horse and the movements of the human body—so it is not surprising that this restless innovator should have been captivated by (and then have capitalized upon) the dramatic three-dimensional effects possible in stereoscopic photography.

If you get the feeling that there is something vaguely odd about most of the shots shown here, you will find that it is because they have been arranged and framed for "3-D" impact and as a result are quite different from the views that Muybridge or any other great photographer would have set up for single-lens work. The rest of that odd impression comes from Muybridge's sure sense of what would go over in a big way in Victorian drawing rooms. Dissections? San Quentin!

STEREOTYPICAL . . . The camera eye caught the popular imagination with the Daguerreian image of the 1850s—but it moved from parlor ornament to parlor game in the 1860s with the development of the paper print from the glass negative and the wonderful stereoscope. The three-dimensional view afforded by commercial cards such as that on the left have never been improved upon and took middle-class Victorians from their drawing rooms to the ends of the earth—Malaya . . . Zanzibar . . . Luxor . . . San Francisco.

VIEWING "THE ROCK" . . . San Francisco's own combination of Gibraltar and Devil's Island excited as much curiosity a hundred years ago as it does today. In the last years of the smoothbore, the guns of Alcatraz commanded the harbor channel, and there were everywhere tasteful stacks of cannonballs sufficient to destroy any fleet that survived the batteries of Fort Point.

Already, in Muybridge's time, the island was gaining its grim reputation of later years: Ashbury Harpending and his Secessionist conspirators were held there, as were some of Captain Jack's Modoc guerrillas, survivors of the little band of Indians that more than once discomfitted the U. S. Army in 1873. Now the island is a park, but those of us who would like to see it returned to the pelicans for which it is named are certain to be disappointed by the much larger faction that would rather see the cell of Al Capone.

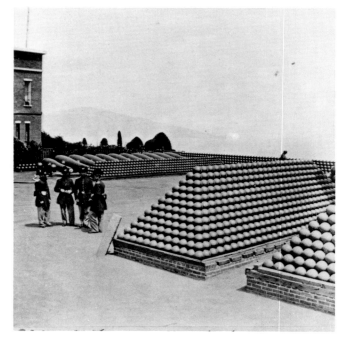

THE MARCH OF INDUSTRY. . . . One of the least-known specialties of Muybridge, a man with a ready eye to novelty, was industrial photography. A thoroughgoing person of substantial wit, he went so far as to document a classic California assembly line. Thus, all hands of the Buena Vista Winery gathered to show how it was done out where there was a limitless demand for champagne and assorted dinner wines, and *Helios*—the Flying Studio—had scored another first.

It was up in the Napa country that Eadweard Muybridge (Edward Muggeridge in his native England) got into a scrape that caused him to suspend temporarily his photographic career by timely flight. He called his wife's lover out of a house and shot him dead. Fortunately for the progress of the photographic art, this act was taken no more seriously as a criminal matter than, say, the assassination of a newspaper editor, but to the sensitive Muybridge the attendant publicity was painful. He did return, and in 1880 at the California School of Fine Arts in San Francisco projected on a screen the world's first motion picture.

Xanadu in San Francisco. . . . The pleasure ground of the family city of the 1860s and '70s was Woodward's Gardens, out in the Mission, where one could indulge an appetite for culture, novelty, and real trees and grass for a trifling admission fee. R. B. Woodward, who appears at the far left with the little girl in Sunday best, opened his Victorian Disneyland in 1866 as the more than worthy successor to such earlier private parks as Russ Gardens and The Willows. There were real animals as well as the stuffed collection, an art gallery as well as an 8'3" Chinese Giant, and balloon ascensions were not unknown. This amiable achievement of private enterprise took the picnic pressure off the cemeteries.

IN THE DAYS OF THE BIG BONANZAS. . . .
When Muybridge made these two
panoramas in the early 1870s, he may
deliberately have sought to catch the un-
lovely sprawl of the working city. Comstock money, railroad money, all the
money in the West might soon be reflected in the Palace and the Baldwin
Hotels, the conspicuous opulence of
Nob Hill, the great business blocks of
Market and Montgomery Streets, but
here we see the plain sinews of the
town. The one view looks down lower
California Street, the other back towards the downtown district from Rincon Hill. The shot tower south of Market is the appropriate landmark of both.

Nothing worth seeing. . . . That literary sightseer of the 1870s, Anthony Trollope, reported breathlessly from San Francisco: "I do not know that in all my travels I ever visited a city less interesting to the normal tourist, who, as a rule, does not care to investigate the ways of trade or to employ himself in ascertaining how the people around him earn their bread. . . . There is an inferior menagerie of wild beasts, and a place called the Cliff House to which strangers are taken to hear seals bark."

Oddly enough, Trollope did accidentally ascertain how brokers of mining stocks traded in everybody's bread and he was suitably astounded. Further investigation of breadwinning as the civic sport and art form would have proved quite interesting.

On May 10, 1869, the Great Work of the Age was done when the rails of the
Central Pacific met those of the Union Pacific at Promontory, Utah. In San Francisco, citizens danced in the streets; choirs sang in the Tabernacle of Salt Lake City;
Philadelphians rejoiced; people in Chicago, St. Louis, and New York looked west
with new interest; even Bostonians lost their composure.

Chapter VI

THE TRADE WINDS OF TIME

WHILE WILLIAM C. RALSTON consolidated his interests on the Comstock into an amalgam of fortified monopoly and Adolph Sutro wove the threads of his tunnel dream, Henry George spent much of the decade of the 1860s simply struggling to survive. With the exaggerated combativeness common to short men (George had to stand on a small platform to set type), he chafed and fretted and bickered so much with his various employers that he found it difficult to hold a job for any great length of time—a situation scarcely improved by the quick arrival of two children after his youthful marriage. Like Sutro bouncing from city to city in his fruitless search for financing, George eked out a living between 1860 and 1865 by alternating between San Francisco, Sacramento, and Oakland, "subbing" for other printers when his own positions vanished. He opened up his own job-printing plant, which quickly failed. He sold clothes-wringers for a time. He patented a new kind of wagon-brake, which buyers trampled over one another in a rush to ignore. He toyed with the notion of starting his own newspaper venture in La Paz, Baja California. He and his wife joined a vague post-Civil War movement to free Mexico from the dread hand of dictatorship under Emperor Maximilian. Enrolling in the Defenders of the Monroe Doctrine, the remarkable couple boarded a gun-runner carrying some ten thousand rifles in 1865 only to have the ship seized by federal revenue cutters before it could get out of the bay. Back in San Francisco, they knelt and kissed the revolutionary flag of Mexico, took a solemn oath on a naked sword, and waited for word to come to them from rebel leader Benito Juarez to join his army in San Luis Potosí. The word never came. Not even George's crusades seemed to work.

Worst of all, George had lost all of his not very substantial savings in silver stock flyers. In his own parlance, he had stretched out for the "gold ring" of the Comstock and ended up with a broken leg. More often than he could comfortably bear, his little family was reduced to a diet of corn meal mush, and one day he grew so frantic with worry that he accosted a perfect stranger on the street and demanded five dollars. The odor of desperation must have been strong about his person, for he got the money. After five years in the golden land of opportunity, George found himself dead up against his own failures,

"Let us not imagine ourselves in a fool's paradise. . . ."

Premonitions: San Francisco burned down six times in the first two years of its existence, but it was substantially shaken up only twice before 1906. At the top, a "well-known" state senator flees the charms of a couple of Portsmouth Square harlots during the quake of October, 1865, as recorded in the steaming pages of the California Police Gazette. *Below that, a warehouse in the wholesale district shows the effect of the excitement of October, 1868. "One is forced irresistably to look upon it as a doomed city," an eastern reporter wrote of San Francisco in 1872. "It needs no gift of prophecy to predict the future, for it is inevitable."*

and out of this dark afternoon of the soul he forged a resolution: he vowed to tone down his instinctive belligerence, get a job and keep it, send no more money down any speculative holes, and write.

Writing suggested itself to him naturally enough. More than ten years of giving other men's words the dignity of print had invested him with a love of language, of stories, of ideas—particularly of ideas. Never bashful about expressing his opinions on any and every subject—a fact which had crippled his employability—he now discovered the incomparable delight of expressing them for publication and being paid for it. The remuneration was especially gratifying, and it came quickly. His first attempts, a series of bombastic little articles written in response to the assassination of Abraham Lincoln, were published on submission to the *Alta California.* His next three, stories built around the theme of spiritualism and supernatural occurences, were published in the *Californian,* a literary journal founded in 1864 by Charles H. Webb. Its regular contributors included Bret Harte, Mark Twain, Ambrose Bierce, Prentice Mulford, and a handful of others who comprised San Francisco's *literati.*

By 1868, George's new resolve had not made his fortune, but it had unquestionably improved the course of his life. His demonstrated talents had lifted him from the composing room to the editorial desk. He was now a journalist, and if his continuing inability to tolerate fools in silence resulted in his shifting from newspaper to newspaper as he had once shifted from job shop to job shop, his grasp on the future seemed firmer than ever before. Paradoxically, his faith in that very future, if not in himself, began to deteriorate as his own life grew in security. His native genius, first stimulated by constant reading, then bent—almost twisted—by the bitterness of poverty, was now enlarged and sharpened by the observation necessary to his new occupation. As he observed, he began to question and as he questioned, he began to doubt.

What he doubted was that the dream, the dream for which San Francisco stood as reflection, the dream that had enlivened the careers of such as Billy Ralston and Adolph Sutro, could survive the future. The harbinger of that future was the transcontinental railroad snaking east and west for a meeting in Utah. San Francisco's entrepreneurs, its bankers, merchants, real estate speculators, stockbrokers, industrialists, and agriculturists, watched the railroad's progress and rubbed their hands in anticipation of the boom that would inevitably follow its completion. Henry George watched it, too, but his anticipation was haunted by the memory not only of having tasted the dream's ashes himself, but of a moment in New York City in early 1868. He had been sent there by John Nugent's *San Francisco Herald* in an attempt (predictably unsuccessful) to break the monopoly on telegraphic news service held by the Associated Press. While standing on a street corner, George later wrote, he had been stricken, as if by a vision, by "the shocking contrast between monstrous wealth and debasing want." That vision never left him, and it was that vision that was still in his mind when he sat down that same year and began writing an essay that was ultimately published in the *Overland Monthly* in October.

The essay was titled "What the Railroad Will Bring Us," and it stands even today as one of the most prescient observations the nineteenth century ever produced. George, almost certainly alone among his contemporaries, saw the coming of the railroad not with feverish expectation but with a cold insight. Life in California, he wrote almost nostagically, had previously displayed "a certain cosmopolitanism, a certain freedom and breadth of common thought and feeling, natural to a community made up from so many different sources . . . a feeling of personal independence and equality, a certain hopefulness and self-reliance, and a certain large-heartedness and open-handedness." In such a milieu, he suggested, men rose or fell according to their abilities or the dictates of circumstance, but were commonly accepted whether in success or failure as part of a system that was within individual human power to control. The railroad, he determined, would bring not only a period of immediate, if short-lived, economic decline, but would prove ruinous to the social and economic flexibility that had characterized the state and the city for nearly twenty years. It would, in fact, introduce the rigidity that was already converting the American East into a bitter warren of class struggle. "And this in general is the tendency of the time," he wrote, "and of the new era opening before us: to the great development of wealth; to concentration; to the differentiation of classes; to less personal independence among the many and the greater power of the few. . . . Connected more closely with the rest of the nation, we will feel more quickly and keenly all that affects it. We will have to deal, in time, with all the social problems that are forcing themselves on older communities.

"The California of the new era will be greater, richer, more powerful than the California of the past," George said, and in this corroborated the highest expectations of San Francisco's financial elite. But: "Will she be still the same California whom her adopted children, gathered from all climes, love better than their own mother lands . . . ? She will have more people; but among those people will there be so large a proportion of full, true men? She will have more wealth; but will it be so evenly distributed? She will have more luxury and refinement and culture; but will she have such general comfort, so little squalor and misery; so little of the grinding, hopeless poverty that chills and cramps the souls of men, and converts them into brutes?"

The prognosis for anything of the sort was poor, he concluded. "Let us not imagine ourselves in a fool's paradise, where the golden apples will drop into our mouths; let us not think that after the stormy seas and head gales of all the ages, *our* ship has at last struck the trade winds of time. The future of our State . . . looks fair and bright; perhaps the future looked so to the philosophers who once sat in the porches of Athens—to the unremembered men who raised the cities whose ruins lie south of us. Our modern civilization strikes broad and deep and looks high. So did the tower which men once built almost unto heaven."

I F A COPY OF George's *Overland Monthly* essay had fallen into the hands of William C. Ralston, it would have impressed the banker not at all. Assuming he got through the first few paragraphs, he would have dismissed it as so much intellectual twaddle, a gloom-ridden screed written by a man soured by his own failures in the world. George's well-honed skepticism would have galled the very nature of Ralston, who was, if nothing else, a definitive optimist. What the railroad would bring was *prosperity*, by God, and no sane man believed otherwise. Ralston would hardly have been alone in such an opinion. When the rails of the Central Pacific and the Union Pacific were finally joined at Promontory, Utah, on May 10, 1869, and the telegrapher signaled "DOT. DOT. DOT. DONE," whistles blew, city offices were vacated, citizens danced in the streets, champagne flowed like rainwater, and at least one group of inebriates pranced along Montgomery Street with a banner that proclaimed "SAN FRANCISCO ANNEXES THE UNITED STATES!"

Even before all this bibulous hilarity, however, Ralston got a hint that the

A variation on transcontinental travel—the "Avitor Hermes, Jr.," a steam-powered balloon invented by Frederick Marriott, publisher and editor of the San Francisco News Letter. *On the morning of July 2, 1869 this remarkable beast actually made the first unmanned, powered flight of a lighter-than-air craft in America at the Shell Mound Race Track in San Mateo County. Marriott promptly formed the Aerial Steam Navigation Company, among whose investors was none other than William Chapman Ralston. Ralston did not get a return on this particular flyer, but he was always game for the possible, even the impossible.*

It took effort, money, and a purely German-Swiss persistence, but the hopeful king of the Comstock finally engineered his ambitious tunnel company in the summer of 1868.

decade of the '70s just might not be all that it was cracked up to be, at least not for the Bank of California. On April 7, 1869, a fire broke out in the Comstock's Yellow Jacket Mine, a bank-owned property. In a matter of hours, forty-five men had died and the Yellow Jacket, together with the adjoining Crown Point and Kentuck mines (both also bank-controlled), had been sealed up to let the fire burn itself out. It would be months before any of the three could be worked again, thus interrupting a good part of the treasure flow on which the bank depended. Moreover, Adolph Sutro, still worrying at his dream like a dog at a bone, pounced on the issue of the fire and used it to good effect. If his tunnel had been built, he pointed out (implying that only the opposition of the "Bank Ring" had prevented its completion before now), all of the dead miners could have been saved. Ever-mindful of the importance of muscular public relations, he had a lurid brochure printed up depicting in one cartoon a pathetic collection of trapped miners being scorched by fire and strangled by smoke and in another a similar group fleeing the smoke and flames in safety and being greeted at the mouth of Sutro's Tunnel by weeping wives and children torn between terror and relief. He hammered away at his theme on street corners and in bars, in newspaper stories and before union meetings, and on August 25 was vindicated by a stock subscription to the tune of $50,000 from the miners of Virginia City themselves. This was more hard cash than his project had yet engendered, and Sutro jubilantly opened up a stock subscription office in Virginia City in September. The money that greeted his ambitious advertising campaigns did not exactly flood the office, but enough had come in by the middle of October for the Sutro Tunnel Company to begin construction.

Sutro's thoroughly unexpected success was more of an affront to Ralston's pride than a raid on his bank vaults would have been. After all, the Bank of California's control of the Comstock remained unchallenged, and even if Sutro kept enough money coming in to complete the tunnel—surely a matter of years—it could in no way dilute the power of the spreadeagle monopoly the bank had created. Still, Sutro's sudden good fortune was an annoyance, just the first in a series that was beginning to cloud Ralston's otherwise clear plans for the future. As the months after May passed by and the end of the year drew close, it became clearer and clearer that no boom was going to come on the heels of the completion of the railroad. Stockpiles of lumber laid in to meet the expected building mania lay unused in their yards; stacks of merchandise in warehouses and stores stood on their shelves gathering dust; "For Sale" signs stayed rooted in San Francisco lots, and township speculations in the hinterland lay quite as empty and ruffled by the wind as they had been when laid out. Worst of all, such eastern centers as Chicago and St. Louis had been laying in their own goods and manufactures in anticipation of the railroad's completion, and a flood of cheap merchandise streamed into San Francisco almost immediately, glutting the market. San Francisco's business interests, hampered by the high cost of raw goods and high wages, simply could not compete, as Asbury Harpending later recalled: "For months we had been living in a fool's paradise over the boom that the railroad would bring. That day came, but what a disappointment! . . . For the business people it spelled ruin. It brought an avalanche of goods . . . at prices our local men could not meet. Many firms failed, some consolidated, some retired from business. Rents dropped like lead, real estate values shriveled to nothing. It was ten years before those values recovered to 1869 levels." (In San Francisco, real estate transactions had averaged $3.5 million a month through most of 1869; in 1870, that average tumbled to $1.3 million.)

Tension and frustration mounted, and the smell of panic was in the air by the end of the summer of 1869. Aggravating the problem was the fact that the United States subtreasury in San Francisco had remained closed during the transition period between the administrations of Andrew Johnson and Ulysses S. Grant and for reasons apparently known only to God and himself, Grant had ignored frantic telegrams from San Francisco's bankers asking him to reopen. At question was the existence of some $14 million worth of coin stored in the treasury, coin which the banks of San Francisco needed badly, coin for which they would gladly trade the bars of gold bullion that stood uselessly in their vaults, if only they could. One afternoon, Asbury Harpending stopped by the Bank of California to discuss conditions with Ralston.

"If things go on as they are," Ralston said, "every bank will be closed by tomorrow afternoon. Not one of us can stand a half day's run, and all will go down in a heap. Then look out for hell in general to break loose."

Ralston had a plan, however, and asked Harpending to help with it; Harpending, who loved conspiracies as other men loved wine, was more than willing. At one o'clock the next morning, Harpending and a friend, Maurice Doré, began padding down the dark streets between the Bank of California and the subtreasury building on Montgomery Street, carrying gold bars which were exchanged for sacks of coin in equal amounts. Before the flush of dawn could expose their little adventure, more than one million dollars worth of coin had been carried to the Bank of California. If Harpending ever discovered how much the "arrangements" with subtreasury officials had cost Ralston, he never reported it.

When the Bank of California opened the next morning, a crowd large enough to comprise a "semi-run" was gathered, just as Ralston had predicted. But when this milling throng of bank-wreckers saw tray after tray heaped with the glitter of coin, their urgency deteriorated and they faded into the street. When a similar crowd gathered at the doors of another bank, Ralston rushed over, stood on a box, and harangued the group. The bank was as solid as granite, he maintained, and they were fools to think otherwise. If they were so hungry for money, he added, then they should stroll over to the Bank of California and he would guarantee their withdrawals. This mob, too, soon disintegrated.

With bravado and moral persuasion Ralston had personally prevented a genuine panic, but it did nothing to relieve the larger economic situation. A bitter drought in the winter of 1869-70 devastated inland farms and ranches, and the anticipated rich harvest of the fall of 1870 simply never materialized, just as the railroad boom never materialized. By the end of 1870, Samuel

In 1873, Andrew S. Hallidie designed and executed one of the most permanent images we have of the city that was and is: a trolley that operated by no visible means of support. It was called a cable car, and in its earliest manifestation it tugged at an artful little dummy behind it, as in this scene of the Clay Street Hill Railroad Company of about 1875.

Another image of the city that was: Joshua A. Norton, Emperor of the United States and Protector of Mexico. Rich in 1849, ruined in a rice speculation of 1853, he disappeared until 1859, when he re-emerged in all the trappings of royalty. For the next twenty years, the city coddled and nurtured this dear, demented old gentleman, giving him an honored place in the tapestry of its life throughout the 1860s and 1870s. He died, with his times, in 1880.

Bowles, a visitor from Massachusetts, reported in a letter home that "All of the great interests of the state are depressed. . . . Several thousand laborers are reported idle in San Francisco alone, and 50,000 to 100,000 in the state. . . ."

Lost in the labyrinth of this recession, of course, was a good deal of the Bank of California's money, investments on which there now could be expected no early return—if any. As noted, it was months after the mine fire of 1869 before the bank's principal Comstock mines—the Kentuck, Yellow Jacket, and Crown Point—could be opened again for working. When they were, they soon began to slip from bonanza to borrasca (barren rock), and by the spring of 1870, the Crown Point had slipped so far that the price of its stock had gone clattering down to an abysmal two dollars a share. At this juncture, the Crown Point's superintendant, John P. Jones, sank an exploratory drift to the 1,200-foot level and encountered streaks of increasingly rich ore. Before long, he was certain that he had discovered an immense pocket of treasure. Contemplating the facts that Crown Point stock had fallen to two dollars a share, that Ralston and Sharon did not yet know of his discovery, and that he was tired of "supering" other men's mines, Jones took his information to Alvinza Hayward, one of the trustees of the Union Mill & Mining Company. Quietly, slowly, so as not to "bull" the price up to unreasonable levels or occasion the suspicion of the Bank of California, the two began buying up blocks of Crown Point stock, and by May of 1871 they had acquired control. During that month, unsurprisingly, Jones admitted publicly that the Crown Point had gone into bonanza. The mine's stock immediately spurted to $180 a share, and by the middle of 1872, had gone to a screaming high of $1,825. Ralston had been neatly dealt out of the game, and Jones and Hayward added injury to injury by organizing the Nevada Mill & Mining Company as a rival to the bank's conglomerate.

Ralston was shaken by this betrayal by two of his own, but not yet disheartened. Operating on the reasonable assumption that the ore body discovered by Jones could also be reached through the adjoining Belcher Mine, he and Sharon sank several hundred thousand dollars into a campaign to control the Belcher. The attempt succeeded, and the gamble paid off when the mine broke into a body of ore even larger than that found in the Crown Point mine. (Before its demise some ten years later, the Belcher would produce nearly thirty-five million dollars in ore.) Inspired by the new flood of treasure, Ralston increased his injection of bank money, as well as large chunks of his personal fortune, into the body of his dream to make San Francisco queen of the continent. Once again, everything seemed not only possible, but probable.

His almost iridescent optimism may be the only explanation that exists for Ralston's subsequent entanglement in one of the most delightful frauds in the history of the West. In January, 1872, two more than slightly uncouth miners walked into the Bank of California and deposited a sackful of diamonds, rubies, sapphires, and emeralds. Their names were John B. Slack and Philip Arnold, and their manner was nervous and insecure, in the fashion of men who have stumbled upon the answer to a prayer. Word was immediately passed to Ralston, who invited them into his office. After some prodding, the pair admitted to having discovered a major deposit of precious gems, notably diamonds. They refused to say where. With great effort, Ralston convinced them that there was a fortune to be made with proper management, and Slack and Arnold finally agreed to let him and a few select individuals in on the venture. Ralston shipped the sackful of gems off to Tiffany's in New York for evaluation and sent two blindfolded mining engineers with Slack and Arnold to investigate the discovery. Tiffany's soon reported that the gems were worth a minimum of

$150,000 and the engineers returned with the stunning report that they had found jewels sticking right out of the earth.

Ralston immediately organized the San Francisco and New York Mining and Commercial Company, capitalized at $2,320,000 with $80,000 contributions from each of twenty-nine investors, including Ralston, Asbury Harpending, Baron Ferdinand Rothschild of London, and Charles Tiffany and Horace Greeley of New York. Still wanting to be absolutely certain that he had bought in on the most spectacular mineral discovery in the history of the United States, Ralston hired a young geologist and mining engineer by the name of Henry Janin to investigate the field himself. Janin's fee was $2,500, expenses, and the option to buy one thousand shares of the company at a nominal fee. In the meantime, Slack and Arnold wondered if it wouldn't be possible to borrow against their own interest in the enterprise; of course it was, Ralston replied, and advanced them $300,000.

Janin, like the engineers before him, returned so enthusiastic that he immediately exercised his stock option. Ralston began plans to launch a major public stock subscription program. All this financial hoopla proved to be too much for the simple prospectors, Slack and Arnold. They respectfully requested that the company buy them out; Ralston obliged, giving them another $300,000 above and beyond what they had already been advanced. Obviously relieved at being allowed to avoid the psychological stress of sophisticated money-men, Slack and Arnold shook hands all around and vanished. Shortly thereafter, Henry Janin sold out his own shares for $40,000.

Then the inevitable bombshell: Clarence King, a mining engineer and geologist quite as young as Henry Janin, took an interest in the ostensible diamond fields, an interest heightened by the fact that he had more than once stated for the record that there were no deposits of precious gems in the American West. Anywhere in the American West. On his own hook, this skeptic calculated from various newspaper reports that the diamond field was in northern Utah, not far from the line of the Union Pacific Railroad (less than two miles, as it turned out), and hauled himself and an assistant off to find it. He did, and found his skepticism vindicated when his assistant held up a diamond and shouted, "Look, Mr. King! This diamond field not only produces diamonds but cuts them also!" King returned to San Francisco, did up a report, and the desert that had sprouted diamonds soon became known for what it was: a fabulous swindle. Slack and Arnold, it developed, had "salted" the region with $25,000 worth of reject gems purchased from German jewel merchants; Tiffany's, unaccustomed to evaluating uncut gems, had grossly overestimated the sackful sent to them; Henry Janin's part in the affair remained obscure, but since only he and the two prospectors walked away from the curious affair with any money, more than one eyebrow was raised among mining men. The investors got back their $80,000 apiece, and Ralston made up the $600,000 paid to Slack and Arnold out of his own pocket. Not without style, Ralston had the receipts for the repayment of the investment money framed and kept them hanging on the wall of his office as a reminder of the essential duplicity of man.

More than style, however, was going to be necessary to get Ralston through the vicissitudes that would follow hard upon his relatively harmless leap into the diamond business. That was a minor miscalculation, but it possessed significant implications; for if he had slipped so far from reality as to seriously accept the notion of diamonds in the desert, if he could be so neatly flimflammed, we can wonder how he thought to survive in a real world that swam with genuine sharks.

This Ed Jump cartoon of 1863 portrays Emperor Norton at a free lunch table with two friends, a pair of independent, rat-killing mutts named Bummer and Lazarus, whose companionship inspired more than one newspaper editorialist to compare them to Damon and Pythius.

"The Chinese Must Go!"

The slogan that the rabble-rousing labor leader Denis Kearney used to such dramatic effect in the San Francisco of the late 1870s commands our attention as perhaps the only catch phrase in American history that ever "solved" a major race problem. For not long after, a great many Chinese did go, with the result that those remaining constituted an increasingly small minority in the population of the city and region.

What was "the Chinese Problem"? In 1876, the year before Denis established his sandlot meetings of San Francisco's workingmen, it appears (from available statistics and educated guesses) that the ratio of unskilled and semi-skilled white workers to potential Chinese competitors was approaching one-to-one.

Chinese had come to California in numbers during the Gold Rush, and there had been anti-Chinese feeling in the mines. But by the late seventies the railroad had brought what Henry George had told Californians the railroad would bring—oversupply of labor, cut-rate competition from eastern manufacturers, and depression. The Chinese added a problem which would not be solved by economic theory, strikes, or troops. For the Chinese worker would live on wages smaller than those an American thought necessary for bare subsistence. And more Chinese flooded from the steerage quarters of the transpacific steamers each month.

continued

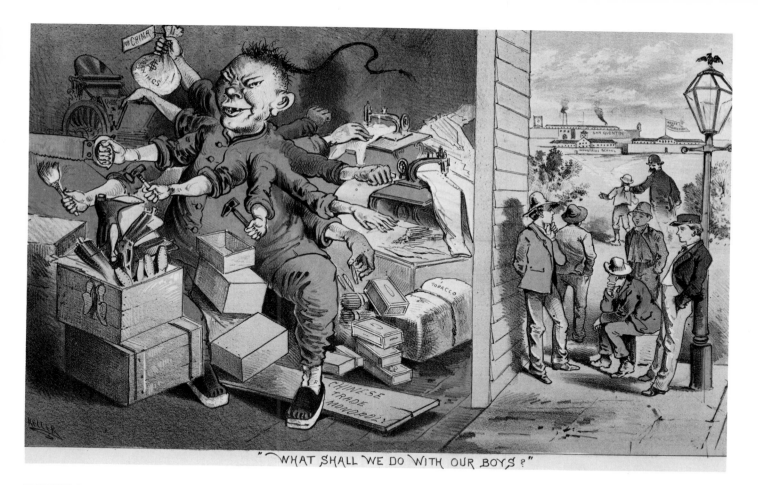

"WHAT SHALL WE DO WITH OUR BOYS?"

"The Chinese Must Go!" was a demand that everyone could understand, whether or not it was in each case relevant to the economic crisis at hand. Thus it was that poor John Chinaman was responsible for the organization of the Workingmen's Party of California, for raising an Irish demagogue in San Francisco who threw a fright into solid folk as far away as Boston, for forcing the Republican and Democratic parties in California to club together for mutual protection from the threat of socialism, and for agitating national politics for a decade.

The position of thoughtful activists was awkward, and the pungent political and satirical journal of those times, the *San Francisco Illustrated Wasp*, reflected the dilemma. The savage drawings of the gifted cartoonist Frederick Keller vacillated between attacks on the Chinese as a real threat to the economic position of white labor and swipes at "General" Kearney (with his ass's head) and the simpleminded racism of many of his supporters.

Not too curiously, for all the fiery and threatening rhetoric that agitated San Francisco, it was not here but in such backwoods communities as Tacoma and Los Angeles that there was mob action against the Chinese. Federal restriction of Chinese immigration came in 1882; in subsequent years those Chinese who had achieved their ambition of accumulating a modest pile and retiring to their native villages did so; the Chinese "threat" to "American" workingmen faded.

THE CITY'S OWN. . . . The Chinese were of course the victims of racial persecution partly because they were different, conspicuous, defenseless, and therefore an easy target for anybody looking for somebody to blame for the troubles of our civilization. They continued to be different and conspicuous after they had ceased to be any real menace to unionization and the white workingman. But now their distinction was that they were "colorful"—as they had seemed in the first year of the Gold Rush. Arnold Genthe, one of San Francisco's greatest photographic artists, made his international reputation around the turn of the century with his Chinatown portraits.

At the right is the artist with a favorite model, everybody's image of a doll. But there is realism beyond a taste for the exotic in Genthe. He saw San Francisco's Chinese as few have seen them and he helped to carve them their rightful and notable and permanent niche in the accepting culture of the city.

THE SHOEMAKER. . . . Shoemaking, cigarmaking, and clothing manufacture were industries that the Chinese took over almost completely in the 1860s and 1870s, and in Genthe's day these trades were still characteristic of the Chinese community. But "the Chinaman" did everything—from building the railroad and harvesting the grain bonanzas of the seventies and eighties to taking in all the dirty wash a city can create. The steady face of Genthe's shoemaker is the face of the patient thousands who worked a hundred years to earn first-class citizenship in an American city.

The Illustrated Wasp's *view of exportable California goods, 1878.*

Chapter VII

ON THE ALTAR OF THE GOLDEN CALF

IN FEBRUARY OF 1873, Darius Ogden Mills and William Ralston clashed in one of their increasingly frequent disputes. Mills, president of the Bank of California's board of trustees, was particularly nettled by the financial condition of two of Ralston's favorite local enterprises, the Kimball Manufacturing Company and the Pacific Woolen Mills. He had opposed loans to these ventures from the beginning, and pointed out now that he had been right; they still did not show a profit, and their remaining debt to the bank amounted to more than $1.5 million. "I consider it most unwise to foster factories of this kind," he announced stolidly. "We must protect ourselves and the country will take care of itself."

The country will take care of itself. Probably no better one-line definition of *laissez-faire* economics has ever been uttered. It was anathema to Ralston, but he found it quite useless, as always, to argue the point. As usual, he effected a compromise whereby he personally assumed a large part of the debt. It was the beginning of a year that did not get much better for Ralston. For one thing, William Sharon, who had amassed a huge personal fortune as manager of the bank's Virginia City branch, announced his resignation and his intention to purchase a senatorship from the Nevada state legislature. Sharon, more than Ralston himself, had been responsible for the bank's Comstock operations, and he would be missed. For another, an unlikely quartet began to muscle in on Ralston's territory. Since 1869, James C. Flood and William S. O'Brien, partners in a popular San Francisco saloon and a sideline brokerage firm, along with James G. Fair and John W. Mackay, former mine superintendents, had been in partnership on the Comstock, patiently gathering up and developing moderately successful properties on the gamble that one of them, sooner or later, would disgorge a fortune. In 1872, for the grand sum of $80,000, they bought control of the adjoining California and Consolidated Virginia mines on the conviction that there was more in those mines than met the eye. They were right. After careful exploration, the partners struck a rich vein early in 1873. The vein widened, then widened again, and by the spring of 1874, it was obvious that they had encountered, according to the *Mining and Scientific Press* of San

> ## "We will not cash any more checks today."

Francisco, "a body of ore absolutely immense, and beyond all comparison superior in every respect to anything ever seen on the Comstock Lode."

This was the "Big Bonanza"—the *big* bonanza—and Ralston got none of it. Those who did were soon dubbed the "Bonanza Kings" or the "Big Four of the Comstock," and they celebrated by swiftly constructing their own mills and laying plans for the organization of the Bank of Nevada to compete with the "Bank Ring's" Virginia City branch. Watching his iron control of the Comstock begin to disintegrate like tissue paper in the rain, Ralston gambled once again. The old Ophir Mine, now controlled by E. J. "Lucky" Baldwin, whose Baldwin Hotel and Theatre would grace the San Francisco of the '80s and '90s, was located not far from the Con-Virginia. Superficial logic suggested that some artful exploration might tap into the big lode. In that expectation, Ralston went after control of the mine, enlisting the partnership of William Sharon. Baldwin, who probably had expectations of his own in regard to the Ophir, fought the two to retain control, but could not match their resources. At the end of the final day of trading on the floor of the Stock and Exchange Board, the mine belonged to Ralston and Sharon. The new owners immediately directed the mine's super to start drifting.

That accomplished, Ralston continued in his program of state and urban renewal. Four million dollars was loaned out to agricultural enterprises in the interior valleys to assure bringing in the wheat crop. Another $5 million went toward a scheme to buy the Spring Valley Water Company, San Francisco's principal water supply, in hopes of turning around and selling it to the city for as much as $10 million. Hundreds of thousands were plowed into the operation of his collection of industries. Most spectacularly, another $3 million was swiftly consumed by the first months of construction on Ralston's supreme gift to the city of San Francisco: the Palace Hotel, the "largest hotel on earth," the "great caravanserai," which fourteen hundred carpenters and three hundred bricklayers were busily erecting at the southeast corner of Market and New Montgomery streets. There was little doubt that Ralston considered this his crowning achievement, a monument, as it were, to the hopes and energies that had driven him. Nearly every day, he could be seen clambering around the construction site, talking to bricklayers, carpenters, and plumbers, conferring with his construction superintendent, Henry King, watching the walls rise toward glory.

It might have been better had he watched instead the Honorable William Sharon, senator of Nevada, his business colleague for more than ten years. Early in 1875, Sharon learned on good authority that not only had the Ophir not yet come close to tapping into the Big Bonanza—more than likely it never would. Surreptitiously, he began dumping his shares on the market. By the time he got his investment back, Ophir stock had dropped from a high of $315 a share to a little over $35. Thanks to Sharon's machinations, Ralston was left holding nearly $3 million worth of stock in an unprofitable mine, which he could not resell for what it had cost him. Once again, he had been done in by one of his own (though it is not known whether he ever discovered Sharon's scurvy little operation). Things were not going to improve.

By the summer of 1875, Ralston had spent more than $12 million of the Bank of California's money on his various projects. True, he had personally guaranteed to the bank's nervous trustees much of what he had spent, but the bank's treasure reserves nevertheless were badly depleted, a situation that was hardly relieved when the Bonanza Kings incorporated the Bank of Nevada, freezing $5 million of its own assets as a treasure reserve, an amount more than

Donkey engine, mules, and masts on the waterfront at Broadway Wharf, ca. 1880.

impressive even to the cashier of the Bank of California. Every depositor, however small, who came up to a teller's window in the Bank of California with a check or withdrawal slip in his hand was bleeding Ralston, and as the months passed, more and more of them came with those insidious slips—no run, yet, but a constant, fearful drain. Public confidence in the bank began to slide, prodded along by innuendoes and outright attacks in some of the local newspapers ("Ralston's Ring is entrenched behind bank-counters and installed in comfortable chairs," said the *San Francisco Bulletin*. "Its dangers smack of the villa, bank, and palace rather than the back-alley and slum. For all that, its bite is more vicious than that of New York's Tweed Ring.").

Rumors cluttered the air, pressures mounted, and Ralston, whose nose for the emotional drift of the financial district remained as sharp as ever, could discern an impending crisis. Cash—that was the thing! He had to have cash. He sold a sixteen-thousand-acre-block of Kern County land for $90,000 and fed it into the bank's reserves. He borrowed on his Spring Valley Water Company stock. He sold out chunks of San Francisco real estate at prices at a level with, and sometimes below, what they had cost him. He sold his interest in the Palace Hotel—his darling—to William Sharon for $1.75 million, only to have Sharon return the deed a few days later on the grounds that he could not raise the cash. Sharon refused an outright loan with the same excuse, though even Darius Ogden Mills came up with $750,000 as a personal loan. The drain continued in spite of everything, and by the last week of August 1875, the bank's reserves were almost gone. By August 25, they were so low that Ralston knew the bank could not survive even another day of regular business, much less any kind of run. But Ralston, ever the optimist, was sure he had the solution. In an attempt to recreate his triumph of 1869, he had hauled $1.4 million worth of bullion out of the bank-controlled Selby Smelting Works near Oakland, turned it over to the United States Mint for coining, and by the morning of August 26, the money trays of the Bank of California glistened with piles of new money. As an added resource, he had authorized William Sharon as his personal agent to sell blocks of bank-owned and Ralston-owned Comstock shares beginning on August 23.

That may have been his worst mistake. The market had been jittery for more than a month. Sharon's selling spree did little to steady it, and by the morning of August 26, the financial district fluttered in the wind of frantic assertions. The Bank of California had gone dead broke. Ralston's businesses were going bankrupt. The Bonanza Kings had ruined him on the Comstock. The Oriental Bank of London had coldly refused the Bank of California credit (this last, *almost* correct; the Oriental Bank had not exactly refused Ralston credit—it had merely ignored his frequent cables). The fever of uncertainty climbed during the day as Sharon continued his methodical sales program, and by two o'clock in the afternoon the run that Ralston had feared for so many months, the run he had hoped to deflect with the glitter of all the gold in his money trays, had begun. Hundreds of depositors crowded through the great bronze doors of the Bank of California, spilled down its steps, clamored at its windows, piled up in the street outside, waving checks and withdrawal slips, chattering with panic. By 2:40, the bank's reserves were down to only $40,000. Ralston, outwardly unruffled by the commotion, walked over to his chief teller. "We will not cash any more checks today," he said calmly. One by one, the tellers' cages closed, deaf to entreaties. Muttering and shouting its frustration, the crowd oozed out of the bank and the huge doors closed with a sound like the knell of mourning.

William Sharon, Senator from Nevada, confidant of Ralston, and a man singularly devoted to the interests of number one.

The date, August 26, 1875; the time, 2:40 P.M.; the place, Montgomery Street, in front of the Bank of California; the occasion, failure.

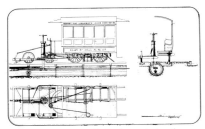

Andrew S. Hallidie's original patent drawing for his cable car system, the first in the country, the first in the world.

The Bank of California had failed.

That night, Ralston told his wife that they would have to close down the estate at Belmont and their town house on Pine Street and move in with friends. She took the news numbly, without questioning. The next morning, the bank's board of directors held a meeting that excluded Ralston. When it was over, Darius Ogden Mills walked into Ralston's office. "We have decided to ask for your resignation," Mills said. "In writing." Silently, Ralston scribbled out the requested letter and handed it to Mills. He then had the bank's notary public legalize a deed of trust conferring upon William Sharon all of Ralston's personal holdings to be used to pay off the bank's unsatisfied depositors, the remainder to go to his wife and children. The business of the day finished, at three o'clock he strolled down for his customary swim in the bay. An hour later, his body was pulled from the water. A coroner's jury pronounced his death as accidental, very likely the result of a stroke. Others were not so sure, including William Sharon. That evening, Sharon turned away after looking briefly into the dead man's face as he lay in state. "Best thing he could have done," he said.

WILLIAM CHAPMAN RALSTON'S body was carried to its grave on Monday, August 30, in a six-mile procession that wound from Calvary Church on Powell Street to the cemetery at Lone Mountain. "By nine o'clock," the *Chronicle* reported, "a dense mass of people had congregated for blocks about Calvary Church . . . and along the route of the procession. There have been one or two other occasions when the people of this city have gathered en masse to pay their respects to death and his guest; but the sincere demonstration of today has not been seen before, nor will it be witnessed again, in San Francisco."

San Franciscans, then as now, displayed a remarkable devotion to the memory of those men—and some women—who seemed to appear larger than life; Billy Ralston certainly qualified, and the public demonstration of grief at the passing of "the man who built San Francisco," as he was frequently eulogized, was unquestionably sincere. Yet it may also have represented something more profound than simple lamentation at the departure of one of the city's heroes. We often speak of the inarticulate, unsystemized strength that accompanies an idea whose time has come. It may well be that the body public of San Francisco who stood on sidewalks to mourn the death of William Ralston was paying mute tribute to an idea whose time had gone.

Even as he consolidated his power into the entity called the Bank of California, even as he fashioned his vision of San Francisco, even as he put a financial hammerlock on the Comstock Lode, even as his success appeared to be unstoppable, Ralston was functioning in a world rapidly expanding beyond his comprehension. His personal crusade to establish what amounted to a Pacific Republic—culturally and economically, if not politically—was hopeless in the face of a world that would not be ignored. It was overwhelmed by the weight of history, which, as Henry George had pointed out, was heading west on the transcontinental railroad. Ralston could not see it; perhaps would not see it. To the end, he operated as if the economic decline that overtook him and his city were a purely local problem amenable to local solution by a few whole-souled, dedicated men—and a lot of money. But the game was being played by different rules now, and his failure to recognize this destroyed him.

Had he lived beyond 1875, he might have learned to recognize it, but the

Steam and sail: the Sacramento sidewheel steamer Chrysopolis *boils out of port on its way to the Carquinez Straits, ca. 1870.*

signs of a new age were apparent even before then. As the national depression of 1873 staggered the East, it sent thousands of unemployed men and their families to California, whose appeal as a land of gold and opportunity had not diminished. Between 1873 and 1875, two hundred sixty-two thousand people arrived in California, most of them by rail, at least sixty thousand of whom were factory hands. What they found when they arrived, of course, were conditions that approached the worst the East could offer. There were not enough mines, mills, factories, foundries, refineries, lumber yards, shipyards, or wheat farms to keep even the state's resident labor force regularly employed, much less the newcomers.

Hardly improving the situation was the presence of the Chinese. The completion of the transcontinental railroad released somewhere between fifteen and twenty thousand Chinese laborers, most of whom drifted back to California. Between 1870 and 1875, another eighty thousand arrived as immigrants. Of this total of something close to one hundred thousand, most were able-bodied males ready and willing to compete for jobs at wages most Caucasian workers not only considered beneath their dignity, but beneath the simplest survival levels. The temptation to employ Chinese, predictably enough, was well-nigh irresistible, and by the latter 1870s, their labor population comprised perhaps 20 percent of the total working population in the city. In San Francisco alone, the Chinese represented 52 percent of the boot- and shoe-makers, 44 percent of the brick-makers, 84 percent of the cigar-makers, and 32 percent of the woolen mill operators.

San Francisco's union community—like the rest of the city's social and economic structure—was simply not equipped to deal with such a phenomenon. Since the end of the Civil War, San Francisco had been, in effect, a "closed-shop" town, whose craft guilds and workers' societies played a major and generally accepted part in the city's economic life, much of it based on the concept (unique at that time anywhere in the United States) of the five-dollar day. There had been strikes here and there—bakers marching out for a ten-hour day, machinists for an hourly increase, that sort of thing—but such strikes were usually short-lived and singularly nonviolent. In San Francisco, there was, to all intents and purposes, no labor "problem." But that condition, like Ralston's free-wheeling financial adventuring, depended in large part on San Francisco's continued isolation from the rest of the country. When the railroad destroyed that isolation and spilled all those unemployed refugees into the state, and when these were added to the flood of Chinese already in San Francisco, the closed shop disintegrated, and the five-dollar day with it.

Thus was created a social substratum previously unknown in San Francisco, one that bubbled with discontent. The bubbling increased when the Bank of California failed, taking many of the city's banks with it (the crowds that had been ushered out of the Bank of California had surged on to others, operating on the traditional assumption that in such moments all banks were entitled to an equal share of guilt). Even though the Bank of California reopened with much self-congratulatory fanfare five weeks later, together with most of the rest of the banks, the fiscal uncertainty represented by its failure did not go away, so that by 1877 the laborers' discontent had developed into a full, rolling boil.

Unemployed workers from all over the state wandered into San Francisco, congregating on streetcorners, in workingmen's saloons, on vacant lots, muttering grimly about their condition and casting baleful glances at the monuments to other men's wealth that rose all around them. On the night of July

An outing of ambitious dimensions pauses and poses beneath Bridalveil Falls in the Yosemite Valley, summer, 1880.

Revolution by picnic: a bill of the Workingmen's Party of 1878.

SUNDAY,
March 31st.
THE OPEN LETTER
PICNIC
—WILL TAKE PLACE AT—
Shell Mound Park
BERKELEY,
Under the Auspices of the
WORKINGMEN'S PARTY OF
CALIFORNIA.

WILLIS' BAND
OF 16 PIECES.

THE TENTH WARD INDEPENDENTS
WILL ACT AS GUARDS OF HONOR.

☞ PROGRAMME. ☜

THE Band will assemble at the Sand Lot at 9:30 o'clock, A. M.
The Board of Directors, Printers, Carriers, Reporters and Editors will head the Procession.

The Band.

Tenth Ward Independents, as Guards of Honor, Capt. Wiggins, Commanding.

Stockholders, Subscribers, Friends and all members of the Workingmen's Party, and all who desire to spend a day in the country, at one of the most delightful Parks in the State.

The following Exercises will take place at the Park, and Mayor Andrus, of Oakland, will preside:

D. Kearney, W. Wellock, H. L. Knight, M. Steinle, Mr. Gans, H. M. Moore, F. Rooney and others, will speak to the question, "The Chinese Must Go."

Fine interludes by the Band.

Little JENNIE WELLOOK............In Recitation.
Labor Shall be King."

Miscellaneous.

Dancing will commence at 2 o'clock P. M. and continue until 5:30 o'clock P. M.

Admission to the Park...................25 cents.
Children.........................Half Price.

If it rains it will be considered postponed, but if the sun shines there will be a legion go.

Special trains run to the grounds direct, at 10:30 A. M. and 12 M.

FARE FOR ROUND TRIP.......   25 cts.

23, 1877, six or seven thousand gathered on a sandlot across from San Francisco's city hall to express sympathy for workers in the great Pennsylvania Railroad strike of that year (yes, indeed, the problems of the nation were the problems of San Francisco by now). Generally peaceful, the meeting took on an ugly tone when some lunatic fired a couple of shots into the crowd, wounding two workers; police apprehended him before he found himself dangling from a rope, but the meeting was finally climaxed when a small contingent of workers split from the larger group and ran amok for a time, burning several Chinese laundries.

The city's business leaders, long apprehensive that a major riot would erupt among the local unemployed, gathered the next afternoon in the offices of the Chamber of Commerce and elected a Committee of Public Safety under the leadership of none other than William T. Coleman, who later dismissed the problems besetting the city as "an agitation among the workingmen of a socialistic nature." With some experience in extra-legal law enforcement, the old vigilante recruited a defense force of five thousand men, armed them with good hickory pickhandles, and sent them out to patrol the city streets. Coleman compared the operation favorably to the vigilance committee of 1856 in his recollections: "In 1877 the same people, in the same place, under different conditions and yet in some regards similar, finding danger from the same elements but on a grander scale in some respects, determined to act in the spirit of the law but in a different mode." Whatever the mode or the spirit, Coleman's "Pickhandle Brigade" came in handy two nights later, when a mob attempted to burn down the docks shared by the Pacific Mail Steamship Company and the Central Pacific's Occidental & Oriental line, the largest overseas carriers of Chinese immigrants. The docks were protected, but four men were killed, several wounded, and a nearby lumber yard sent up in flames. No further rioting occurred, however, and a few days later the committee's army was disbanded, replaced by one hundred fifty special police financed by agitated property owners.

Over the next few months, the city's disenchanted gradually coalesced into an organization of their own. Dubbed the Workingmen's Party of California, the new group largely represented the organizational efforts of an Irishman named Denis Kearney, once a mate on a British square-rigger, now owner of a small drayage concern, and, strangely enough, a recent soldier in Coleman's Pickhandle Brigade. With much red-faced, arm-waving oratory and the repeated cry of "The Chinese must go!" Kearney addressed meeting after meeting on the sandlots of San Francisco throughout the summer and fall of 1877. He was once arrested and jailed for inciting to riot (although, unfortunately for the authorities, no riot had occurred), was released a martyr, and when the Workingmen's Party was formally organized, emerged as its president. "We will have a new party," Kearney rhapsodized, "the Workingmen's Party. No great capitalist, no political trickster, no swindler or thief shall enter it. We will fill the offices with honest poor men who will make laws to protect themselves. We will send the Chinese home, distribute the land of the grabber, tax the millionaire, make a law to hang thieves of high as well as low degree, elevate the poor, and once more return to the simple virtue of honest republicanism." The new party achieved almost instant popularity, and affiliate groups were soon scattered over the state.

The medium through which Kearney's version of the millennium might be introduced presented itself in the constitutional convention of 1879, a response to the steady criticism that the state constitution of 1849 was too brief and general for the needs of a more complicated society. In the June 1878 election to choose delegates to this convention, the Workingmen's Party managed to capture 51 seats out of 152. By the sheer weight of numbers, the party managed to effect many reforms, including tax equalization, railroad regulation, the regulation of corporations and banks, a compulsory education law, and the prohibition of the use of Chinese labor in public works. Yet, as time would prove, these were "paper" reforms for the most part, easy to formulate but almost impossible to enforce. Moreover, the compromises involved in getting them into the constitution so disaffected party membership that it soon began to disintegrate into various partisan factions. And even the Oriental question, which had given the party its one theme of unity, was rendered pointless by the national Chinese Exclusion Act of 1882, which ended immigration from China. By then, the Workingmen's Party, the first major expression of protest on the part of San Francisco's new society, was a dead dream.

The Workingmen's Party was neither broad enough nor coherent enough to alter effectively the course of California's descent into the pit of industrial society. According to Henry George, it would not have made any difference even if the party had been broader in scope and deeper in purpose, for neither it nor any other political entity of the day recognized the one great need that faced not only San Francisco and California, but the entire nation: an economic revision of revolutionary proportions. Since his *Overland Monthly* essay of 1868, George had spent more and more of his mind's time on the question of why, as society progressed, the lot of the few became better while the lot of the many deteriorated. The answer, he finally determined, lay in the land—or, rather, our use of the land. In a pamphlet published in 1871, *Our Land and Land Policy, National and State*, George first articulated his theory. The story of land in California, he wrote, was one of "greed, of perjury, of corruption, of spoliation and high-handed robbery, for which it will be difficult to find a parallel." Everywhere, he said, land was valued not as a resource, but as a commodity; not as a fruitful and productive gift of nature, but as an income-producing agent. Land was money, not life, and because land was treated as money it was withdrawn from those who would use it as God intended. Even San Francisco, with the "opportunity to build up a great city, in which tenement houses and blind alleys would be unknown; in which there would be less poverty, suffering, crime, and social and political corruption of any city of our time . . ." had abandoned its responsibility, sold its public lands to speculators who laid down a dismal, grid-like pattern of lots designed to satisfy the demands of maximum profit.

George's idea would not go away. In 1875, out of a job as editor (and in a small way, part owner) of the *San Francisco Post*, George accepted the position of State Gas Meter Inspector, a splendid sinecure that gave him time to rationalize his land theories. They appeared, finally, in *Progress and Poverty: An Inquiry into the Cause of Industrial Depression and of Increase of Want with Increase of Wealth*. While the book's scope was quite as expansive as its title, it still expressed, as Kevin Starr has written, "a specifically Californian anger that the land had been denied the people. . . ." The book abounded with bitter images of an empty, misused land, and of a people denied their legacy. "And on uncultivated tracts of land in the new State of California," George wrote at one point in the book, "may be seen the blackened chimneys of homes from which settlers have been driven by force of laws which ignore natural right, and great stretches of land which might be populous are desolate, because the recognition of exclusive ownership has put it in the power of one human

Denis Kearney, the "immigrant Irish drayman" who gave voice to the short-lived, if cantankerous, Workingmen's Party, articulating frustration in sandlot perorations.

The "Terrible Disappointment of the Ass" (Denis Kearney), as portrayed by Edward Keller in The Illustrated Wasp, 1878.

creature to forbid his fellows from using it." And that monopoly, he went on, was the key to understanding the paradox of progress and poverty, for "the ownership of land is the great fundamental fact which ultimately determines the social, the political, and consequently the intellectual and moral condition of a people."

Unlike *Our Land and Land Policy*, which only hinted broadly at it, *Progress and Poverty* went on to propose in considerable detail a solution that would "remove want and fear of want," that would "give all classes leisure, and comfort, and independence, the decencies and refinements of life, the opportunities of mental and moral development. . . ." The solution was the Single Tax. For generations, he maintained, individuals had been using land as if it were money gathering interest in a bank. This "interest" came in one of two ways: either as exploitation in the form of rent charged to those who would use the land productively, or as a kind of usury in the form of holding land unused until such time as purely external conditions increased its value and it could be sold at a profit—the "unearned increment." Yet both rents and the unearned increment were values imposed by the needs and the presence of the whole community, not by the land itself, nor by anyone who might happen to own it without either using it or improving it. Those values should be returned to the community which created them. And the form by which this could be accomplished was the Single Tax, a tax based on the rental value or the unearned increment of land as it increased in value. Such a tax would be the *only* tax imposed by the state; it would support government and public institutions, destroy land speculation and monopoly, and inevitably return the land to those who would nurture it in the manner dictated by reason, nature, and logic.

Formed out of the crucible of George's experiences and observations of the 1860s and 1870s in San Francisco, the ideas expressed in *Progress and Poverty* found an audience that ultimately came to include much of the western world. Before George's death, *Progress and Poverty* would sell more than two million copies, the most impressive record achieved by a serious economic treatise. For millions of people, he became "the prophet from San Francisco," and if the Single Tax itself was never seriously put into practice, the insights and arguments of his book qualified him as the most original economic thinker the United States had ever produced, a thinker whose influence was such that one economist, Sidney Webb, went so far as to say that "the event which, more than any other, stimulated the revival of socialism in Great Britain was the publication of an American book, Henry George's *Progress and Poverty*." It was the world that called his attention now, and in 1880 the printer from San Francisco packed up and moved to New York, that rabbit hutch of social injustice whose "shocking contrast between monstrous wealth and debasing want" had altered the course of his life in 1868. He died while running for mayor of New York—and a likely winner, too.

These are the sort of things our great-grandmothers wore. Well, not all of them, but enough to cause us to wonder precisely how it was that so many of them ever got to be great-grandmothers.

I**N THE SPRING OF 1859**, these three men—William C. Ralston, Adolph Sutro, and Henry George—had mortgaged their hopes on a city trembling between the end of one era and the beginning of another. Now only Sutro was left. His Comstock tunnel, begun with marginal financing in 1869, had struggled through nearly nine years and four miles of mountain before completion on June 30, 1878, Sutro scrambling around for money all the while. And sure enough, the tunnel worked; it began draining the mines immediately, and continued to do so for more than fifty years. But it came too late. The great ore bodies that had excited the imagination of the world swiftly degenerated into ore of less and less value, until by the end of 1880, the total annual output amounted to less than $2 million. In twenty years, the Comstock had been stripped, gutted, of more than $300 million worth of treasure.

There were many who believed that another bonanza could yet be found, who stretched their hopes thin toward that expectation, but Sutro was not one of them. In 1880, he sold out his interests in the Sutro Tunnel Company for an estimated $900,000 and turned his back on the project that had defined his life for fifteen years. He returned to San Francisco, invested his money both in the city's "outside lands" by Ocean Beach and in downtown property (ultimately acquiring nearly one-twelfth of the city's land area), ran for mayor and won, built monuments on his own land for the delight and edification of the public (and, reasonably enough, for the continued enrichment of "A. Sutro, his heirs and assigns"), and accumulated a superb library, which he ultimately bequeathed to the state of California.

That was Sutro's legacy to the city that had made him. Henry George's legacy was in the book whose impact has continued into our own day. What, then, of the legacy of William C. Ralston? It was inherited by men whose simple greed was as cold as the voice of Darius Ogden Mills, the thousandaire-made-millionaire by the good offices of Ralston's manipulations, when he walked into Ralston's office and demanded his resignation ("in writing"). It was inherited by men whose unenlightened self-interest was as singlemindedly devoid of compassion and social concern as Collis P. Huntington's methodical construction of a railroad empire. It was inherited by men with as little sense of obligation to posterity as the Bonanza Kings, who succeeded beyond all reason in the greatest game of all—the game of power—and left nothing of value to either the state or the city that had been their arena. It was inherited, finally, by men with the arrogant hypocrisy of a William Sharon, a man who could solemnly lift a toast to the memory of the departed Ralston at a civic function, then proceed to use his trust as Ralston's executor to bilk his widow and children out of their fair share of his estate, and ultimately acquire full ownership not only of the estate at Belmont, but of Ralston's most enduring monument, the Palace Hotel. Ralston's dream had fallen into the hands of trolls.

But it was not Ralston's dream alone. It was the dream that had colored an entire generation, that had spilled over into another, in however diluted or distorted a form. It was the dream that had enlivened a horde of strapping, hopeful young men thirty years before, that had sent them bravely across the continent, or through the jungles of Central America, or around Cape Horn in the single greatest adventure in the history of the nineteenth century. "And where are they now?" Mark Twain inquired of these boys who had pursued the quests of men. "Scattered to the ends of the earth—or prematurely aged and decrepit—or shot or stabbed in street affrays—or dead of disappointed hopes and broken hearts—all gone, or nearly all—victims devoted upon the altar of the golden calf—the noblest holocaust that ever wafted its sacrificial incense heavenward. It is pitiful to think upon." And with them now was William Ralston, who had sought, however imperfectly, to translate the basest metal of the dream into something of purpose and permanence for his city.

What was it they were thinking, those thousands of San Franciscans who had gathered on a summer Monday morning to watch the passage of Ralston's body to Lone Mountain? What was it to which they were saying goodbye—Billy Ralston, or a part of themselves?

Young America, young San Francisco—a moment in time when Joe Harris and his waterfront saloon were caught and fixed in the emulsion of a glass plate.

On the Loose in the Eighties . . .

With the development of the dry-coated glass negative packed and sold in boxes, it became possible for the professional and amateur photographer alike to make snapshots in the field. At the time these plates of the 1880s were exposed, anybody could catch the flight of a cannonball or of a sparrow, so had the art progressed from the days when the portrait artist had gripped the head of his model in a kind of iron coatrack to ensure a sharp picture.

Muybridge had pioneered the art of instantaneous photography; the "Merry Tramps" of Frank B. Rodolph, a commercial photographer of Oakland, could take to the field (or to the backyard) and capture the life and times as they saw it themselves.

Rodolph lived in Oakland, and his friends were part of the suburban class that commutes to the glass towers of downtown San Francisco today. So here was the life that we casual San Franciscans have lost. It was a life wherein a modest income could provide the amenities that both that age and our own admire. Yet we must realize that many amenities were created by the Merry Tramps themselves, as they strayed from the front porch to the tennis court and beyond.

THE MERRY TRAMPS TAKE AN OUTING. . . .
In an age where we look askance at most gang
activities, we can scarcely credit the enthusiasm
of the Victorians for charging about the countryside in great groups. But they did—and the
modern Sierra Club outing is one of the last
holdovers of these bygone times.

At the right, Rodolph may have combined
work with pleasure as he shoots a group
aboard a South Pacific Coast handcar. Below,
the Merry Tramps are out in force for an excursion to Sausalito. The date is 1884, the occasion
obscured by time. No doubt the group came
to Marin by way of the Oakland ferry and the
Sausalito boats—a great way to go that is
now essentially gone to us. It would have
taken an early start and a late return for such
a picnic day, but half the fun was in the coming
and going and the spirit of group adventure.

TRAMPING THE MARGINS OF THE BAY. . . . Poised at Land's End, two lady photographers of the Rodolph group get set to shoot the Marin Headlands. This barren countryside is now covered by groves of handsome trees that frame one view after another far better than could the amateur photographers from Oakland. Below is a grand outing to Angel Island, probably performed with the aid of a friend's yacht. Then, as now, Angel Island had the magical appeal of a tropic isle dropped into a great urban setting.

WHEN GRASS GREW IN THE STREETS. . . . The Amador Market was an institution by the time that Rodolph shot this scene of a score of butchers and buyers, passers-by, children, and dogs. Fresh game was a staple of the place and its atmosphere was as primitive as the games-playing children in their Sunday best working out the sportive possibilities of a pond in suburban Oakland. What on earth are they all *doing* around this mudhole, and why did Rodolph see fit to catch the action?

HIGH SUMMER. . . . And the little girls of Oakland are out to pick blackberries in the tiny jungles of a civilized landscape. If you are bemused by the ever-present hiking boots on today's youth, then take a look at the footgear of this group. These were our grandmothers or even great-grandmothers, people scarcely known to us but not so far removed from our times and thoughts as we may think. Then, as now, the childhood years were measured off in summers, and the summers themselves measured off in outings sometimes recorded by the camera.

This picture may have been made when the Rodolphs and several other families had set out for the hills of present-day Tilden Park. In any event, the girls, from post-toddler to pre-adolescent, arranged themselves at the roadside for the generation-bridging camera.

PACKING IN. . . . With bedrolls, baggage, weaponry, and photographic equipment, the advance guard of the Merry Tramps penetrates the wilds of the Santa Cruz Mountains. The bagged critter carried by the hunters is probably a leg of mutton imported from the Amador Market, for it is too big for a rabbit and too small for a bear.

A leafy bower in a bosky dell did not suggest to our Victorian ancestors the idea of sleeping on the ground or scrambling about in cut-off Levis. Settled down in a comfortable tent equipped with proper cots, they spent vacation time improving the surroundings.

END OF THE LONG SUMMER. . .
Below is "Our Chowder Party,
August 30, 1885." This festive
gathering seems to have been
not far from the picnic site seen
at the left—an embayment near
the Golden Gate. The chowder
party at the beach or on Angel
Island dates back at least as far
as the grand Angel Island
festivity of Captain Moody's
yachting friends in the late
1850s as recorded in *Hutchings'
California Magazine*. Hail to fresh
chowder and the fruit of the
vine!

HoIST HIGH THE FLAG AND SING OF LIBERTY. . . . While the yachtsmen and Master Mariners turned out for sailing races on the Bay, while militia companies and fraternal organizations marched through the city streets, while patriotic orations reverberated from the fronts of downtown business blocks, the Merry Tramps bedecked their retreat in the redwoods (and even the harness of the horse that carted in their stores) with Old Glory's stars and stripes.

In fact a dray must have been needed to pack in the initial vacation equipment, such as the cast-iron stove presided over by the Chinese cook and his helper.

Yet if there was a hired cook in this era when help was cheap, there was also no laundromat next to a supermarket down the road a piece. Instead, there were the women of the contingent, who scrubbed up and hung out—cheerfully now!—more than anyone today would care to contemplate.

Then, as now, relaxation in the out-of-doors involved working like a mule. "Days of ticks and nights of fleas,/swollen feet and rock-barked knees./Far away from our employment,/in the wilds we find enjoyment."

Chapter VIII

PORTRAIT OF A MEMORY

THE BRIDGING OF TIME is a shadowy business at best, an uncertain mix of fact, speculation, and memory. For the serious historian of San Francisco the problem is compounded when he encounters the city of the 1880s, 1890s, and that brief period just past the turn of the century—the Mauve Decades, the Gilded Age, the Victorian Era, call it what you will. The San Francisco of those years, encrusted with real and imagined memory, is one of the most permanent images we have of the city's past. There are those still around—a diminishing handful—who can remember the city as it was then, and for the most part they remember it as Will Irwin remembered it when he gave San Francisco its classic eulogy in 1906 as "the gayest, lightest hearted, and most pleasure loving city of the western continent, and in many ways the most interesting and romantic. . . ." Such recollections vigorously maintain that the dream which had given the city birth and seduced the attention of the world shone undimmed in these years, as bright with the promise of tomorrow as it had ever been. Yet if we have the tendency to make saints of dead men who are not around to defend themselves, we are equally capable of doing the same to a city whose reality may have been more—or less—than what it is remembered to have been. Sheer common sense would suggest a certain darkness lurking behind all the bright memories, a darkness populated by the ghosts of irony and counterpoint, and any thoughtful portrait of the city-that-was cannot ignore them.

First, let us consider those shells of elegance, the palaces of the great. They were impressive. Even those who disliked them, who deplored their seemingly mindless eclecticism or their incongruous Greco-Roman-Italianate magnificence, could not deny that. Like fortresses, they crowned that windy eminence which by 1880 had long since been christened Nob Hill, the "nob" a corruption of nabob, the "nabob" a half-envious, half-contemptuous term for those whose tickets had paid off in the lottery of the American dream. The largest of these homely castles was the Hopkins mansion at the southeast corner of Mason and California streets, a sprawling, turreted architectural conglomerate that might

"San Francisco breeds all sorts. A few are born with a drop of iron in their souls. . . ."

151

Chinese New Year in San Francisco, 1877.

The Stanford mansion at California and Powell streets in about 1880—the burnt umber celebration of a railroad mogul.

Interior of the Stanford mansion, 1880; appearances to the contrary notwithstanding, it was not a museum, but a place in which people actually lived. This is a view of the sitting room.

have been designed by a quarreling team of Albanian draftsmen. It was said that on a clear day this monster could be seen from as far away as the hills behind San Mateo, twenty-five miles south of San Francisco. Next door, painted a gloomy brown, sat the barn-like Stanford mansion, whose mansard roof hung over its walls like the brim of an immense derby. Diagonally across California Street from these two was the ornate Flood mansion, a massive hulk of eastern brownstone whose grounds were marked off by a $30,000 brass fence kept polished to a glittering sheen by a faithful retainer who had no other duty. Down the block at California and Taylor streets were the Colton and Crocker mansions, the first a comparatively modest reminder of the Hopkins residence, the second a heavily Roman structure behind which rose a sixty-foot "spite fence." The fence surrounded the three sides of the home of a luckless Chinese undertaker who had refused to sell his portion of the lot to Charles Crocker; Crocker wanted it all, and determined to get it by the simple expedient of cutting off his neighbor's sunlight with a wall. A little distance down the slope of Nob Hill, on Pine Street, stood the much less ambitious residence of Senator James G. Fair. To rectify his somewhat demeaning position in the hierarchy of the hill, however, the Senator had surrounded another slab of property on Mason Street between Sacramento and California with a high stone wall, and planned to erect a mansion on the spot so splendiferous that it would make even the Hopkins place look flimsy. (He died before starting the mansion and his daughters built the neo-Renaissance Fairmont Hotel on the property instead.)

If all this suggested the presence of a kind of royal enclave in the midst of the bastion of democracy called San Francisco, it was by no means an illusion—nor did it go unrecognized for what it was. The men who had contrived these urban castles were not merely wealthy; there were plenty of wealthy people in San Francisco in 1880. No, these men were *rich*, rich on that level at which money ceases to have real meaning. They were encrusted with wealth, weighted down by it, given a ponderous dignity by it; they wore it like armor and its possession defined their lives. Was the intellectual capacity of Leland Stanford submarginal at best? Illuminated by his money, those painful, minutes-long pauses in ordinary conversation while the former governor desperately rummaged around in his mind for words became the thoughtful ruminations of wisdom, and the phrases that sooner or later oozed from his lips were not simply listened to, they were embraced, treasured, written down, carried home to be told to wives over the dessert wine. Was James G. Fair a doddering libertine, as sexually irresponsible as he was morally bankrupt? Gilded by his Comstock fortune, his sordid excesses became charming peccadilloes, followed by much of the city's populace with all the amused and admiring attention that a London mob might have given the antics of Charles II. Was Charles Crocker vindictive, arrogant, and spit-on-the-floor crude? Blessed with the glitter of money, he became a diamond in the rough.

Such were the men who had inherited the dream. They toiled not; neither did they spin. They produced nothing, enriched nothing. They had acquired their wealth through means so purely exploitive that the mind is astonished at the ease and simplicity of it all. Fair and James L. Flood had assembled their monumental "pokes" not just by gutting the mountains of Nevada of their treasure, but much more significantly by their convoluted stock manipulations, coldblooded and brilliant. When the Comstock went "bust" in 1880, it was not such as Fair and Flood who were damaged. It was the thousands of small investors—the miners, shopkeepers, bartenders, shoe clerks, and domestic workers—whose blind faith in the mines had bloated the value of the nabobs' certificates and whose patrimonies had been steadily sucked away through all the years of assessments for exploratory tunneling, for new equipment, for rising milling costs, while those in control calmly and cheerfully raked everything off the top.

Stanford, Crocker, and Hopkins (three of the Big Four that included Collis P. Huntington, who now spent most of his days in New York and Washington administering the political needs of the company) had first assumed the mantle of royalty during the construction of the Central Pacific. The means were devious but effective. The Big Four had hit upon the notion of organizing their own construction company—an organization ostensibly independent of the railroad itself—calling it the Contract Finance Corporation, and using it to siphon off so much of the federal loans authorized by the Pacific Railroad Act of 1862 that the railroad was kept in a state of near bankruptcy. In the end, the Contract Finance Corporation charged its own railroad an estimated $120 million for the construction of a line that had in reality cost less than $58 million, a clear profit to the associates of at least $62 million. Stanford, Crocker, and Hopkins would have been satisfied with that; they wanted, in fact, to sell the railroad outright and rest on the cushion of their fortunes. Huntington, a determined, foresightful, and persuasive man, talked them out of it.

Under his careful, patient supervision, the Central Pacific gathered unto itself a total of nine individual railroads in the state (which is to say *all* of the railroads worthy of the name), then purchased the California Steam Naviagion Company (giving the associates control over the state's northern internal waterway system). It started its own Pacific steamship line, the Occidental & Oriental (whose competition proved so ruinous to the Pacific Mail Steamship Company that it was ultimately absorbed by the Big Four). It effectively locked up across-the-bay transportation with an extensive ferry system which continued to operate until after the construction of the San Francisco–Oakland Bay Bridge and the Golden Gate Bridge, and acquired interests in several of San Francisco's various street railroad companies (including a California Street cable car line which, it was said, was constructed so that the associates would be able to get from Market Street to Nob Hill without difficulty). Finally, the organization reincorporated in 1884 as the Southern Pacific Railway Company, a Kentucky corporation (Kentucky's corporation laws being lenient to the point of nonexistence), and proceeded to run its transportation empire where, when, and for how much it chose, setting and changing its freight and passenger rates with a whim of steel and without visible interference on the part of any regulatory body. The whole system, given its beginning by millions of dollars in federal loans (which the company was not forced to pay back until 1910, and then only in part), and supported by federal land grants that ultimately amounted to more than twenty million acres (whose timber, agricultural development, and land sales generated—and generate—a substantial part of the company's income), was a vast machine for making money.

To ensure that his splendid, multi-leveled monopoly would not be tampered with, Huntington methodically bought politicians and bureaucrats as if they had been so many maidens on an Arabian auction block, either through outright bribes or by promises of financial and arm-twisting help during elections—and the corollary threat of powerful opposition. Until his death in 1878, the company's political strong-arm boy in California was David D. Colton (the "half" of what critical newspaper editorials were wont to call the "Big Four- and-a-half"); from 1878 to 1893, the job was performed by W. W. Stow, until he resigned to become director of Golden Gate Park; from 1893 on, the

Leland Stanford, Mrs. Stanford, and Leland Stanford, Jr., whose name was given by his mother and father to the second major university founded in California.

position was filled by William F. Herrin, who so refined and improved it that virtually no corner of California's political world was left untouched by the "Octopus." If we see this now as corruption on a grand scale, as cold and efficient as the company's transportation network itself, the men who practiced it and profited from it saw the whole business as nothing less than survival. As David Lavender has written, "Self-defense and the survival of the fittest, their attitudes proclaimed, were the first law of economics as well as nature. In fulfillment of that law they would do, with no sense of wrong, whatever was necessary to protect their great achievement against erosion by politicians . . . competitors, or raiding speculators, just as they would have protected their homes against robbers or wild animals. If this involved breaking unjust laws (and the associates could define justice to suit themselves), then they would do it."

The castles of the great were inhabited by Darwinian mutants whose motto, if any, would have echoed the words of Darius Ogden Mills: "We must protect ourselves and the country will take care of itself." Of them all and out of the hundreds of millions of dollars they represented, only Stanford presented a substantial legacy to the city and state which had provided him with the trappings of power, and we are allowed to wonder if that legacy—the creation and endowment of Leland Stanford Junior University—would ever have been undertaken had Stanford's son not died, draining his father's life of hope. For all their power, for all their influence, for all their wealth, these residents of Nob Hill occupied a place and represented a time out of joint with the city around them. Relics of a past whose dreams they had appropriated, they sat in aloof splendor, making few contributions to the growth and development of San Francisco; like all royalty in essentially democratic societies, they were largely vestigial, even ornamental. The corridors of their lives, like the halls and great rooms of the mansions they had erected—too ambitious to be called houses, too empty of meaning to be called homes—echoed with a certain hollowness; and the reverberations were the sound of irrelevance.

The Hopkins mansion, Nob Hill, San Francisco, in the 1890s—a feudal fortress whose towers could be seen to the horizon.

BELOW THEM, some five blocks down the hill to the east, was another city. We can call it the city of hope, for unlike the arid enclave of Nob Hill, which memorialized the exploited past, the area that spread in a rough triangle from Kearny Street down to the waterfront at East Street (now the Embarcadero) and from Clay Street south to Market—and another rough triangle bounded by Post, Powell, and Market—spoke of a commitment to the future, even if that future might only be tomorrow afternoon. It is not enough to describe this section of almost one hundred square blocks as the business heart of the city; it was that—but a good deal more. From the brick and galvanized-iron warehouses of the filled-in and built-upon waterfront to the square, granite office buildings of the financial district, from the sturdy relics of the gold rush years on upper Montgomery to the skyscrapers that began going up on Market in the 1890s, the section embodied much, if not most, of what generations to come would remember as the genuine city-that-was.

It was the city of banks and financial institutions, among them still most assuredly the Bank of California, whose Florentine facade reflected memories of Billy Ralston; the Bank of Nevada, Ralston's adversary, whose ornate block building attempted to out-rococo the Bank of California; the Wells Fargo Bank, which gathered the Bank of Nevada into its fold in 1893; the Hibernia Savings & Loan, begun as an Irish workingman's institution and soon one of the largest and most successful banks in the city; the small ground-floor offices of A. P. Giannini's Bank of Italy, the embryo of what would become the Bank of America, the largest in the world; and the Merchant's Exchange, whose crowding, shoving, chattering brokers dealt more often now with transactions in wheat and other commodities than with gold and silver stocks.

It was the city of merchandisers, from the Emporium on Market Street, which catered to the working class, to the City of Paris and the White House on the edge of Union Square, which filled the needs of the affluent. Kearny Street, from California to Market, may be said to have been the main artery of store-window commerce, however. It was a shopper's delight, a thoroughfare crowded with art galleries and notions stores, milliners and dressmakers, druggists, hairpiece makers, tailors, jewelers, high-class grocers, vintners, a place where anything from a cast-iron toy to an original gown from the *beau monde de Paris* could be bought. During the day it clamored with pedestrians and horsecars, buggies and broughams, and even at night the hearty bustle continued:

"After the gas is lighted," B. E. Lloyd wrote in *Lights and Shades in San Francisco*, "Montgomery Street is almost deserted, but Kearny is gayer than before. Those who have been confined in the workshop and office during the day, seek recreation on the street at night. The stores are brilliantly lighted, and look more gorgeous than in the light of day. Thousands of pedestrians move slowly through the street—a motley stream of humanity. . . . On almost every corner is observed one of the numerous curbstone dealers, crying out his business to the passing throng—'Pea-nuts, pea-nuts, fresh roasted pea-nuts, five cents a glass!' 'Oranges, sweet oranges, two-bits a dozen!' 'Peaches and apricots, ten cents a bag!'—accompanied by the piping tones of the hand-organ, as the 'Marseillaise,' 'America,' or 'Star Spangled Banner,' are ground slowly out in measured staves; while, in the middle of the street, perched upon a box, the patent medicine dealer delivers his lecture. Aside from these criers there is little noise on the street. The army of promenaders pass and repass, and only a low hum of voices is heard. A sound of revelry may break forth from the brilliantly-lighted saloons, or subdued notes of music may be heard as they float up from the concert cellars, but there is seldom any boisterous outburst to grate upon the ear. Until ten o'clock there is no perceptible diminution in the number of persons on the street; but soon after that hour, aching limbs and tired feet begin to call for rest, and gradually the throng disperses. . . . The lights no longer burn in the stores, and the tramp of the lonely policeman, as he treads his weary beat, echoes in the stillness of the night."

It was the city of hotels and restaurants and theaters and elegant parlor houses. Of the Lick House, the hostelry created by James Lick, a piano-maker who stumbled ashore in San Francisco in 1847 with $35,000, immediately began purchasing real estate, and before his death had run his fortune into the millions—almost all of which was bequeathed to the future in the form of the Lick Observatory on Mount Hamilton, the Mechanics Library on Post Street, and a dozen similarly benevolent projects. Of the Baldwin Hotel on Market and Powell, the splendid child of E. J. "Lucky" Baldwin, Comstock speculator, racing fancier, creator of the Santa Anita racetrack of Southern California, and helpless spectator when his magnificent—and uninsured—San Francisco hotel burned before the turn of the century, utterly ruining him. Of the Russ House, the Grand, the Occidental, the Cosmopolitan, the American Exchange, the Morton, the Commercial—and above all, of the Palace, the "great caravan-

If gold in the 1850s fed the imagination of the world, it was the California wheat of the great Central Valley that fed its stomach in the 1880s and 1890s; this scene of about 1885 shows a steam thresher in the wheat fields east of Martinez.

The Annie L., *one of that crowded fleet of "square-toed packets" called scow schooners that hauled the produce of the great Central Valley to the port of San Francisco during the last quarter of the nineteenth century and a few years of the twentieth.*

From the beginning, San Francisco was a town of transients, hotel-dwellers, boardinghouse denizens, and apartment renters, and "eating out" was a tradition that leapt across the generations right into our own. Above, a family samples the toothsome offerings of Spreckel's Rotisserie on the fifteenth floor of the Call Building in the 1890s.

If eating out was a tradition by the 1890s, so, too, was the Poodle Dog Cafe, an institution that moved around the city as if it were a person, claiming several addresses before the fire of 1906. Wherever it went, it offered a generous menu and a seemly upstairs privacy for the sort of revels documented by the National Police Gazette *in the drawing below.*

serai'' of Billy Ralston's dream, owned now by William Sharon and host to the great and near-great of the nation and even the world: from King Kalakaua of Hawaii to Emperor Dom Pedro of Brazil; from former President Ulysses S. Grant in 1879 to current President Theodore Roosevelt in 1903. Of the Maison Dorée, the Poodle Dog, and Marchand's, where the "gloved and glossy young men about town" and their female companions ingested the best of French cuisine in curtained and cushioned booths and discreet upstairs bedroom suites, and of Campi's, where they were graced with the toothsome and expensive pastas of the Italians; of the United States Restaurant, the Tadich Grill (the "Original Cold Day Restaurant"), Hoffman's, and a couple of dozen other steak, fish, chop, and oyster houses that fed the hungry armies of the business district at lunch and dinner; of the What Cheer House, the Sailor's Delight, the Fair Wind, and the scores of cheap restaurants that filled the bellies of the proletariat. Of the California Theatre (Ralston's legacy), Maguire's Opera House, the Tivoli Opera House, and Wade's Opera House (in all of which genuine operas were in fact occasionally presented), and the Columbia Theatre (whose sprightly band came under the baton of the popular Eugene E. Schmitz in the 1890s). Of the lush bagnios of the "Uptown Tenderloin," of "Diamond Jessie" Mellon's places on Ellis and Eddy streets or those of Bertha Kahn and Johanna Werner on Sacramento Street, and a couple of dozen more scattered through Turk and Polk and Pine streets—"gilded palaces of sin," as B. E. Lloyd called them.

It was the city of the free lunch saloon, perhaps the noblest institution of the city's memory. San Francisco, suckled in its infancy on the raw *aguardiente* of the Mission fathers and weaned on the authoritative whiskies of the golden era, was still a drinking town. "Temperance societies are not very popular institutions in San Francisco," a schoolboy is alleged to have written as a classroom essay in the mid-1870s. "They interfere too much with business. There is lots of money made in San Francisco by saloons. If it wasn't for our papa's selling beer and whiskey along with other groceries, quite a number of us boys couldn't dress as good as we do, and get money to buy cigarettes. . . . But then there's two boys I know who have to wear ragged clothes and work, and have to smoke old cigar stumps, just because there are saloons in town where their fathers spend all the money they make for whiskey. I tell you I don't see through it. . . . I went down to see the License Collector, and he told me there was over two thousand saloons in San Francisco. That seems like a good many for a place of this size. That's all I can think of now, except that I don't think I'll ever drink." In 1889, Rudyard Kipling found the situation quite the same: "As you know . . . the American does not drink at meals as a sensible man should. . . . Also he has no decent notions about the sun being over the yard-arm or below the horizon. He pours his vanity into himself at unholy hours, and indeed he can hardly help it. You have no notion what 'treating' means on the Western slope. It is more than an institution; it is a religion, though men tell me that it is nothing to what it was. Take a very common instance. At 10:30 A.M. a man is smitten with a desire for stimulants. He is in the company of two friends. All three adjourn to the nearest bar,—seldom more than twenty yards away,—and take three straight whiskeys. They talk for two minutes. The second and third man then treat in order; thus each walks into the street, two of them the poorer by three goes of whiskey under their belt and one with two more liquors than he wanted. It is not etiquette yet to refuse a treat. The result is peculiar. I have never yet, I confess, seen a drunken man in the streets, but I have heard more about drunkenness among white men, and seen more decent men above or below themselves with drink, than I care to think about."

While pouring his "vanity" into himself at ungodly hours, the typical San Francisco male also was stuffing himself quite adequately between the hours of 11:00 A.M. and 2:00 P.M., for these were the happy hours of the free lunch, a phenomenon that crossed all social, economic, and political lines. At every unpretentious corner "grocery" the workingman with a nickel in his fist for a mug of beer could fill himself with plain but ample portions of cheese, bologna, dried beef, sausage, crackers, pickles, and mustard, and for some it was the most nutritious meal of their day—all free, free as air. At the "bit" saloons, hard-working shoe clerks and brokers' runners could toss back cheap whiskey and feed on a somewhat more varied menu. And in the most elegant of the saloons, those with cut-glass and crystal chandeliers, with tables of mahogany and marble, with walls adorned with paintings of meaty, Rubenesque women, with back bars that sparkled in a glory of mirrored glass, the brokers and bankers and merchants could sip their brandies and champagne and button punches and pisco punches with ready access to a free menu whose proportions and variety would have shamed New York's Delmonico's. The Palace of Fine Arts, on the ground floor of the Lick House, would offer on any given day the following selection of munchables as its free lunch: radishes, crab salad, celery, pig's head, Bolinas Bay clams, clam juice, head cheese, *saucisses à la famille*, beef *à la chili colorado*, chili con carne, Honolulu beans, chicken croquettes, veal croquettes, terrapin stew, fried clams, sardines, boiled ham, Saratoga chips (potato chips), corned beef, cold tongue, beef stew, pork and beans, chipped beef, smoked salmon, cheese, crackers, cracked crab, Holland herring, almonds, popcorn, and apples. Bilious and somewhat bleary, San Franciscans staggered back from the bars and free lunch tables to shuffle the papers and push the buttons that made the city go.

When drinking was an art, not an indulgence: This view of the interior of the barroom of "Lucky" Baldwin's hotel in 1878 suggests something of the seriousness with which San Francisco's male population approached the heady matter of deciding between a "Martinez" and a straight whiskey, with or without water back.

IT WAS NO ACCIDENT that in 1891 the ample Daniel O'Connell (he tipped the scales at close to three hundred pounds), who had joined with Henry George to found the *San Francisco Evening Post*, wrote a guidebook with the splendid title of *The Inner Man: Good Things to Eat and Drink and Where to Get Them*, for if this city of memory was one of banking and brokering, of hotels and theaters and restaurants and merchandise stores and saloons and free lunch, it was also the center of San Francisco journalism, big and little, and of the self-consciously bohemian *literati* that spread out around it like ripples in a pond. The freewheeling and sometimes murderous journalism of the city's early years had long since been transformed into something a little more stable, if still colorful. If the sight of an editor being horsewhipped or shot in the street was no longer a common part of the city's traditions by the turn of the century, it had in fact happened as recently as 1879, when Charles de Young, co-publisher of the *Chronicle*, was gunned to death by the son of then Mayor Isaac S. Kalloch in retaliation for de Young's having taken some shots at the mayor. And if the memory of that were not color enough, William Randolph Hearst's *Examiner* could offer Ambrose Bierce, whose "Town Crier" column, written with a pen dipped half in vitriol, half in wormwood, caused more than one San Francisco socialite to mutter that the man *ought* to be shot. Still, journalism in the city was big business now, a fact substantiated in the 1890s, when the city's first skyscraper started going up on Market Street on the corner of Third: it was the *Call* Building, still one of the most eloquent reminders of an age in which a skyscraper was a celebration of a person's ingenuity, not a comment on his anonymity. The *Call*, the *Bulletin*, the *Examiner*, and the *Chronicle*, all of them grouped on or near Market Street, were by then substantial enterprises.

Daniel O'Connell himself stood as a kind of link between this level of journalism and the more fragile expressions of the art, of which there was an abundance. His own *Post* never became more than marginally successful (and in fact ended its days as the mouthpiece of the Southern Pacific Railroad), but it cannot be said that the fact bothered him much. He was born in Ireland and educated by Jesuits, and the good life—which in his view included good food, good drink, good talk, and the pursuit of Truth, Art, and Knowledge—was to him far more important than building newspaper empires. In 1872, he joined with a few other like-minded journalists to form the Bohemian Club, with rooms in the Astor House on Sacramento Street. The organization soon became the focus not only of what might be called the underworld of journalism, but of much of the city's literary and artistic life. In time, its members came to include such diverse types as poets Charles Warren Stoddard, Gelette Burgess, George Sterling, Edward Robeson Taylor, and Joaquin Miller; newspapermen Frank Norris, Will and Wallace Irwin, and Prentice Mulford; painters William Keith, Virgil Williams, and Jules Tavernier; economist Henry George (before his departure to the East) and naturalist John Muir (who in 1892 formed another organization, the Sierra Club, the first in the country to be consciously dedicated to the preservation of wilderness); the abrasive Ambrose Bierce, the viticulturist Arpad Harazthy, the printer Edward Bosqui, and the millionaire-philanthropist-onetime-mayor (and later United States Senator) James Duval Phelan.

The Astor House gathering place of the Bohemian Club was a rather formal expression of the city's cultural life in these years; it was a genteel sort of exuberance, a respectable bohemianism. If the "High Jinks" theatricals in which the club specialized were usually hilarious, they were not often rowdy. Yet within walking distance of the Astor House stood another expression of the city's bohemian life, this one perhaps closer to the essence of the style. Most of those who belonged to the Bohemian Club were familiar with this other, but at the same time it encompassed a wide circle of those who would never have occasion to enter the elegant doors of the Astor House—the poets and writers whose work would never be read, much less printed, the painters whose work would never be shown, much less sold. The building in question was the Montgomery Block at the corner of Clay and Montgomery streets, on the very edge of the financial district. Affectionately dubbed the "Monkey Block" by those who knew it, the massive brick-and-granite building had been constructed in 1853 by James Halleck as a purely commercial enterprise, but by the middle of the 1880s, while it served its commercial purposes well enough, it had become something more than just one more downtown office building. It had its share of jewelry shops, milliners, lawyers' and doctors' offices, and on one corner the Bank Exchange, one of the oldest and most elegant saloons in the city. It also had on its upper floors a veritable warren of cheap apartments mixed with reasonable studio space and fairly expensive suites. It was in the Montgomery Block that Adolph Sutro stored most of his library collection for many years, and where painters William Keith and Jules Tavernier maintained studios. It was in the basement of the building that vineyard entrepreneur Arpad Harazthy had at one time or another stored vats of some of his best vintages, for protection against fire, and for the same reason the basement vaults of the place were for a long time popular repositories of gold and silver

George Sterling, who called San Francisco the "cool, grey city of love," the home of his heart. He took his life with a vial of cyanide to escape what the city told him of his lost youth and beauty, his talent spun out into the futility of late nights and empty talk.

coin and bars. And it was in the upper floors of the building that such as Mark Twain, Bret Harte, Mary Austin, George Sterling, Prentice Mulford, Ina Coolbrith, and scores of much more minor lights of the city's literary world had made their homes at various times, scribbling their poetry and essays and stories, cooking by the flame of gas rings, passing bottles of cheap red wine around in a circle of friends and colleagues while the talk bounced from the walls of tiny apartments until sunrise—a bohemian saraband, as ritualized as it was common to similar enclaves all over the country. It was not a club, the Montgomery Block, but a way of life for generations of real and would-be artists. It was the informal hostelry for a milling army of the destitute and the successful, who pursued various muses in the morning, and in the afternoon and evening congregated in Coppa's ground-floor restaurant, where Giuseppe "Papa" Coppa dispensed pasta and wine and credit, fuel for the pursuit of glory. Here, upcoming issues of the short-lived literary quarterly, *The Lark*, might be outlined; here, the almost daily contributions to the little newspaper, the *Wave*, from Frank Norris and the Irwin brothers would be praised or ridiculed; here, life had a glow of the same hope that energized the rest of the city.

Yet, just as among the shells of elegance that topped Nob Hill, there was a hollowness to be found in the Montgomery Block's masonry of hope, a darkness that hovered at the edge of dream. For some, the weakest and those most disturbed by the thinness of their talents and the failure that greeted even their best efforts, escape from the shadows that haunted them came with drink or opium or both, and for some, suicide. Both George Sterling and his wife Carrie ultimately took cyanide (though not simultaneously) to end the dream-become-nightmare. Even those of greater psychic strength—those like Mary Austin, the Irwin brothers, Gertrude Atherton, Frank Norris, Gelette Burgess, Mark Twain himself—had to flee the city in order to accomplish work of more than passing merit. In her novel *Ancestors* (1907), Atherton had one of her characters, Philip Stone, a failed painter, explain the problem: " 'San Francisco breeds all sorts. A few are born with a drop of iron in their souls. They resist the climate, and the enchantment of the easy luxurious semi-idle life you can command out here on next to nothing, and clear out. . . . Where they get the iron from God knows. It's all electricity with the rest of us. There are hundreds of my sort. You've seen them at the real Bohemian restaurants; young men mad with life and the sense of their own powers; all of them writing, painting, composing, editing—mostly talking. Then at other tables the old-young men who have shrugged their shoulders and simmered down like myself; lucky if they haven't taken to drink or drugs to drown regrets. Still other tables—the young-old men, quite happy and generally drunk. . . . Never was such a high percentage of brains in any one city. But they must get out. And if they don't go young they don't go at all. San Francisco is a disease.' "

Too easy an explanation, one supposes, but the image of the old-young, young-old artists spinning out their lives in talk and wine and not much else speaks of something false in the life of the city-that-was, for all its color, its gaudy, go-ahead enterprise, its banks and hotels and emporiums and theaters and skyscrapers which so aggressively proclaimed the future. Nor was this image alone. There was another, a symbol, we may call it, one as physically visible as it was mutely eloquent. It was to be the seat of government for the city of San Francisco, this symbol, and it stank of failed dreams.

An informal gathering of literary woodsprites in the Bohemian Grove along the Russian River in northern California, ca. 1900. It was here that the members of the Bohemian Club escaped—and still escape—the pressures of cityside concrete and conferences.

An afternoon ferryboat excursion of about 1895. What splendid mischief are those two delightful boys about to pursue?

"At the Ends of Our Streets Are Spars. . ."

Ships in admiralty law are persons, in common understanding, female persons, and in the eye of our late nineteenth century San Francisco photographer they were as numerous and distinct as the ladies of the Palace Court, the Kearny Street promenade, and the Barbary Coast.

CITIZENS OF THE SEA. . . . The sisterhood of ships and the brotherhood of seamen added more than color to San Francisco in its passage to maturity—they ratified the claim to metropolitan status that gold had optioned but that all the parvenu magnificence of cast-iron business blocks and gingerbread mansions could not itself buy.

In 1885, when the yachtsmen who exposed the plates seen on these pages cruised the Bay, over 500 square-riggers loaded central California wheat for the ports of Great Britain and northern Europe, and more than a few of their 15,000 crewmen stayed to work the coastal ships or take a job where their feet stayed dry. At the upper left, the rust-streaked "limejuicer" *Barfillan*, a four- or five-month Cape Horn voyage behind her, glides past Alcatraz under upper topsails as her crew tucks a furl in the fore royal and the main topgallant and the Whitehall boats of boardinghouse runners hover about her flanks.

Above, a "Dago fish-boat," immigrant built and manned, departs Fisherman's Wharf in quest of Pacific salmon. At the left is not a waterfront disaster but an almost anachronistic glimpse of an old technique: the "downeast" bark *Majestic* is hove down on her beam-ends so that shipwrights can recopper her wooden bottom.

A PEG TO FIT EACH HOLE. . . . The configuration of ships and boats was as varied and precisely efficient as that of the specialized vehicles one sees about a big construction project in our own day. Lumber schooners like the *Big River* (left) were designed to beat up the coast against the prevailing northwesterly winds without the nuisance of ballast in their holds, and carry back their weight in lumber from the "doghole" ports of Mendocino. They, and the three- and four-masters that sailed to Puget Sound, were as distinctive to the sailor's eye as a brewery truck would be to a landsman. A San Francisco development of the 1880s that even a locomotive driver would have spotted as unusual was the "steam schooner," a coastwise carrier exemplified by the little *Jewel* in an early form, when the masts still carried auxiliary sail to give the machinery a boost in a favoring breeze.

TIMBER-TOTING TEAKETTLES. . . . *Jewel* has a deckload of something in sacks which the skipper wants to keep dry, but it was lumber for the burgeoning cities of California that kept the steam schooners puffing from Bellingham to San Diego. And from Hoquiam or North Bend or dozens of other ports the thrifty traveler bought steam schooner passage to San Francisco.

OF NOTE OR NOTORIETY. . . . If the Italian fishermen had feluccas, the Chinese shrimpers would also have vessels to their own tastes and needs, as interpreted by August Schultze, master carpenter of Hunters Point. Below, the elegant *Annie*, once the agency of "Boss" William Marcy Tweed's flight from New York to Havana, sails past Fort Point as the tug *Sea Queen* hastens back to port after towing a laden Cape Horner to sea. At the right is a view of the Marin ferry *San Rafael* in her days of glory. She went to the bottom on the night of November 30, 1901, victim of a collision celebrated in the opening pages of Jack London's *The Sea Wolf.* London relates, "our pilot, white with rage, shouted, 'Now you've done it!' "

SAILING FOR OLD GLORY. . . . The regatta of the Master Mariners' Benevolent Association was the premier sporting event of the Fourth of July in the 1870s and again in the mid-'80s. The lumber schooners of the redwood coast and the hay scows of San Francisco Bay turned out in force, with other entrants ranging from the little sloops that fetched melons down Sonoma Creek up to such unlikely closed-course racers as the 500-ton barkentine *Makah*, seen below as she bears off toward the Fort Point stakeboat with splendid condescension toward the inside rights of the handy scow schooner in the foreground. The proud "Champion" banner of the Association was the trophy sought by these holiday sailors, but waterfront merchants put up all kinds of prizes for outstanding performance in the various classes, down to such useful annual mementos as a ton of coal for the galley stove. At the left, the scows *Granger* and *Garibaldi* reach neck and neck, while below the handsome "outside" schooner *General Banning* bounds home a winner on the last leg from the Presidio down to Meiggs Wharf.

A TOAST TO GOOD DAYS . . . AND
YESTERDAYS. . . . Photographer William
Letts Oliver, Commodore Gutte, and their
San Francisco Yacht Club cronies hoist a
glass aboard the Commodore's hospitable
Chispa in celebration of a time when even
sportsmen shared the common heritage of
the sea and the afterguard of a yacht
would have been at home on the poop of a
lumber schooner. Below, Oliver and his
gang hoist sail and anchor to get the
Emerald under way—while at the right two
of these yachtsmen-photographers and
their ladies visit a whaler of Herman
Melville's era, a relic preserved in San
Francisco's Arctic fishery and represented
in the rows of sailing ships wintering in
the quiet waters of Oakland Creek.

The National Police Gazette, *1885: "Saved from a Flaming Fate By the Bubbly: How Quick Thinking and Mumm's Extra Dry Prevented Tragedy in the Poodle Dog Cafe in San Francisco."*

Chapter IX

THE INHERITORS

FOR NEARLY THIRTY YEARS it stood unfinished, a towering, skeletal hulk, its stucco peeling, most of the girders of its great dome open to the sky, like a great crumbling tombstone on a triangular plot of land bounded by Market, Larkin, and McAllister streets—the site, in fact, of little Yerba Buena's original cemetery. It was San Francisco's splendid new city hall, destined, according to those who promoted it, to be "not only the largest and most durable structure in the city, but . . . the largest edifice of this description in the United States." The city had contracted for the building in 1871 with the architectural and construction firm of Shea & Shea; it was to have been completed within two years at a cost not to exceed $1 million. By the middle of the 1880s, the more cynical citizens of the town were calling it the "new City Hall ruin," taking a perverse kind of pride in its bony incompleteness. The building's exterior would not be finished until 1898 and it would not be occupied until 1900. The final cost was not $1 million, but $8 million—a pioneering exercise in the delights of the cost-overrun. Appropriately enough, soon after the building was occupied, it was discovered that for some unaccountable reason all of the structure's internal sewerage gathered in a reeking pool in its basement.

One would be hard pressed to discover a symbol that spoke more eloquently of the character and quality of San Francisco's city government throughout most of the 1880s and 1890s, a government that almost sardonically refuted all the hope that had been loosed by the grand explosion of the Gold Rush. The fact was that for all its youth, San Francisco by the 1880s had become as thoroughly corrupt as any city in the country. When the firm of Shea & Shea approached the city administrators year after year for almost thirty years, one hand out asking for more money, please, the other ready to deal a few bills off the top as kickback, it was by no means acting in splendid isolation; it was participating in a well-established and generally sophisticated tangle of venality whose sticky filaments attached themselves to nearly every manifestation of the city's life.

Ostensibly, until the transfer of offices to the "new City Hall ruin," the machinery of government was oiled and set in motion from rooms of an old masonry building on the corner of Kearny and Washington streets, the site in 1846 of Brown's Hotel, later of the Parker House, and still later the Jenny Lind Theatre, the El Dorado House, the Union Hotel, and the city's original Hall of Records. Throughout the 1870s, in fact, the government did operate here, under the tender ministrations of Republican political bosses Martin Kelly and

"I could not manage the politicians. . . ."

San Francisco's new City Hall (left rear) and Hall of Records (foreground), seen here shortly after they finally opened for business. The sewer stink in the basement was not the only smell to emanate from the interior of the structure.

Throughout most of its existence, the Barbary Coast was in fact a genuine sink of degradation— although this lively scene of the Bella Union theatre in operation suggests more innocence than outrageous depravity.

Phil Crimmons and Democrats Owen Brady and John Mannix. But in 1880 the seat of city government moved—spiritually, if not physically—next door to a prosperous tavern called the Snug Cafe (founded and owned by the legendary Duncan Nichols before he sold out and moved down the street to become a partner in the fashionable Bank Exchange in the Montgomery Block). The new owner was Christopher A. Buckley, one of Nichols's bartenders, who soon indulged himself in his own whiskey so enthusiastically that he was stricken ill and became blind. Recovered in bodily health, Buckley forthwith swore eternal temperance and dedicated himself to the political arts. By all accounts a slender, dapper, charming, and totally amoral being, Buckley utilized his position in the Workingmen's Party in 1879 to wrestle control of the Democratic Party in the city from Brady and Mannix, whose power had been steadily undermined by Kelly and Crimmons. With an instinct for the avenues of power and the weaknesses of his opponents that can only be called genius, in less than a year Buckley had reconstructed the Democratic Party into a muscular and all but unchallenged prominence, and his own position into something approaching one-man rule. With the debonair insouciance of a Tammany graduate, he sat in the back room of his saloon for fifteen years, memorizing voices and the grip of handshakes, receiving petitioners, passing out doles, licenses, and city contracts, transferring bribes, accepting bribes, dictating the names of municipal appointees, formulating party policy, cheerfully delivering the San Francisco delegation in state elections to whoever came up with the necessary wherewithal (more often than not, the Southern Pacific Railroad, under W. W. Stow and later William F. Herrin). He was "Blind Chris" Buckley.

Aside from such considerations as streetcar franchises or utility contracts, the greatest part of Buckley's power was generated in an area within walking distance of the Snug Cafe. From Washington Street on the south to Green Street on the north, from Powell Street on the west to East Street on the east, it encompassed a loose rectangle of nearly fifty square blocks divided into two separate enclaves—city-states, as it were—whose interests and occupations were nevertheless frequently intertwined. The first of these was the Barbary Coast, an area that extended roughly from Kearny Street down to East Street on the waterfront, whose main thoroughfare was Pacific Street, and which was perhaps most passionately described by B. E. Lloyd in his *Lights and Shades in San Francisco* in 1876:

"The Barbary Coast is the haunt of the low and vile of every kind. The petty thief, the house burglar, the tramp, the whoremonger, lewd women, cut-throats and murderers, all are found here. Dancehouses and concert saloons, where bleareyed men and faded women drink vile liquor, smoke offensive tobacco, engage in vulgar conduct, sing obscene songs, and say and do everything to heap upon themselves more degradation, unrest, and misery, are numerous. Low gambling houses thronged with riot-loving rowdies in all stages of intoxication are there. Opium dens, where heathen Chinese and God-forsaken women and men are sprawled in miscellaneous confusion, disgustingly drowsy, or completely overcome by inhaling the vapors of the nauseous narcotic, are there. Licentiousness, debauchery, pollution, loathsome disease, insanity from dissipation, misery, poverty, wealth, profanity, blasphemy, and death, are there. And Hell, yawning to receive the putrid mass, is there also." Also there were fetid brothels, which dispensed delight and disease in about equal portions; saw-horse-tabled saloons, which featured Mickey Finns and trapdoors for purposes of shanghaiing; and sailors' boarding houses ruled by crimps who specialized in providing warm bodies for that form of involuntary servitude known as the seaman's trade. Altogether, it was a place where a man could lose his senses, his virtue, his money, his health, his freedom, and his life, in more or less that order. And over it all was the comforting mantle of Blind Chris Buckley and his machine, assuring, for a suitable stipend, the renewal of liquor licenses, the disinterest of the police, the indifference of health authorities, and the impotence of reformers.

The second enclave was no less sordid, if somewhat more exotic, but enjoyed the distinction even then of being a major tourist attraction. It was called Chinatown; it held an estimated fifty thousand Chinese (although no reliable census of the city's Chinese population had ever been made), and not even the righteous B. E. Lloyd could fully escape the fabled seduction of the Far East: "Chinatown proper, that is, the portion of the city where the Chinese constitute almost the entire population, consists of sections of two blocks each of Sacramento, Clay, Washington, Jackson, and Pacific Streets, between Kearny and Stockton Streets; and Dupont [later Grant] Street from Sacramento to Pacific Streets. . . . In this territory a few whites are to be found, engaged in some small business, but the Chinese have monopolized almost all the business rooms, as well as the residence houses, and only that it is in the Occident, is it distinguished from an Oriental city. The few white stragglers that are met upon the streets are scarcely more numerous than would be found in any open seaport town in China, and they gaze about them with the same curiosity as do those who are visiting for the first time the cities of the Celestial Empire. Thus, in San Francisco, it is but a step from the monuments and living evidences of the highest type of American civilization, and of Christianity, to the unhallowed precincts of a heathen race, where unmistakable signs of a contrasting civilization, are seen on every side."

It was not merely raw xenophobia that colored Lloyd's description of the area, for there *was* an otherworldly air about Chinatown that spoke of people driven by both instinct and circumstance to gather together into a kind of ancestral ghetto that both cut them off from the opportunities of the larger society and protected them from its blind excesses. Unfortunately, it also left them helpless against the excesses of their own kind, and this city-within-a-city was, on its own level, and in its own manner, quite as mean and corrupt as San Francisco proper. This was the world whose legitimate commercial life was ruled by the Six Companies—the Sam Yup, Yung Wo, Kong Chow, Wing Yung, Hop Wo, and Yan Wo—which until the Chinese Exclusion Act of 1882 had financed the immigration costs of individual Chinese in exchange for periods of what amounted to indentured servitude and with this labor supply established themselves as the economic heart of Chinatown. This was the world whose illegitimate commercial life was ruled by organized gangs called tongs—among them the Kwong Docks, Suey Sings, Sum Yops, and Hop Sings—groups fully as competitive as any Chicago gang of the 1930s and equipped with the same sort of hired murderers and armies of fighting men, called *boo how doy*. This was the world of that pigeon coop of fornication called the "crib," the twelve-by-fourteen-foot arena of the Chinese slave girl.

Like dark little railroad cars, the cribs were strung throughout Chinatown, along Dupont Street, Stockton Street, Jackson Street, Waverly Place, Bartlett, Stout, Church, China, and Brooklyn alleys. The girls and young women who occupied these squalid cubicles—many of them in their early teens and some, so legend had it, not even that old—had been purchased or kidnapped from their parents in the coastal provinces of China by the agents of local dealers. Upon arrival in San Francisco, they were auctioned off to the operators of

No photographer of the day captured the quality of life in Chinatown with so much skill and feeling as Arnold Genthe. Below is this particularly luminous shot of a cobbler plying his trade in Ross Alley, probably taken in 1890.

bagnios. The purchase price was paid directly to the young woman who then handed it over to her dealer and was forced to sign a document similar to the following: "For the consideration of __, paid into my hands this day, I, _____, promise to prostitute my body for the term of __ years. If, in that time, I am sick one day, two weeks shall be added to my time; and if more than one day, my term of prostitution shall continue an additional month. But if I run away, or escape from the custody of my keeper, then I am to be held as a slave for life." The last clause was hardly necessary, since a woman's menstrual period was considered an illness, thus adding a month to her term for every month she stayed alive. This was not long, usually no more than six years, by which time if she had not done herself in, she was so hagged-out and disease-ridden as to be useless to her owner and was carried off to a Chinese "hospital," given enough food and water to last a couple of days, and left to die.

This was the world of the hophead and the dope fiend, the opium addict, a creature by no means confined to the Chinese population. "A Chinese opium den," wrote B. E. Lloyd, "is one of the offensive sights that the vistor discovers during a stroll through Chinatown. . . . This 'den' may be a very small room (and it is apparently all the more popular if it is) but there is always 'room for one more.' There are shelves on all sides, one above the other, upon which are spread blankets, and perhaps an occasional mattress for the more fastidious smoker. Upon these are sprawled out in all manner of pose, and in all stages of stupor or idiocy, the opium smokers, each clinging to his pipe endeavoring to get one more full 'whiff,' with the tenacity of a drowning man hanging to a floating wreck." Even worse: "In some of the more secluded opium dens, and those kept under strict privacy by the proprietors, at any hour of the night he who is admitted will find a number of young men and women—*not Chinese*—distributed about the room on lounges and beds in miscellaneous confusion, all under the influence of the drug. Of course most of these women are of the disreputable class, but the young men, though really no better, are our respectable sons and brothers, who move in good society, and are of 'good repute.' " In 1885, it was estimated that there were twenty-six opium dens open to the public, Caucasian as well as Oriental, with a total of 320 bunks, and at least that many limited strictly to a Chinese clientele. And if many of the public dens were in fact fabrications staged for the delectation of tourists by the Chinatown Guides Association, those which were genuine existed as a significant blotch on the city's social body.

This was the world of Fung Jing Toy—"Little Pete"—chieftain of the Sum Yop tong, who for more than ten years reigned over Chinatown by force and murder, his bejeweled fingers in every available pie of corruption. Only once between 1880 and 1897 (when he was assassinated by killers hired by the rival Sue Yop tong) was his rule interrupted, and then only because he overstepped the boundaries of good taste, not to mention good sense, by attempting to bribe a white jury in a murder case in order to get one of his henchmen acquitted. He was sentenced to five years in San Quentin prison, but he was so rich and powerful that even in jail he was able to keep his organization intact and upon his release stepped back into the district's kaleidoscope of crime as if he had never left, strolling grandly through the streets, his body protected by chain mail, his head protected by a hat lined with steel, his progress accompanied by both white and Chinese bodyguards, his *boo how doy* never out of calling distance.

For the most part, San Francisco's white society assumed an attitude of blithe remove from the wretched clutter of Chinatown, piously ascribing its

An opium-eater from the haut monde, *as depicted with a certain relish in the pages of Frank Leslie's New York-based* Illustrated Weekly *in 1877. Then, as now, the antics of the city by the western gate were of more than passing interest to the denizens of the settled East.*

excesses to the natural depravity of the Oriental mind—deplorable, of course, but what could one do?—and so long as the district's miasma of degradation did not measurably affect the rest of the city it was regarded with an almost amused disdain in no way weakened by the number of tourist dollars it attracted. It was perhaps not widely known—and most certainly almost never admitted—that it was Caucasian money that nurtured many of the brothels and gambling hells and opium dens, and it was Caucasian politicians who blanketed the district with protection from those who might otherwise have attempted to do something about it. Chief among the latter, needless to say, was Christopher A. Buckley, who possessed no unseemly concern over the source of the money that fed his machine. Little Pete, with visible resentment, called him "that Blind White Devil," but he paid his dues with a regularity that kept him in power longer than any other of Chinatown's tong leaders.

"Winged Victory," a favorite landmark of the 1890s. It came into rather unusual use at the end of the war in 1945 (see page 250).

T HE "COOL, GRAY CITY OF LOVE," as poet George Sterling described San Francisco, was demonstrably a good deal more complex than this phrase or glittering legends or handouts from the Chamber of Commerce would have led the idle tourist to expect. This is not to say that San Francisco's tapestry of corruption went entirely unnoticed in these years. In 1885, the Board of Supervisors was actually persuaded to assign a commission to investigate crime and prostitution in the city; the commission did its duty competently enough, filed a report according to custom, and conveniently disbanded; the report itself got tabled for what was called "further study." And in 1889, Jeremiah Lynch, one of the town's state senators, issued a pamphlet called *Buckleyism* in which he declared that Buckley "debauches all those he touches and then takes from them half the price of their crime." The pamphlet stirred up a brief flurry of concern which Blind Chris was able to stifle in a quick smother of bills, and the machine continued to percolate quite nicely for the next several years.

But time was catching up with him. In San Francisco—and in America generally—one of the preconditions of any significant movement for reform was depression. After all, when most of those who accounted for anything in society were each getting a healthy slice of the economic pie, there were few interested in examining too closely the techniques and ingredients the baker might have been using. Throughout the 1880s, and on into the early 1890s, San Francisco was an economically healthy—almost booming—town. If the failure of the Comstock in 1880 had cut off its source of ready silver, the deep mines of the Sierra Nevada continued to gouge millions of dollars of gold out of the mountains every year ($2.1 billion by 1900), and the immense wheat farms of the great Central Valley—most of them owned or financed by San Francisco interests—grew so remarkably that by 1885, California had become the greatest wheat-producing region in the world (and by 1890, the state's farms were yielding forty million bushels a year on 2.75 million acres). Not since the glory days of the Gold Rush or the first bloom of the Comstock had the city enjoyed so much prosperity, and such considerations as the leprous condition of city government were easily ignored.

That period of bliss came to an end with the great depression of 1893, which saw the failure of 580 banks and more than sixteen thousand businesses across the country, with proportional casualties in California. Nationally as well as locally, the crash of 1893 fanned the embers of discontent until they flamed into the creation of the People's Party, or Populism, the first major threat to two-party politics in American history, and the embryo of the first

(Continued on page 184)

The City That Was . . .

"O that one who has mingled the wine of her bounding life with the wine of his youth should live to write the obituary of Old San Francisco!" So wrote Will Irwin at the conclusion of his *New York Sun* essay on the city that perished in three days of April, 1906. The prose of Irwin's classic has worn less well than the Kodak images of the hitherto uncelebrated artist that claim our attention on these few pages.

To be young in Old San Francisco! is a theme that did not escape the Brown Bag Phantom (as we call the photographer) even before catastrophe induced reflection. In 1905, his lunchtime and weekend forays more often than not caught youth or childhood in the precious frame of a time that disappeared so utterly on April 18, 1906. Yet the timing was nothing but a stroke of luck—the important thing is that the eye of this enthusiast with a folding camera would have improved the work of a dozen of the more celebrated San Francisco photographers before his time and not a few since.

At the threshold of a new age. . . . Pondering the old San Francisco that he knew so well and the new San Francisco that he foresaw, the greatest historian of western America, Hubert Howe Bancroft, wrote shortly after the 1906 conflagration: "In this day of great wealth and wonderful inventions we realize more and more the value of the city to mankind. . . . Cities are not merely marts of commerce; they stand for civility; they are civilization itself. The city street is the school of philosophy, of art, of letters; city society is the home of refinement. In their reciprocal relations the city is as men make it, while from the citizen one may determine the quality of the city. The atmosphere of the city is an eternal force."

The eternal force was usually lively in San Francisco, though it had been dozing in the decade immediately before the turn of the century. A generation that had reveled in the genteel *kitsch* of Woodward's Gardens now gave way to one that bought instant adventure for a nickle at the Chutes on Haight Street. If this monument to *civitas* went unproclaimed by Bancroft, he could well indulge in lofty reflection in considering Golden Gate Park. Here, the sand dunes which the thrifty city fathers of the 1860s had dedicated as the playground of future generations were rapidly yielding to the indefatigable zeal of John McLaren and already outstripped in scope, permanence, utility, amenity, and civility the monuments of Billy Ralston, the man alleged to have built the town.

Meanwhile, down at Lotta's Fountain, "Workingmen of the World Unite" was a slogan that appeared almost respectable, if we are to judge by the dress of the interested crowd. In a way, it *was* respectable, for down at City Hall a mayor and all sixteen supervisors claimed allegiance to a labor party (even while they looted the treasury in the last great raid of the age of saloon politics). Bancroft no doubt disapproved of the politics even more than the graft, since the former threatened the cheap labor supply he thought essential to float the leviathan of Progress, while the latter was but a passing wave that induced temporary nausea.

A CITY OF DREAMS. . . . Here we see some people doing—not much, for the most part—but, in fact, engaged very personally in the urban scene. The blind fiddler, observed by city strollers, imposes tangible life and activity in his space. A fellow reflects as he finishes feeding the pigeons. A child's desires center on a miniature version of the nineteenth-century equestrian world—a goat-cart-and-pony fantasy. And a hero in shirtsleeves slashes a base hit through a picnic-afternoon sporting break. The style of a city is indeed a city way of doing things.

TIME STOPPED ON SUTTER STREET. . . . The definitive cable car with its definitive passengers is frozen in six-mile-per-hour majesty in a casually reflective moment not long before the fire wiped out all of these bay-windowed shops and residences, reduced most of the cable cars to bare, heat-twisted wheel-trucks, and introduced perhaps one or two of these very riders to the novelties of household tenting in the park.

Like Andrew S. Hallidie's original Clay Street franchise of 1873, the Sutter Street line employed "dummies" as traction units with trailers scarcely different from horse-cars for the bulk of the passengers. The Sutter dummies were as pretty a piece of equipment as ever rattled along an American street, even in an age when a five-cent fare bought some fancy rides. When the management of the present-day Muni system perceives that an electric line using the railroad tracks from the Ferry Building almost to Fort Point will outdo even the overloaded remnants of the cable car system as the most popular traction in America, we will gather courage to suggest the virtues of dummy-and-trailer units inspired by the design of No. 46. Unfortunately, neither the tourists nor, alas, the natives will enhance these trolleys so much as the customers in an era that admired decorum as highly as decor.

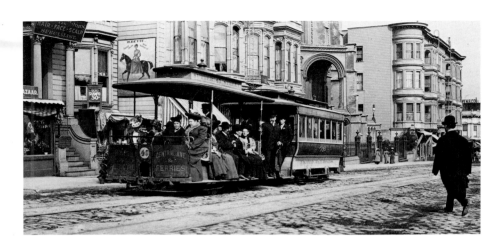

TAKE ONE LAST LOOK. . . . In any age an accounting of the time spent by males of the Younger Generation in just hanging around would prove startling. We are not sure just what you can prove by photographic examination of structured idleness—except that by 1905 the pocket camera had reached a point where it was possible to capture this ancient activity with complete detachment.

Yet a vague but powerfully evocative scent of the times wafts from these images. "Manure, spray, and piston oil," you may observe, "with a whiff of cheap tobacco." If so, then maybe you have forgotten the smell of sunlight when you too were young enough to hang around.

The Mechanics' Monument is still where it was, a memorial to the life and lifestyle of Peter Donahue as filtered through the tastes of his son, a railroad magnate a generation older than these youths gathered for a noon lounge. By this time the name of Peter Donahue's gold rush manufactory on the beach at Happy Valley was perpetuated in the Union Iron Works, constructor of battleships at the Potrero. By our time, the Mechanics' Monument just doesn't smell the same.

And does the Ocean Beach smell different, too? (Gobs of bunker oil ignored?) Most likely. Eternal memories parse into ephemeral images. When will they again give us the smell of long-unwashed wool saturated with salt spray?

One of Adolph Sutro's many legacies to the city that had made him was Sutro's Baths, seen above in about 1900 from the vantage point of Sutro Heights, looking across the Golden Gate to Marin.

Silhouettes: a magic moment caught on the Oakland-San Francisco ferry run in about 1895.

determined reform movement in San Francisco since the Vigilance Committee of 1856. Noses suddenly cleansed of too much prosperity began to detect the stink of corruption in the city by the bay. Records and other evidence that had been gathering dust for years were opened up and looked at and published in the local newspapers, particularly the *San Francisco Examiner,* whose owner, William Randolph Hearst, son of San Francisco mining man George Hearst, was busily forging the beginnings of a political career that he confidently expected would see him in the White House before he was done. The immediate target of this new reform movement was to win the mayoralty election of 1895, and in July of 1894 two delegates of the People's Party paid a call on the man who the party had decided could most successfully carry its standard.

That man was Adolph Sutro, the sixty-four-year-old veteran of the Comstock wars with the Bank of California. Superficially, the choice was a good one, for the aging warrior was immensely popular in San Francisco. He had developed the Cliff House above Ocean Beach into a successful resort and was in the process of creating his most enduring monument, Sutro's Baths (it was completed in 1896 and remained until its destruction by fire in 1965). He had converted his own estate on Sutro Heights into a manicured park complete with landscaped gardens, fountains, and statuary, and opened it up to the public, free of charge. Even more to the point, he had singlehandedly taken on the Southern Pacific Railroad. Until 1893, the Powell Street trolley line, which served Sutro Heights, had charged a five-cent round-trip fee to the park. In that year, the line was absorbed by the Market Street Railroad Company, a subsidiary of the Southern Pacific, and the fare was raised to ten cents. Sutro was quite sincerely outraged over what he considered an unfair increase, one that would discourage the common people from enjoying his park. He promptly fenced off his property and began charging twenty-five cents admission of anyone who used the Southern Pacific cars, letting all others in free. He then obtained a franchise from the city to build his own competing line and began construction. (We do not *know* that Sutro paid Christopher Buckley more to obtain the franchise than the Southern Pacific was willing to put up to block it, but it would be a not unreasonable guess.) Finally, when Collis P. Huntington began attempting to force legislation through Congress that would have given the railroad as much as another century to repay the federal loans it had received for the construction of the Central Pacific (which loans fell due in 1899), and then at a much reduced rate of interest, Sutro added his not inconsiderable voice to the chorus of objection that sounded throughout the state.

All this made him a most attractive candidate—a self-made man, a benefactor, a foe of monopoly wherever he found it. It was certainly enough to convince Sutro himself to run for the office, and it was in fact enough to enable him to win with 31,254 votes, more than all other contenders combined. But the whole idea was a tragic mistake, not only for the reform movement but for the old man himself. Sutro was neither politician nor administrator; he was a general superintendent, a boss. All his working life he had given orders and had seen them obeyed. Stubborn, inflexible, and utterly convinced that he knew what was best under any given circumstances, Sutro attempted to run the city of San Francisco as he would have run a stamp mill, and with predictable results. "He passed his term," the *Examiner* said, "in a state of exasperation," and nothing along the lines of reform emerged from the almost constant bickering with the Board of Supervisors and other bureaucrats that characterized the two years of his mayoralty. Just about the only positive note that could be heard in these years, in fact, was sounded the year of his election (and with which Sutro himself had nothing to do): the city's Democrats, refusing to be bought for the first time in fifteen years, ousted Christopher Buckley from the leadership of the party by a margin of thirty votes; Buckley sighed, packed his bags with money, and retired to Vallejo, heavy with the fruits of wisdom and corruption; he lived until 1922. In 1896, Sutro was pointedly not asked to run again (nor had he expressed any desire to), and shortly before leaving office he summed up his two years: "What have I accomplished as Mayor? Very little. The Mayor is little more than a figurehead. . . . I have always been master of a situation; I have always had a number of men under my employ, and they did as I told them. I could not manage the politicians." Less than two years later, his body was carried to the crematorium of the Odd Fellows' Cemetery. His political adventure in San Francisco was a sad and profitless finale to an otherwise remarkable career, one that had spanned more than forty years of the city's life and given much to that life along the way.

Sutro's successor was, by his own lights, quite as reform-minded as the old German, if a much different man. He was James Duval Phelan, a thirty-eight-year-old native San Franciscan, a trained and practiced lawyer, a banker, a sometime poet, past president of the Bohemian Club, and a man as committed to the promise of San Francisco as William C. Ralston had once been. He was one with that special class of men which the latter half of the nineteenth century had managed to produce in spite of the frequently brutal single-mindedness of industrial capitalism—refined, astonishingly well-read, pragmatic in action but philosophical in thought, and earnestly dedicated to the principle of public service (service, mind you, not profit or the hope of profit, nor power for the sake of power). On the national level, such men—among them Secretary of the Interior Carl Schurz; Major John Wesley Powell, creator of the U.S. Geological Service and the Bureau of Ethnology; and Theodore Roosevelt, soon to be president of the United States—would effect major reforms in land use, Indian treatment, and civil service. On the state level—led by such as Chester Rowell, editor of the *Fresno Morning Republican*, and Thomas R. Bard, pioneering oil man and Ventura rancher—this same breed would create the progressive Lincoln-Roosevelt League, far and away the most influential single coterie of reformists in California history.

Phelan's approach to San Francisco was colored by a combination of European models and what he saw as America's finest political traditions. As literary historian Kevin Starr has written, "He wanted San Francisco to learn from the great cities of the Continent, for to his way of thinking they, and not the cities of the American East, provided the appropriate models of development. The Roman Catholic side of his imagination made Phelan sensitive to the cities of Southern Europe, Rome most of all. An Italianate quality, sun-splashed and baroque, would ever cling to Phelan's vision of the ideal San Francisco. . . . A Democrat who had more Hamilton than Jefferson in his make-up . . . Phelan adhered throughout his life to a classical republicanism which he considered the true legacy of the Founding Fathers, a belief that the gifted, the educated—and the wealthy—should lead the Republic in a spirit of service and reform." A man of far greater tact and personal charm than Sutro, Phelan was able to handle the politicians—enough, at least, to initiate some geniune changes in the city, among them the passage of a streamlined city charter, the beautification of streets and parks (particularly Golden Gate Park, which John McClaren was still in the process of developing), and the beginning movement for the municipal ownership of transportation lines and utilities. In 1899, he was re-elected by a handsome margin, and on the face of it might have continued as

City scenes, 1895: Above, one of the several statues which pioneer dentist Henry D. Cogswell erected to memorialize himself and to promote the notion of temperance in perhaps the least temperate town in the country. In the old boy's hand is a glass; in the glass is water. Below, a casual moment on the waterfront fixed forever on glass. We do not know who the men are, but we cherish their fine, strong faces.

All the bustle, clatter and rumble of turn-of-the-century San Francisco is visible in this Market Street scene. In the middle distance is the city's first genuine skyscraper, the Spreckels Building, also called the Call Building, and, more recently, the Central Tower.

Wuxtry! Wuxtry! Gityer Call *right here! Or your* Post, *or* Bulletin, *or* News, *or* Chronicle, *or* Examiner *in an age that still possessed a variety of newspapers hawked by such wonderful street gamins as the lad below, seen at the Ferry Building during the afternoon commuter rush.*

mayor of San Francisco for as long as he cared to hold the position.

Yet that class which Phelan so eloquently represented, for all its sincerity, education, conviction, even selflessness, possessed a blind spot that assured the ultimate failure of its most progressive dreams. It took for granted a base of power which did not really exist and all but ignored that one segment of American society which, if courted and cultivated, might well have provided the broad foundation on which to build all its castles of perfection: the working class and the labor movement which articulated its hopes.

"THE PRACTICAL EQUALITY of all the members of a community," Bayard Taylor had written of the San Francisco of 1849, "whatever might be the wealth, intelligence, or profession of each, was never before so thoroughly demonstrated. Dress was no gauge of respectability, and no honest occupation, however menial in character, affected a man's standing. Lawyers, physicians, and ex-professors dug cellars, drove ox-teams, sawed wood and carried luggage; while men who had been army privates, sailors, cooks or day laborers were at the head of profitable enterprises. . . . A man who would consider his fellow beneath him, on account of his appearance or occupation, would have had some difficulty in living peaceably in California. . . . The security of the country is owing, in no small degree, to this plain, practical development of what the French reverence as an abstraction, under the name of *Fraternité*. To sum up all in three words, *labor is respectable*: may it never be otherwise while a grain of gold is left to glitter in California soil!"

The grains of gold continued, but that careless fraternity which Taylor celebrated did not long survive the first two or three years of the Gold Rush. For a time, the working man could seduce himself into the belief that his station in life was a temporary condition preceding that moment when he, too, would come up with a handful of opportunity. For most, it simply did not turn out that way, and as early as 1850 working men in various trades began forming guilds, associations, and unions. For many years, these organizations were more social than functional because both wages and working conditions in San Francisco gave little cause for all but occasional, isolated, and very brief strikes—the five-dollar, ten-hour day was a standard in San Francisco at a time when most workers in the country were laboring twelve-hour days for three dollars or less. That happy circumstance was permanently altered in the 1870s, when both an abundance of Chinese and a substantial influx of laborers from the eastern states created an oversupply of labor in the city and the state and a consequent decline in the daily wage.

The first expression of the resulting discontent had been the Workingmen's Party (see Chapter 7), but it is important to remember that this was a political movement far more than a labor movement. Denis Kearney, after all, was an *employer* of labor, not a bona fide worker, and during the party's first state convention in 1878, neither he nor the other leaders of the organization gave any official recognition to the delegates from the unions of San Francisco. Disgruntled, a number of these delegates, led by Frank Roney, a member of the Iron Moulders Union and a transplanted Irish rebel, formed the "Representative Assembly of Trades and Labor Unions," popularly known as the Trades Assembly, which continued to function until 1886 and was later replaced by the San Francisco Labor Council. Throughout the 1880s, aided and abetted by the national Knights of Labor, Roney and his colleagues conducted an organizational campaign that by 1890 had won the membership of most of the workers in most of the trades in San Francisco. And if the strikes scattered through the 1880s and 1890s (some of them of long duration and some of them violent) in the end accomplished very little in the way of improved pay, hours, and working conditions, they did demonstrate that San Francisco was well on its way to becoming one of the leading union towns in the country.

The men who did the organizing, who officered the unions, who led the strikes, were radicals by the standards of the time. Even Frank Roney, who considered himself a moderate and often declared that a strike was something to be resorted to only as a last alternative, was a Marxist socialist. Others were far more radical, chief among them Burnett G. Haskell, founder of the Coast Seamen's Union (which in 1891 merged with a union of steamship sailors to create the Sailors' Union of the Pacific under Andrew Furuseth), a passionate anarchist who at one time or another in his career had advocated the use of dynamite and other forms of particularly forceful expression. The employers of the town, who had themselves joined together into an Employers' Association to combat union organization, pointed with considerable alarm at the creeping socialism of the city's unions and declared that any and all means were justified in nipping this un-American movement in the bud—including the violation of civil rights, blacklisting, and police and military suppression.

Caught between these two forces (by no means confined to San Francisco or even California), progressives like James Duval Phelan found themselves in a near-vacuum. The movement they spearheaded was in a very real sense a response to what they considered an appalling division in American society between the conglomerate rich and the swelling mass of industrialized workers. These two segments, in the progressive view, spelled ruin for America. "A pox on both your houses!" might have been the gut response, but in reality the progressive was inclined to fear the excesses of the working man somewhat more than those of corporation capital. For all the evils of entrenched wealth he saw all around him, the average progressive, possessed of enormous respect for private property and the inherent virtue of legitimately acquired money, found it considerably easier to identify with, say, a William F. Herrin of the Southern Pacific than with a foundry worker with a foreign-sounding name and a pronounced weakness for socialism—or even dread anarchy. Organized labor could be tolerated reluctantly as a short-term "war measure to provide relative justice to a few," as Chester Rowell once noted, but when it attempted to exercise muscle, particularly when it espoused the anti-individualistic idea of the closed shop, it became, again in Rowell's words, "anti-social, dangerous, and intrinsically wrong." However much the enlightened progressive movement liked to think of itself as a buffer between the two great coagulating streams of society, its influence along these lines was in fact only minimal. It gave to the middle class an avenue through which its grievances might be satisfied, but it was constitutionally incapable of doing the same for the working class, and that incapacity, if it did not directly cause, certainly contributed to an era of periodic violence throughout the state and nation—and, in San Francisco, to the demise of the most splendid visions of Mayor Phelan and the beginning of yet another period of glistening corruption.

The end and the beginning came in the summer of 1901. On July 20, the Brotherhood of Teamsters called a strike in response to being locked out of a major drayage firm, and immediately asked the support of the thirteen thousand-member City Front Federation, an association of waterfront unions. On July 29, that support was announced by the association's leadership: "The full membership of the City Front Federation refuses to work at the docks of

Arrival: In 1898, the U. S. Army transport Sherman *brought home some of the veterans of the "splendid little war" with Spain. They had just captured the Philippines for the American Empire and the* Chronicle's *newsboat was on hand to learn all about it.*

San Francisco, Oakland, Port Costa, and Mission Rock [today, China Basin]. The steamers *Bonita* and *Walla Walla*, with mail and passengers now in the stream, will be allowed to go to sea.'' It was the largest strike in the city's history up to that time and one of the longest ever. It lasted nearly three months, cost four lives and more than three hundred injuries, and changed the course of San Francisco history. Phelan, a good man caught in an impossible situation, fumbled through as best he could. When the Employers' Association demanded that he call in state or even federal troops to put down the strikers, Phelan refused, appalled at the prospect of military rule in San Francisco. On the other hand, he did assign city policemen to accompany and protect strike-breaking teamsters and other workers hired by the Employers' Association.

Convinced that his refusal to bring in state troops marked him as a man too weak to control the city in times of stress, San Francisco's business interests withdrew their political support of Phelan; he was not asked to run again in 1901. Equally convinced that his use of the police to protect strikebreakers put Phelan and the rest of the city government in the pocket of the Employers' Association, the labor movement—spurred on by a militant priest, Father Peter Yorke—concluded that its only hope for the future lay in forming its own party and capturing the political control of San Francisco. To that end, in September 1901, union delegates gathered at a convention to form the Union Labor Party, draw up a platform that upheld labor's rights, and nominate candidates for the upcoming city election.

Enter Abraham Ruef. Ruef, the son of a French merchant who had come to San Francisco in 1862, was a native San Franciscan. In 1883, at the age of eighteen, he graduated from the almost brand-new University of California and was admitted to the California bar in 1886. Supremely idealistic in his youth (his senior thesis in college had been entitled "Purity in Politics"), Ruef acquired a fine veneer of cynicism after more than a decade of participation in the murkier levels of Republican party manipulations under the tutelage of political thugs Martin Kelly and Phil Crimmons as they constantly jockeyed for position (albeit vainly) with Blind Chris Buckley. The precocious Ruef was a quick study, and between 1886 and 1888 rose from lowly precinct captain to boss of the North Beach district. On that solid base he developed a lucrative law practice, a profound respect for power, and a certain knowledge of how power could be made to work—for him.

At the Union Labor Party convention he was given his chance. Most of the delegates to the convention were rank amateurs in political games, lost and confused in a parliamentary labyrinth. Ruef had little difficulty in gaining control of the new party's machinery. The next step was to choose a candidate for the coming mayoralty election, and Ruef went about it with a cool, percep-tive calculation that would rival any of today's public relations firms. The man he chose was Eugene E. Schmitz, and the selection was brilliant—in spite of the fact that Schmitz's only previous claim to public attention had been conducting the orchestra at the fashionable Columbia Theatre. Nevertheless, Schmitz had two things going for him: he was the son of an Irish mother and a German father, giving him one foot in each of two of the city's major ethnic camps; and perhaps even more important, he was a most attractive man. As Ruef later recalled: "The psychology of the mass of voters is like that of a crowd of small boys or primitive men. Other things being equal, of two candidates they will amost invariably follow the fine, strongly-built man."

Schmitz's Republican and Democratic opponents were pale and lifeless by comparison, and with an expectedly strong showing in the city's working-class

Departure: Even as the veterans of the Spanish-American War were coming home, thousands of San Franciscans were scrambling for passage to the gold fields of the Klondike. The first ship out of port and on its way to Skagway was the steam schooner Excelsior.

districts, he won the election with more than twenty-one thousand votes. From that time forward, Ruef began weaving the strands of a little behind-the-scenes empire in San Francisco—and if union labor did indeed seem to prosper during the years of his dominance, almost succeeding in its goal of a closed-shop town, so did Ruef and those he let in for a piece of the action. Not since the 1880s had the wheels of municipal government been so well lubricated with the oil of graft, of payoffs and bribes and special favors, of fraudulent "retainers," all accompanied by the almost constant sound of mutual back-scratching. By 1905, an extremely intricate web of greed and corruption had been spun through nearly every level of the city's commercial and political life. Unfortunately, the more it was spun, the more obvious that web became, particularly those filaments in the hands of Ruef's Board of Supervisors, most of whom he had planted. These men, a gaggle of former saloon keepers, draymen, and lower-echelon political functionaries, were so eager to better their condition in life that even Ruef said that they were prepared to "eat the paint off a house." That fact calls into question Ruef's standing among the traditional big-city "bosses" of the nineteenth and early twentieth centuries, for the most apparent characteristics of an urban boss and his machine were discipline and control. Ruef, a professional grafter surrounded by enthusiastic amateurs, was never able to fully control the greed of his cohorts, a failure that would help to destroy him.

The movement dedicated to precisely that end had begun to gather force by 1905, faced with the prospect of another successful Schmitz election in November. It was led by James Duval Phelan, who must have found it hard to believe what had happened to the municipal dream he had hoped to make reality in the late 1890s; Rudolph Spreckels, the son of sugar king Claus Spreckels and a man to whom Ruef had recently had the effrontery to offer an especially sordid deal; Michael de Young, publisher and editor of the *San Francisco Chronicle* and a man with political ambitions of his own; and Fremont Older, editor of the *Bulletin*, the definitive crusading editor. Most of the other newspapers in town followed the lead of Older and de Young, though it would have been difficult to match the outraged prose of the *Chronicle* as election day approached: "Schmitz hardly counts. What he is told to do he does. Ruef is by all odds the most dangerous boss this city has hitherto endured. . . . For four years it has been known that if one wanted anything which the administration was not compelled to grant, he must see Ruef. If you wish for a job for yourself or your friend, you must see Ruef. If you wish for a license for a grog-shop or a theatre, you must see Ruef. If you desire to construct a building in defiance of the fire ordinances, you must see Ruef. . . . His baleful influence covers our city like a pall."

The *Chronicle* and the rest of the growing cadre of anti-Ruef forces confidently expected that months of steady exposure had eroded Ruef's power and assured Schmitz's defeat in November. They underestimated either the genius of Ruef or the gullibility of the public, for on the morning following election day it was announced that not only had Schmitz won the mayoralty again, this time with forty thousand votes, but that every Ruef-picked Union Labor candidate had won. From its Market Street building, the *Chronicle* fired a red star-bomb in despair (in the process accidentally setting fire to its own clock-tower), and the minions of reform considered the dimensions of the problem that confronted them.

Before they could do more than begin to explore possibilities, however, the gods had prepared an interruption—the last living expression of the city-that-was.

Prophecy in the park: we do not know what occasion inspired this springtime picnic in Golden Gate Park, nor what predictions the bags may have contained. We do know that it occurred almost precisely one year before the earth shrugged and cleared the boards of all such traces of that age of splendid innocence.

Gone in Three Days . . .

In the lexicography of elderly San Franciscans, the monstrous event commencing at 5:12 A.M., April 18, 1906, is "The Fire," perhaps "The Earthquake and Fire," never "the earthquake." The conventional explanation of this usage is that during the reconstruction years the term "earthquake" was bad news to investors sensitive to the possible consequences of recurrent phenomena. We prefer an explanation that appears at once more obscure and more convincing: the fire was historic, a serial event comprised of the collective experiences and narratives of those who went through three fearful days; the earthquake was apocalyptic, an instantly shared revelation that diminished in impact to the extent that it was described in detail.

Indeed, the definitive history of the earthquake and fire is reduced to passing along to us such eyewitness description as "and then began a series of the liveliest motions imaginable. . . ." Yet it may be possible to capture verbally some flavor of the shock—by indirection, to be sure. Here is what happened to the family of publisher Alex Robertson. The big house down the Peninsula lurched off its foundations and the brick chimneys crashed through the roof and second floor, the family stumbled down the stairs and out into the front yard. It was dead quiet in the first light, except for the chirping of a few birds. Then, from beyond the oleander hedge that cut off the view of the street, came the authoritative clip-clop ring of the shoes of the milkman's horse. Robertson's wife spoke the first words. She said, "Can this have happened only to us?"

Yes. It had happened discretely, even though to everybody.

A few seconds before Jennie Robertson defined the earthquake, Dennis O'Sullivan, Fire Chief of San Francisco, was falling through the air toward a pile of bricks, the debris of a chimney that had collapsed straight down through the floor of his wife's bedroom. His wife was down there in the basement, still safe in her bed, but O'Sullivan was mortally injured when he plunged after her. As time started up again, the few hundred firemen who might have kept disaster short of complete catastrophe were in deep trouble. The Chief was as good as dead, the water mains were broken—and the gas mains, too, and the chimney flues.

The men of the fire department were to fight it out from one outpost to another for three days—while a whole generation of San Franciscans stored up anecdotes.

WATCHING IT ALL GO UP. . . . Dozens of fires broke out in the gaslit city even while most of its citizens still stood in the streets outside the lodgings they had fled. Soon, columns of smoke rose from South of the Slot and the produce district north of Market. A lady at Gough and Hayes started to fix a bite of breakfast and her broken stovepipe kindled the "ham and eggs" fire that swept a whole section of the city. By 9:00 A.M. it was becoming clear that the fires would wreak immense damage; by noon it was *the fire,* advancing on three broad fronts.

Yet while the fire sometimes raced through blocks of flimsy structures South of Market and while the view from Nob Hill was that of a boiling rose-and-yellow-tinted curtain of smoke a mile and one-half long, on the fire lines the inferno most often seemed to creep methodically from building to building, block to block.

While thousands fled—at one pace or another—before the flames, other thousands gathered to see the sights. Arnold Genthe photographed the fire line and its spectators atop Russian Hill. At the upper left we see the fire approaching Market along Fifth Street, but mostly we see a cop and two troopers and a bunch of men in their usual Wednesday morning clothes. On Market Street the Emporium is gone, the *Call* tower is an inferno, the *Examiner* is blazing, but the flag still flies from the Palace Hotel. Mayor Schmitz has closed down the saloons, and sightseers gather to witness this unlikely event. From the photograph, it appears that a lot of good booze ran down the drain, but contemporary reporters assure us that the tipplers managed to guzzle quite enough.

THE SPECTACLE CONSUMES IT-
SELF. . . . As the fires became the
firestorm, the street-corner vignette
at the heart of the action became a
memory of a time that had ended a
few hours ago. Not a half-dozen photographs suggest the close-up intensity of the flames that melted steel
and created new ceramic shapes. In
this one, we see an ordinary building
burning with more energy than is
contained in all of its materials; there
are no chatting spectators, no troops,
no firemen—only the implication of a
cameraman shielding his face. From
the bay, the cityscape familiar to a
generation of transcontinental travelers is a line of pierheads fringing a
monstrous backdrop of living smoke,
a theater of catastrophe where the
special effects overwhelm the drama.

THE SCENE AND A SECOND VISIT. . . . The Brown Bag Phantom, photographer of "The City That Was," had a roll of film in his camera on the morning of April 18, but only one negative survived. However, it is this view that he sought to duplicate a few months later—though with no roof left to stand on. The relationship of the *Call* and Mutual towers (center) remains almost exactly the same. Both of these buildings were rebuilt and stand today. The charred tree that adds symbolic punch to the lower picture appears in its last foliage at the lower left in the April 18 view.

FLIGHT TO THE FERRIES. . . . Those who had friends in the East Bay—and many who did not—got out of town before the embers cooled. Over 250,000 people were homeless. A whole new way of living was starting to spring up in the remains of the city.

TENTING TONIGHT. . . . Ragged villages appeared in open spaces everywhere, together with formal tent cities laid out by the Army in the parks. It seemed that everybody was thrown together with everybody else.

THE BIGGEST COOKOUT. . . .
Even those who had a
house lived differently. No
plumbing. No gas. And it
was months before the
flues could be repaired
and pass inspection. So
the street kitchen became a
temporary institution of
the Western Addition.

MOVING AGAIN. . . . From
the Ferry Building tower,
the signs of revival are
clear: the trolleys are running and so are the beer
wagons. There is some-
thing to commute to, even
if it is an office in a frame
shack. Oakland is not to be
the new metropolis of the
West.

REBIRTH IN MID-CAREER. . . . It is a lively coincidence that the establishment of the presidio and mission at San Francisco matches the bicentennial date of the Republic. Another coincidence is that it was just 70 years from the completion of the first "new" frame building at Yerba Buena Cove to the destruction of the city in the most celebrated natural disaster of our era, and a second 70 years of rebirth and development down to this anniversary year, 1976.

At this midpoint between the vision of Jacob Leese and the collective visions of today there stood a magnificently formidable pile of ruins—"the damndest finest ruins ever gazed on anywhere," in the mock-inspirational ballad of Lawrence Harris. The colossal City Hall that had been 30 years in the building was a total loss; at the first jolt, it had collapsed in a manner fitting its construction material—thinly varnished graft. At Portsmouth Square, the more authoritative Hall of Justice stood the shock, but showed the intensity of firestorm heat. Its worthy shell was fitted out again, and only recently was swept away by Progress. The Mechanics' Monument stood before and stands today and will until all of the past that we share is scrapped.

"Put me somewhere west of East Street, where there's nothin' left but dust,/ Where the lads are all a'bustlin' and where everythin's gone bust. . . ." was the scene Lawrence Harris had in mind when the Brown Bag Phantom of our 1905 pictorial caught the yard locomotive, the reconstruction of the gutted *Call* tower and the purposeful bystanders for whom he had so much affinity. He also went out to Van Ness Avenue, where he proved the point that lumber was king of San Francisco in the spring and summer of 1906. The white mansion with its jerry-built extension was now the headquarters of the Emporium, "California's largest and America's greatest department store."

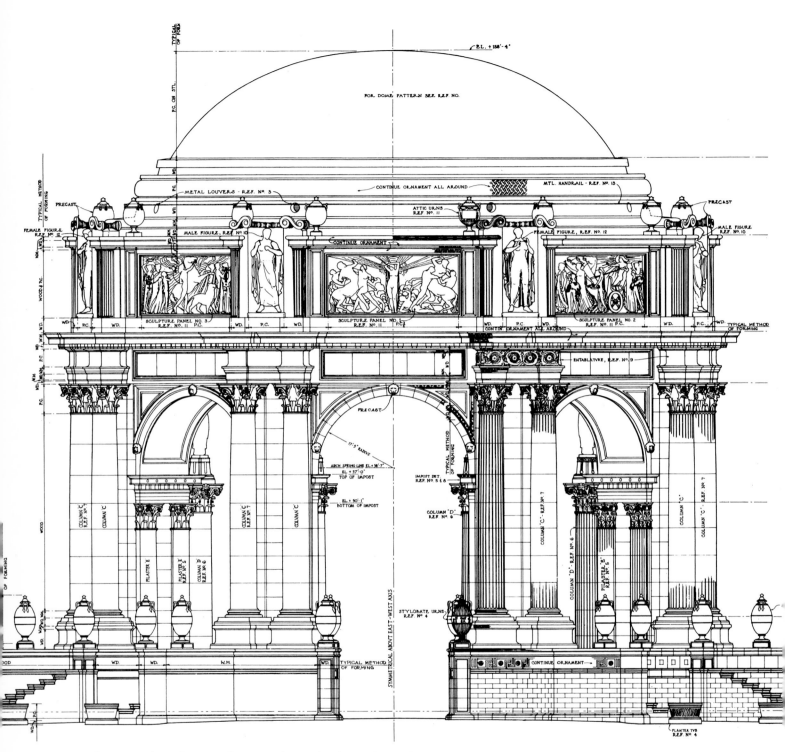

An architectural rendering of Bernard Maybeck's Palace of Fine Arts, the only expression now remaining of the Panama-Pacific International Exposition of 1915. Of this brooding edifice, a promotional booklet of the time declared, "After the little, breathless shock that follows the first vision of perfect loveliness, half the world and his wife looking across the Fine Arts Lagoon in San Francisco, ask: 'Who did it? Why have we had to come here to see the most divinely beautiful building ever reared in America?'"

Chapter X

DIMINISHING RETURNS

AS THE MIDDLE FEW DAYS of April 1906 did their work and the San Francisco that had captured the imagination of the world shuddered and flamed into memory, the citizens of the town were saddled with dual responsibilities: first, the future, with which the city was now forced to deal on a more direct and immediate level than at any time since the first year of its existence; second, the past, a burden of both joy and frustration, one weighted with stylistic and philosophical imperatives that clamored for expression, that insisted that even in rebuilding from the ground up San Francisco must not become just another turn-of-the-century metropolis. And had the citizens been tempted to forget this last, there were plenty of outsiders eager to remind them, for the city had long since become a common inheritence. "San Francisco will rise from its ruins and its ashes, grander, more beautiful, more influential than before," the *Los Angeles Times* grandly announced on April 19. "The men who have made the Pacific Coast what it is are not the men to be disheartened by the disaster. . . . They will continue to go forward in the magnificent work to which they have set their hands."

But would they? Could they? Others were not so certain. Sitting at his desk in the city room of the *New York Sun*, shuffling through the Associated Press reports that described the inexorable ruin of the San Francisco he had known and loved, Will Irwin, ex-reporter for the San Francisco *Wave* and Fremont Older's *Bulletin*, former member of the Bohemian Club and regular at the spaghetti-and-dago-red dinners of "Poppa" Coppa's, sadly and lovingly wrote a feature story called "The City that Was," and began it by declaring that it would never be the same again: "The old San Francisco is dead. . . . It may rebuild; it probably will; but those who have known that peculiar city by the Golden Gate, have caught its flavor of the Arabian Nights, feel it can never be the same. It is as though a pretty, frivolous woman has passed through a great tragedy. She survives, but she is sobered and different. If it rises out of the ashes it must be a modern city, much like other cities and without its old atmosphere."

"The crying need of San Francisco today. . . is business."

In the end it was not the editorial writer for the *Los Angeles Times* but Will Irwin who correctly articulated the future. The city did rise from the ashes of its fire and out of the scattered shards of its destruction, but one by one its finest hopes were shredded by the winds of expedience. The resulting difference was a good deal more than physical, although it was that, too; it was spiritual, the matter of a loss of faith, a measurable decline in the strength of possibilities. For more than twenty years after the earthquake and fire, San Francisco was no longer the name of a dream. It was just another city, one whose geography may have suggested Naples or Copenhagen, but whose instincts, for the most part, were indistinguishable from those of Anytown, USA.

FOR SOME, THE EARTHQUAKE AND FIRE, for all its tragedy, was justly deserved retribution from above. "God rules in the storm, the volcanic eruption, the tidal wave and the earthquake," the Roman Catholic journal *The New World* noted; "We remember that only a few years ago on Good Friday night of all the nights of the year many of the wealthy citizens of San Francisco assembled together with lewd women in one of the most luxurious mansions of the city and carried their hellish orgies so far that they kicked the globes off the chandeliers. . . ." For others, it was an opportunity, the chance to make San Francisco the physical equivalent of all the dreams that had attached themselves to the name.

Almost from the city's founding there had been a steady chorus of criticism directed at the city's physical plan—or, more accurately, its lack of intelligent planning. Writing in 1854, the authors of the *Annals* complained that "Over all these square miles of contemplated thoroughfares there seems no provision made by the projectors for a public park—the true 'lungs' of a large city. The existing plaza, or Portsmouth Square, and other two or three diminutive squares . . . seem the only breathing-holes intended for the future population of hundreds of thousands. This is a strange mistake, and can only be attributed to the jealous avarice of the city projectors in turning every square vara of the site to an available building lot. . . ." In spite of such sniping, the avarice continued through the years, until, by the time the Board of Supervisors got around to the notion of creating a genuine park, the only available land was Ocean Beach property well outside the boundaries of the city proper.

This strip of land, three miles deep and half a mile wide, largely a matter of wind-blown sand dunes and scrub brush, was acquired in 1868, christened Golden Gate Park, and in 1871 turned over to the supervision of William H. Hall, who before his retirement in 1887 managed to create seven lakelets, a number of grottoes and arbors, two miles of roads and paths, and the planting of more than one hundred seventy thousand trees and shrubs. He was succeeded by John McClaren, a long-lived, park-committed, and delightfully stubborn Scot who held his job until 1943. During his long tenure McClaren did not take kindly to anyone who had the temerity to meddle with his park. He violently opposed the use of part of it as the site of the Midwinter Fair of 1894; he lost his fight, but when the fair was over, cheerfully razed most of its buildings—most notably exluding the Japanese Tea Garden—and expeditiously planted over the sites. Similarly, when cast-iron statues of everyone from Greek philosophers to Civil War generals were foisted off on him, he shrouded them with greenery so that today the idle tourist rarely sees them.

Golden Gate Park provided a "breathing-hole" of respectable dimensions, but it did little to aid the problems of the central city, whose character changed

It took almost thirty years to complete San Francisco's splendiferous City Hall, but on April 18, 1906, it took only thirty seconds for the heaving earth to reduce it to a skeleton. Of some interest was the fact that after the rubble had been cleared away, it was discovered that old newspapers and other trash had been included in the building materials.

little in the years following the 1850s. A generation after the *Annals*, Helen Hunt (later Helen Hunt Jackson, author of *Ramona* and *A Century of Dishonor*) visited the city. She was not impressed: "When I first stepped out of the door of the Occidental Hotel, on Montgomery Street, I looked up and down in disappointment. 'Is this all?' I exclaimed. 'It is New York,—a little lower of story, narrower of street, and stiller, perhaps. Have I crossed the continent only to land in Lower Broadway on a dull day?'" After an hour's tour, her opinion was revised only slightly: "Many of the houses on the highest seaward streets are handsome, and have pleasant grounds about them. But going only a few steps further seaward, you come to or look down on crowded lanes of dingy, tumbling, forlorn buildings, which seem as if they must be forever slipping into the water. . . . If San Francisco had known it was to be a city, and if (poor, luckless place that it is, in spite of all its luck) it had not burned down almost faster than it could build up, it might have set upon its myriad hills a city which the world could hardly equal. But, as it is, it is hopelessly crowded and mixed, and can never look . . . like anything but a toppling town."

For most of San Francisco's leading citizens, of course, who were as always too busy building to build beautifully, the city's physical presence was a matter of profound indifference. But not for James Duval Phelan. During his brief reign as mayor (as noted in Chapter 9), Phelan had made sporadic attempts to beautify the city with street plantings and such, but the City Front strike of 1901 had cut his career and his efforts short. His vision of the city beautiful did not die, however, and in 1904 he organized the Association for the Improvement and Adornment of San Francisco, whose purposes were "to promote in every practical way the beautifying of the streets, public buildings, parks, squares, and places of San Francisco; to bring to the attention of the officials and the people of the city the best methods for instituting artistic municipal betterments; to stimulate the sentiment of civic pride in the improvement and care of private property; to suggest quasi-public enterprises; and, in short, to make San Francisco a more agreeable city in which to live." With these purposes in mind, the Association swiftly moved to ask Daniel Hudson Burnham, of the Chicago architectural firm of Burnham & Root, to put together a master plan for San Francisco, one that would articulate the greatness which Phelan and his colleagues sensed for the future.

The choice was logical, possibly inevitable. "Make no little plans," Burnham had once written. "They have no magic to stir men's blood and probably will not be realized. Make big plans. . . ." One of the biggest of his plans had been the Chicago World's Fair of 1893, which as Director of Works he had designed as a "Great White City" of neoclassical splendor. Another had been his contribution—with Frederick Law Olmsted and Charles McKim—to the 1901 plan for the city of Washington, D.C., and he applied appropriately substantial designs to all or parts of such other cities as Cleveland, Minneapolis, and Manila. "My idea," he was fond of saying, "is to work up a big business, to handle big things, deal with big businessmen, and to build up a big organization, for you can't handle big things unless you have an organization." Burnham, in short, was a man whose largeness of vision most accurately matched the aspirations of the Association for the Improvement and Adornment of San Francisco, and his plan, produced after months of work in a studio on Twin Peaks and presented to the Board of Supervisors on September 27, 1905, did not disappoint these aspirations.

"We must remember," Burnham noted in the introduction to his plan, "that a meagre plan will fall short of perfect achievement, while a great one will

Even after the earthquake and fire, the city's waterfront still had the sight, smell, and feel of salt spray and sails. But tomorrow was right around the corner, and more than a slight suggestion of what it meant was the arrival in 1908 of the battleships and destroyers of Theodore Roosevelt's Great White Fleet, sailing 'round the world to display American power. They cruised softly, but carried big guns, and their presence announced our determination to place the United States firmly into the arena of world power politics.

Here is a small glimpse of Daniel H. Burnham's almost otherworldly vision of what Telegraph Hill would be like with the application of imagination, energy, and a good deal of money. But there was more money and energy than imagination loose in the post-earthquake city, and the dream never came close to reality.

San Francisco going up, again: a reconstruction scene on lower Sacramento Street, ca. 1907.

yield large results, even if it is never fully realized.'' The plan was not ''meagre.'' What Burnham presented in his precise draftsman's maps and highly impressionistic architectural renderings was nothing less than a vision of Camelot that hovered at the very horizon of the imagination, a city of ivoried walls and temples and fountains and parks, of community gardens, of public housing that linked style and purpose to the life of beauty, of broad tree-bordered streets and circular parkways (including an ancestral version of today's Bayshore Freeway), of municipal offices in a great civic center at Van Ness and Market, of towers and colonnades and walking paths on Telegraph Hill, of parks and open space at Hunter's Point, Buena Vista Heights, Visitacion Valley, Lone Mountain, Twin Peaks, the Presidio, and Lake Merced (whose proposed park Burnham envisioned as being three times the size of Golden Gate Park). Here was the idea and ideal of urban beauty given expression, and given that expression in perhaps the one city in America where hope had not yet been totally eroded by time and circumstance. A writer for the *Overland Monthly* gazed upon the vision and spoke for some of the best of a generation: ''Do not let it be simply—a dream, and a forgetting.''

It was not forgotten, at least not immediately. On the afternoon of April 17, 1906, to the accompaniment of rhapsodic newspaper editorials and much pointing of pride by architects and politicians, printed and bound copies of Burnham's *Report on a Plan for San Francisco* were carefully stacked in the concrete recesses of the new city hall, ready for distribution.

Three days later, they were rescued from the rubble of City Hall and while the flames still licked away at the town were distributed to the Committee of Forty whose duty it would be to oversee the rebuilding of the city; Burnham himself rushed back from Paris to lobby for his plan, and for a few weeks every newspaper and nearly every prominent citizen in San Francisco supported it; even old Hubert Howe Bancroft, proprietor of the ''History Factory'' whose multi-volumed histories had documented the growth of the city and state more thoroughly than any of the age (or since), put in his oar when he declared, characteristically, ''Let us have the city beautiful by all means,—it will pay.''

Perhaps it would have paid, but not soon enough. It was not long before most of those who had supported the plan before and after the cataclysm began feeling the pinch of second thoughts. The plan was all very well and good and unquestionably beautiful—and perhaps it *was* a definition of what the city should have been—but time was on the assault. To continue to exist, it was believed, the city must rebuild now, and quickly, and however it could. By the end of May, the Downtown Business Men's Association had withdrawn its support of the Burnham Plan, reflecting the change of heart expressed by the *Chronicle*: ''The crying need of San Francisco today is not more parks and boulevards; it is business.'' Business had its day, and the great plan swiftly faded into the past as the city put its energies into cleaning up and starting over. Shells were dynamited and razed, streets were cleared and repaired, gas and electric lines replaced, streetcar tracks rebuilt, millions of tons of rubble carried off by the carload and dumped into Mission Bay and into the ocean off Mile Rock, and within three years the ''damnedest finest ruins'' had been more or less re-erected—twenty thousand buildings, including a completely rebuilt Chinatown, and in the downtown area the restoration of twenty-seven buildings that had survived and the construction of seventy-seven more. By the end of 1909, San Francisco possessed more than half of all the steel and concrete buildings in the United States.

This astonishing rebirth was, by any measure, a monumental achievement, one in which the city took—and takes—considerable pride. Yet something had been lost along the way, and it may well be, as Kevin Starr has suggested in *Americans and the California Dream*, that when the city proceeded to get itself selected as the site of the Panama-Pacific International Exposition it was as much an act of expiation as one of self-confidence: "The ideal remained, giving rise to anxiety over failure to realize Burnham's projects, an anxiety compounded by awareness that the new city had neither the rascally charm of old San Francisco, nor the marmoreal grandeur of Burnham's vision. San Francisco seemed neither ramshackle frontier outpost nor baroque imperial city, but just another provincial business town. . . . If gray, looming skyscrapers said something about one San Francisco, the Exposition might give utterance to the city of the mind which yet haunted Bay Area Californians. And it would pay."

The canal exposition was an idea that had been promoted as early as 1904. The earthquake and fire had aborted these early plans, but by the end of 1909 they had been reborn and were embraced enthusiastically. Some $4 million for the project was pledged in one two-hour mass meeting, and another $2 million was pledged over a period of two months. A statewide bond issue garnered another $5 million, and San Franciscans voted to raise their own taxes an additional $5 million. Money was one thing; congressional approval of San Francisco as the official site of the Exposition was another. A bid by San Diego was quickly done away with, but New Orleans proved more stubborn as a competitor, and it was not until January 31, 1911, that Congress was persuaded. "Thank you, Uncle Sam," a banner in the city proclaimed. "We'll do you proud."

And so they did. The spot chosen for the fairgrounds was a two-mile stretch of partially filled tidelands on the shore of the Bay at the northern edge of the city, just inside the Golden Gate. After months of filling and grading, what they built was an enormous fairyland, a wonderfully eclectic mix of Florentine, Venetian, Moorish, Spanish Byzantine, and Greco-Roman styles. "If the plan of the Exposition were reduced in scale to the size of a golden brooch and the buildings made in Venetian cloisonné jewelry," Berkeley architect Bernard Maybeck remarked, "that brooch would pass as jewelry without causing the suspicion that it represented a plan for a World's Fair." The most splendid building of them all was Maybeck's own Palace of Fine Arts, which loomed in brooding magnificence over its curving lagoon, symbolizing, in the architect's words, "the mortality of grandeur and the vanity of human wishes." (The grandeur of Maybeck's creation was less mortal than he probably intended; painstakingly restored in the 1960s, the Palace of Fine Arts stands alive and well today, the only remnant of the entire celebration.)

Equally impressive, on a different level, was the Tower of Jewels, the largest building of the Exposition. Ornamented with fifty thousand varicolored bits of glass hung from its edges and cornices, the tower winked and glittered enchantingly—particularly at night, when it and the rest of the buildings were washed in the light of thirty-six colored searchlights. The spectacle (which reportedly brought tears to his eyes) inspired poet Edwin Markham to utter the following paean: "I have seen tonight the greatest revelation of beauty that was ever seen on this earth. I may say this meaning it literally and with full regard for all that is known of ancient art and architecture and all that the modern world has heretofore seen of glory and grandeur. I have seen beauty that will give the world new standards of art, and a joy in loveliness never before reached. That is what I have seen."

Even as late as 1910, San Francisco was still a city of street entertainment. One of the greatest of them all took place on Christmas Eve that year when international opera star Luisa Tetrazzini drew a crowd of more than ten thousand on Market Street.

Somebody's "Daddy at the Fair," 1915. Top, in front of Stella, a mechanical exhibit whose breasts heaved realistically; below, in the Grand Concourse; and, bottom, in front of the Tower of Jewels.

Well, it *was* a success, the Exposition. It opened at ten o'clock on the morning of February 20, 1915, and from then until its closing less than ten months later on the night of December 4, an estimated two million people tasted its delights: the works of art in the great palace; the huge working model of the Panama Canal; the Fountain of Energy; the plants and flowers of the Palace of Horticulture; the mechanical gadgetry of the Palace of Machinery; the rides and shows and restaurants of the Joy Zone. What is more, it *did* pay, most handsomely. Within months after its closing, the Exposition's land was stripped of all its buildings save the Palace of Fine Arts, carved up into splendid little lots, and sold off in one of the most profitable real estate ventures in the history of the city. If the Exposition can be said to stand as the last febrile expression of the best architectural hopes the old San Francisco had generated, then it also can be said that the old San Francisco ended as it had in part begun: as a real estate speculation.

IF THE PHYSICAL NATURE of the new San Francisco demonstrated with a certain precision the gulf that had widened between the two centuries, conveniently divided by the scorched earth of the fire, there were other less tangible but no less real indications. The first was the progress and ultimate demise of the "good government movement" that had developed in response to the rule of the little kingpin of San Francisco politics, Abraham Ruef, his captive mayor, Eugene Schmitz, and an ambitious gaggle of boodlers otherwise known as the San Francisco Board of Supervisors.

The November elections of 1905, during which Ruef's gang ran up an impressive majority, had discouraged those who would have put him out of business, but it had not deterred them, nor had the disaster of April 1906, during which Schmitz had deported himself remarkably well, earning a considerable portion of public respect. Armed with financial promises from Rudolph Spreckels and James Duval Phelan and their assurances that the "better elements" in the city's business community would back an investigation and prosecution no matter how far or how high they might go, the *Bulletin*'s editor, Fremont Older, journeyed to Washington in search of a suitably tough-minded special prosecutor. The man in his sights was Francis J. Heney, who had gained a reputation for tenacity and integrity while heading up recent investigations into timberland frauds in Oregon for the administration of Theodore Roosevelt. Heney agreed to take charge in San Francisco, provided he could bring with him William J. Burns, head of the Treasury Department's Secret Service and one of the most renowned detectives in the world. After some negotiations with Roosevelt's people, who were reluctant to be deprived of the services of two of their best, the proposition was settled— and was promised, remarkably enough, the full support of San Francisco's district attorney, William H. Langdon, probably the only honest man among those who had been elected in November 1905.

By June 1906, Heney's investigation was well under way, accompanied by almost daily reports of payoffs and bribes in the pages of the *Bulletin*, which exposés were roundly and repeatedly denied by Ruef and Schmitz in blustering rebuttals printed in the *Bulletin* and most of the rest of the city's newspapers. (Whatever other problems San Franciscans faced in the months of reconstruction, they did not suffer from a dull press.) And Ruef, out of what resources of arrogance we can only imagine, did his cause little good in September 1906. Early in that month, delegates of the Republican party gathered in Santa Cruz to select a gubernatorial candidate. On hand were a number of reform delegates, most of them committed to the renomination of Governor George C. Pardee. Their influence was gutted by the efficient teamwork of a group of Southern Pacific lobbyists led by Walter A. Parker of Los Angeles and dedicated to the nomination of Congressman James N. Gillett, who had proved himself a good and true friend of the railroad. On hand also was Ruef, who controlled the largest single body of votes—the San Francisco delegates. After a few days of the kind of wheeling and dealing its Political Bureau had raised to the level of a refined art, the Southern Pacific faction managed to gain control over a substantial bloc of delegate votes. More were needed, and Ruef's contingent was available—eminently available. The matter of a $14,000 payment was discussed, and when the first ballot vote was taken on September 10, Gillett, the railroad's champion, was nominated by a vote of 591½ to 233½. Shortly afterward, the men who had negotiated the nomination gathered for a sumptuous victory banquet, and to document the bibulous occasion, a photographer snapped a most remarkable picture: seated in the center of the group, fittingly enough, was Ruef, flanked on either side by the Southern Pacific's representatives; and standing directly behind Ruef, with one hand gently resting in tender gratitude upon his shoulder, was the gubernatorial nominee himself.

That photograph, printed and reprinted, became a kind of talisman for the reform movement in San Francisco, the visible expression of the blight that Older and his colleagues felt had reduced the city's politics to a nearly terminal condition. Its implications, announced with a "we-told-you-so" glee in the pages of the *Bulletin*, were not lost on the public, nor on the judicial body which represented that public in criminal matters—the grand jury of San Francisco. In November 1906, presented with Heney's first installment of evidence, that body issued indictments against Ruef and Schmitz for accepting as much as $10,000 in payoffs from various of the city's eating-places-cum-high-class-houses-of-assignation, the French restaurants, in exchange for police protection and the renewal of liquor licenses. Before long, Heney was able to trap Supervisor Thomas Lonergan into taking a bribe. In exchange for a promise of immunity, Lonergan promptly confessed to his own peccadillos as well as to those of the rest of the supervisors; and again in a bargain for immunity the remaining members fell over one another in their eagerness to testify—against themselves, against Ruef, against Schmitz, against one another, against anyone else they could think of. That included a lot of people, among them the executives of the gas and telephone companies, who, it was charged, had bribed Ruef to obtain favorable franchises and rates for their utilities. Most significantly, it included Patrick Calhoun, president of the United Railroads, the dominant streetcar system in San Francisco, and his chief counsel, Tirey L. Ford, former attorney general of California. With the full knowledge of Calhoun, it was alleged, Ford had given Ruef $200,000 ($80,000 of which was fairly distributed among the supervisors) in exchange for permission to convert all the company's cable-car lines to an overhead trolley system—less esthetic, thus violently opposed by those in the city–beautiful movement, but infinitely cheaper, which was the only thing that mattered to Calhoun. Also included in the package had been acquisition of a twenty-five-year franchise for the company, the longest such franchise in the city's history.

Almost buried under this mass of testimony, Ruef himself succumbed to Heney's generous offer of immunity if he made a full confession and would testify against Calhoun and the other corporation executives, as well as against Mayor Schmitz. Another rash of indictments was issued, some of them reach-

Eugene E. Schmitz, mayor of San Francisco, protégé of Abraham Ruef, bassoon player, orchestra leader, a genuine good fellow, and the handsomest mayor in the land of The Big Machine.

ing into the hallowed walls of the Pacific Union Club and as far away as Los Angeles. Schmitz came to trial on June 5, 1907, and on June 13 was convicted of accepting bribes—and of extortion to get them in the first place. He immediately appealed (his conviction was later reversed by the district court of appeals), but in the meantime was removed from office. After brief substitutions by Supervisors Gallagher and Charles Boxton, the man selected to replace him as mayor was Edward Robeson Taylor, the old poet and Bohemian Club member whose talents for much of anything were not admired by the *Oakland Tribune*, among other newspapers: "The truth is, that Mayor Taylor is a near success at many things, but falls short of excellence in anything. He discourses on medicine learnedly—for a poet; discusses legal principles profoundly—for a doctor; and writes fairly good verse—for a lawyer. But when we take him separately as physician, poet, or lawyer, he is merely a trick artist having the same resemblance to the real thing that an astrologer does to an astronomer or a talkative parrot to a wise philosopher." Regardless, in the elections of November 1907, Taylor and a new, hand-picked board of supervisors were given the approval of the voters.

After Schmitz's conviction the graft prosecution began a slow disintegration from which it never recovered, and it must be said that one of the main reasons was a certain hubris on the part of the reformers. Shortly after the Schmitz conviction's reversal by the higher court, Ruef recanted on his promise to testify against the "higher-ups" who had paid him his bribes, arguing that for him to declare in court that he had certain knowledge that such as Ford and Calhoun had *known* that his "attorney's fees" were in fact bribes would be to perjure himself, inasmuch as the real meaning and purpose of the payments had never been discussed. Furious, Heney withdrew his offer of immunity and scheduled Ruef for trial, and, unimpressed by Ruef's legal argument (which in fact was a good one), announced his intention to bring all the charged executives to trial in spite of Ruef's recantation. What is more, he let it be known that he was going to go even further: one way or another, he said, he was going to involve not only William F. Herrin, head of the Southern Pacific's Political Bureau, but the president of the company, Edward H. Harriman, who had absorbed the Southern Pacific into his railroad empire (which included the Union Pacific) after the death of Collis P. Huntington.

This was going altogether too far. If Heney's brightest hopes were fulfilled, he would have jailed a good number of the most respected businessmen in San Francisco—not to mention Harriman, one of the richest men in America. With increasing rapidity, those businessmen whom Phelan and Spreckels had painstakingly gathered into the fold of the reform movement fell away; not only fell away, but began objecting out loud to the whole proceeding, maintaining that the prosecution was giving San Francisco a bad name and was therefore bad for business. Of particular concern to most of these backslid reformers was Heney's assault on Patrick Calhoun, who had established himself as the White Knight of San Francisco's reconstruction in the spring of 1907. Almost singlehandedly, it was popularly believed, Calhoun had forced a settlement in a crippling strike against his streetcar lines in May, a strike marked by violence between union carmen and strikebreakers and one that disrupted the city's transportation system at an especially crucial time. Calhoun's courageous and successful efforts to keep things moving in spite of sabotage and rioting had endeared him to the Downtown Businessmen's Association, and Heney's insistence on prosecuting him appeared to its members to be a travesty of justice.   [*Continued on page 212*]

Abraham Ruef's lawyer imparts a confidence to his client. Whatever it may have been, it did little good, for Ruef was the one who paid for all the graft which had oiled the politics of his Union Labor Party.

Saloon Politics. . .

It was a gladhanded sort of politics that Abe Ruef and Eugene Schmitz practiced, a matter of free beer and open-air, street-corner rallies. There was a workingman's confident strut to it and an insouciant disregard for the niceties of ethics which absolutely infuriated Fremont Older, among others. "In the face of accusations and proofs," Older stormed in the pages of his *Bulletin*, "Ruef remains more than serene, —he is jaunty. Schmitz is a rascal, a very avaricious, coarse, and determined one, so fond of money he is willing to undergo disgrace in order to procure it, but truth demands the admission that he is a better man than Ruef. . . . Schmitz will make the journey to San Quentin crushed, bowed, and in dejection, a picture of unnerved wretchedness. . . . But Ruef will take the stage for the prison smiling without and calm within, cursing his ill luck, no doubt, but a chipper, impudent, and swaggering moral idiot to the last."

Impudence!—that was what drove Older to venom in his editorials, and it was impudence that

finally led to Ruef's downfall. In the end, he was the only one of the city's gang of boodlers to be bundled off for the dismal comforts of San Quentin in 1911—and, true to Older's prediction, he did in fact go off to prison with a certain debonair lack of concern. Nearly five years later, older, grayer, and suitably contrite, he was paroled, largely through the influence of the man who had done so much to put him in prison: Fremont Older. Still dapper, if somewhat subdued, in 1916 the aging "Boss" of San Francisco posed for the charming photograph on the previous page.

And Eugene Schmitz, the "bassoon mayor" whose name annotates these saloon shots of 1905? He ran for mayor of San Francisco in 1915 against "Sunny Jim" Rolph and was beaten two-to-one. But in 1921, the city with the short memory elected him a supervisor, and to a second term after that. In 1928, "the smallest man mentally and meanest man morally that ever occupied the mayor's chair" died and was given a splendid funeral—though not at city expense.

The prosecution team, before indifference and violence crippled reform. From left to right: William J. Burns, Fremont Older, Cora Older, Francis Heney, Charles W. Coff (one of Heney's assistants), and Rudolph Spreckels.

Yet, according to Fremont Older, who believed it to the end of his days, the entire strike had been a set-up designed to enhance Calhoun's standing in the community. In *My Own Story*, published in 1919, Older charged that Calhoun had met with the secretary-treasurer of the Carmen's Union in Mayor Schmitz's house and by the payment of a suitable fee had arranged the strike and had settled it similarly, all of this to make successful prosecution of him impossible. "Calhoun knew the City," Older wrote. "He knew what would influence the powerful men of the City. He knew that San Francisco was in ruins and that the businessmen above all wanted the streetcars to run, otherwise they would be utterly ruined. . . . He loomed as the savior of the City, once ruined by fire and threatened again by labor unionism. His indictment made no dent at all upon his popularity. The prominent men of San Francisco stood before him and said: 'Let's see you convict him!' "

Whatever the truth of Older's claim (and it was never proved), the strike had the desired results. When Older asked an unnamed businessman whether Calhoun should be convicted if proved guilty, the reply was unequivocal: "No! If I were on the jury I'd vote to acquit him if he were as *guilty as hell*! He's the man that *saved San Francisco*!" The man who "saved San Francisco" was in fact acquitted, as was each of the bribe-givers brought to trial (some of which trials ground on until 1912). Of the sixty-five indictments which Heney had pried out of the grand jury in 1906 and 1907, only one resulted in a successful conviction: on December 10, 1908, Abraham Ruef was found guilty, and after the usual run of appeals was sentenced to a term in San Quentin prison. Even Ruef's conviction was not without its agonies for Heney. In the middle of the trial, he was shot in the face by a juror he had rejected because of a prior felony conviction. (The unsuccessful assassin, Morris Haas, was later found in his cell with a bullet hole in the center of his forehead; the official verdict was suicide, but there were those who wondered if he had not been done in to ensure his silence.) Heney recovered, but the trials, drained of energy and support, did not. By 1912, when the last of the indictments were dismissed, the trials had long since been relegated to the inside pages of even the *Bulletin*, and when Abraham Ruef was released from San Quentin in 1915, after serving only half his sentence—and released largely through the efforts of Fremont Older, who had done so much to put him behind bars—it was as if the glory days of boodling had never existed, so thoroughly had the memory of San Francisco been cleansed of all that his rise and fall had represented. In 1915, Abraham Ruef was history; in 1915, the march of business had no time for history.

A disaster on Mission Street, July 18, 1911. There were those who claimed that an even worse disaster took place a few months later in that same year: the inaugural election of James Rolph, Jr., as mayor of San Francisco.

AND BUSINESS DID MARCH—led in its parade by an unlikely Babbitt named James "Sunny Jim" Rolph, Jr. Born in the Mission District of poor but earnest parentage, Rolph steadily picked his way through a career that at various times included a partnership in a shipping concern, the presidency of two "South-of-the-Slot" banks, the ownership of the Rolph Navigation & Coal Company, the Rolph Shipbuilding Company, and James Rolph & Company, directorships in the Ship Owners and Merchants Tugboat Company and the San Francisco Chamber of Commerce, the vice-presidency of the Panama-Pacific International Exposition, and the presidency of the Merchants Exchange and the Ship Owners Association of the Pacific Coast—and, not incidentally, nineteen years as mayor of San Francisco, a longer reign than any man before or since. However, neither his varied business career nor his long-lived political career, which continued until his death (he left the mayoralty in 1931 to become Governor of California and died in office in 1934), could be attributed to any astonishing feats of intelligence or acumen. As a businessman, his most noteworthy achievement came when he contrived to lose more than $3 million as a shipbuilder after World War I, a disaster from which it took him ten years to recover. And as a politician, he displayed all the social and administrative instincts of a doorknob; during his nineteen years in office the accomplishment that came closest to what might be called socially progressive was the establishment of a Municipal Clinic for the regular examination and treatment of prostitutes—and even that genuinely laudable effort came to an end in 1917, when the California Red Light Abatement Act was enforced in San Francisco for the first time, driving most of the "crib girls" and streetwalkers from the city and most of the rest into parlor houses and call-girl establishments, removing the possibility of any kind of intelligent regulation.

But Rolph was "Sunny Jim," by all accounts a dapper, ebullient, and utterly charming man whose careless personal and professional morality and casual interest in the functions of municipal government precisely mirrored the foibles of an age committed to little more than the pursuit of the cash register. In her autobiography, *The Lady of the House* (1966), entrepreneur Sally Stanford, a close friend of his for many years, outlined Rolph's easygoing qualities: "Sunny Jim's attitudes were the most significant thing about him. First and foremost, he was for Live and Let Live, Let Sleeping Dogs Lie, and Don't Stir Up Muddy Waters. Also, If You Haven't Tried It, Don't Knock It." Those who wished more than most to be left alone to live, of course, were those of the business community, and the sleeping dog they would just as soon not arouse was the labor movement.

Market Street on Armistice Day, November 11, 1918. The masks are there to protect against the great swine flu epidemic of that year, a scourge that killed 500,000 Americans and more than twenty million people all over the world.

Indeed, the man Rolph defeated in his first bid for the mayor's office in 1911 was Patrick H. McCarthy (called "Pin Head" McCarthy by his adversaries), the Union Labor party candidate—and their last successful candidate, for by 1911 the labor movement in San Francisco was in deep trouble. Between 1901 and 1907, flushed with the encouragement of political success, the movement had made San Francisco the most completely unionized city in the country; deterioration of that power had begun with the revelations of graft and the subsequent efforts at prosecution, the city's business element pointing out at every given opportunity that this was the sort of thing one could expect when unions were allowed to get out of hand. Enough strength remained after the graft trials to assure McCarthy's election in 1909, but even that degree of power (McCarthy himself was considered highly conservative, and thus relatively safe, by the business community) was dissipated soon after his election—not only by the continuing disenchantment with unionism as a political force, but by developments taking place some four hundred fifty miles to the south.

For fifteen years, the Los Angeles Merchants and Manufacturers Association, led by "General" Harrison Gray Otis, publisher and editor of the *Los Angeles Times,* had conducted a vigorous and sometimes brutal campaign to keep its city an open-shop town, with considerable success: by the middle of the first decade of the twentieth century, wages in Los Angeles were as much as 20, 30, and even 40 percent below those prevailing in San Francisco. For some time, the merchants and industrialists of San Francisco had been eyeing the lower wages of Los Angeles with both fear and envy, and in 1908 finally delivered an ultimatum to their local unions: either see to it that Los Angeles wages were brought up to San Francisco levels or face wage cuts across the board. This was the kind of language any good union man could understand,

and San Francisco's labor movement was soon contributing both money and leadership to organizing activities in Los Angeles.

The battle lines in Los Angeles were sharpened by the appearance and sudden rise of socialism, which waxed fat on the city's increasing ideological antagonisms. Socialist parades featuring as many as twenty thousand workers marched through the streets, terrifying the city's conservative element and enraging in particular the *Los Angeles Times*. In this more than slightly charged atmosphere, a series of strikes commenced in the spring of 1910, beginning with brewery workers and soon spreading to the metal trades. In response, the Merchants and Manufacturers Association persuaded the Los Angeles city council to pass a broad anti-picketing ordinance, which swiftly resulted in the arrest of 470 workers. These arrests simply intensified the conflict, and by the end of summer the streets of Los Angeles echoed with the ring of violence. Then in the pre-dawn hours of October 1, a well-placed bomb ripped out one wall of the *Times* building, killing twenty employees and starting a fire that gutted the structure. "O you anarchic scum," cried Otis in a hastily printed edition of the *Times*, "you cowardly murderers, you leeches upon honest labor, you midnight assassins. . . ."

After a nationwide manhunt under the supervision of William J. Burns (who will be remembered for his part in the graft prosecution in San Francisco), three alleged culprits were captured in Indianapolis and whisked off to Los Angeles without benefit of extradition: Ortie McManigal, a confessed professional dynamiter, and John J. and James B. McNamara, brothers with close ties to the militant International Association of Bridge and Structural Iron Workers. While Ortie McManigal, giving state's evidence, fully implicated both McNamaras in the explosion, the labor movement in San Francisco and the rest of the country put its prestige and credibility on the line, giving out with cries of "kidnapping" and "frameup," and hiring the eminent Clarence Darrow to defend the two brothers. As the trial dragged on through the spring, summer, fall, and finally early winter of 1911, the labor movement increasingly found and proclaimed its self-definition in these men being railroaded by a heartless and self-serving business establishment. And then on December 1, 1911, the McNamara brothers changed their pleas from not guilty to guilty. Faced with a damning body of evidence and probable death sentences, Darrow had advised his clients to plead guilty in exchange for reduced sentences—John to receive life imprisonment, James to receive fifteen years.

The McNamara brothers, now officially guilty by their own admission, saved their lives, but in so doing thoroughly discredited the labor movement across the country, almost totally destroying it in Los Angeles and giving it in San Francisco a blow from which it did not recover for more than twenty years. The business community of the city, believing it had solid evidence now that the labor element was not only politically corrupt but riddled with anarchists and murderers, did not hesitate to capitalize on its advantage. With increasing frequency and confidence, employers refused to meet union demands for wage increases, improved hours and working conditions, or the closed shop; deprived after 1911 of any significant political expression, the unions responded with the old recourse of the strike and the picket line; and for the next five years San Francisco became accustomed to clashes between strikers and strikebreakers, to violence and the sporadic disruption of trade.

The culmination of this rapid shift in the city's power structure came in 1916. On June 1, the city's waterfront workers walked off their jobs as part of a coastwide shipping strike, and the inevitable conflicts between pickets and

The speedy Mizpah, *one of a small army of rumrunners which cruised between San Francisco and the ports of Canada and Mexico in the dread, dry days of Prohibition. Unlike most, the* Mitzpah *fell afoul of the Feds in 1925.*

strikebreakers resulted in the beatings of several scabs and the gunshot death of a striker. On June 22, the San Francisco Chamber of Commerce declared a state of war: "The Chamber of Commerce favors the open shop and insists upon the right to employ union or non-union workers, in whole or in part, as the parties involved may elect. . . . Therefore, the Chamber of Commerce pledges its entire organization and the resources it represents to the maintenance of these principles and will oppose any attempt on the part of any interest, business, or organization which tries to throttle the commercial freedom of San Francisco." A little less than two weeks later, the Chamber sent representatives to Mayor Rolph's office demanding that he allow them to deputize five hundred special police to patrol the waterfront, a curious reminder of William T. Coleman's Pickhandle Brigade of 1877; to his everlasting credit, Rolph turned down the proposal. Undaunted, on the night of July 10 the Chamber held a public meeting in the Merchants' Exchange; some two thousand businessmen attended the meeting, and at its end a Law and Order Committee had been formed to collect money and supervise the elimination of "class warfare" in the city. As shipping tycoon Robert Dollar, one of the speakers at the meeting, expressed it, "Let's fight! If a peaceful workingman is beaten up by strikers, then beat up two strikers in return." A war chest of $200,000 was subscribed that night, and within a week would swell to $600,000.

Enter, now, the specter of war. By the summer of 1916 it was becoming more and more likely that the United States would soon be committed to the war in Europe, and planned celebrations of patriotism called "Preparedness Parades" had become all the rage in the cities of the country. San Francisco's own had been scheduled for July 22; to assure a good turnout, most of the city's employers had ordered their employees to march, knowing full well that most of the labor movement was bitterly opposed to American entry into the war. A mass protest meeting on the evening of July 20, attended by more than five thousand people (among them avowed pacifists Fremont Older and Rudolph Spreckels), failed to stifle the enthusiasm of the business and political community, and at half past one o'clock on the afternoon of July 22 the parade started at Market and the Embarcadero, led by Sunny Jim himself, done up in a frock coat with a flower in his buttonhole, gold-heeled boots, a ten-gallon Stetson hat, and a small American flag in his hand.

And at 2:06, near the corner of Steuart and Market, a pipe bomb exploded, scattering metal fragments and live cartridges through spectators and paraders alike, killing ten and wounding more than forty.

In the days of ensuing hysteria, the authorities zeroed in on Tom Mooney, local secretary of the International Workers' Defense League and leader or instigator of a number of recent strikes, including an abortive carmen's walkout in the spring of 1916; Mooney's wife, Rena; Warren K. Billings, a young associate of theirs who had been convicted of transporting dynamite in 1913; and two other minor labor radicals. No other suspects were seriously investigated, and while Rena Mooney was acquitted and the charges against the other two were ultimately dropped, Tom Mooney and Warren Billings were convicted in separate trials, Billings sentenced to life imprisonment and Mooney to execution. President Woodrow Wilson, fearing the repercussions of what had become an international incident, forced the commutation of Mooney's sentence from death to life imprisonment. Though both remained in prison for more than twenty years, Mooney and Billings could take some bitter satisfaction in watching the cases against them disintegrate with the passage of time. Every major prosecution witness ultimately recanted his tes-

The age of flight brought with it a touch of romance not unlike that of the great days of sail, and San Francisco embraced its wondrous machines with enthusiasm. At the top of the page, an intrepid airman pioneers in seagoing flight from the deck of the U.S.S. Pennsylvania in San Francisco Bay, 1910. Below that, another airman and his female copilot prepare to challenge the updrafts of Ocean Beach in 1915.

Death and destruction on Market Street, July 22, 1916—a day billed as Preparedness Day.

timony. Every member of the prosecution team, save District Attorney Charles M. Fickert and his assistant, whose political futures were at stake, asked that Mooney and Billings be given new trials; the presiding judge in the Mooney prosecution, Franklin A. Griffin, almost immediately asked the State Supreme Court for another trial, and as late as 1929 went on record to the effect that "The Mooney case is one of the dirtiest jobs ever put over and I resent the fact that my court was used for such a contemptible piece of work." Fremont Older, at first convinced that the two had been responsible, quickly changed his mind and for the last fifteen years of his life agitated for their release, sacrificing his position on the *Bulletin* in the process and moving over to William Randolph Hearst's *Call.* As the years passed, the evidence against the prosecution mounted: the falsification of documents, the outright lies, the subornation by perjury, the suppression of evidence, the bribes, and the consistent and deliberate perversion of the judicial process, until the trials of Mooney and Billings stood as two of the most disgraceful episodes in American legal history.

Yet the two men remained in prison until it was politically convenient to let them go (in January 1939, Governor Culbert Olson pardoned Mooney, and in October reduced Billings's sentence to time served). The reason was quite as simple as it was, in its own twisted way, logical. In the words of the *Colfax Record:* "The reason Mooney and Billings are in prison is because a majority of the people of the state of California want them there. . . . It is quite beside the point whether or not they are guilty of the particular crime of which they were charged and convicted. The question is: Are Mooney and Billings the sort of people we want to run at large? We have decided this in the negative and we have them locked up. We intend to keep them there."

Colfax, California, was a long way from San Francisco, but the sentiments aired by its little newspaper might just as well have been quoted from one handout or another issued by the San Francisco Chamber of Commerce. To this estimable body, Mooney and Billings were definitely not the sort of people who should be left to run loose, nor was the movement they represented, however tangentially, something that should be tolerated. Radicalism was Anarchism was Bolshevism; the labor movement, since it challenged the conventions of free enterprise, was *ipso facto* a danger to society, and what better proof of this existed than the Preparedness Day bombing of 1916? The business community was not sluggardly about making its position known. The night of the bombing, the Chamber of Commerce called its Law and Order Committee (which by then had grown to some six thousand members, with a hand-picked "Advisory Committee of One Hundred") into session, featuring, among other speakers, Mayor Rolph, who now found it expedient to ally himself with those most likely to butter his bread. Edward Hurlbut, a feature writer for the *Call* and (coincidentally) publicity director for the Law and Order Committee, gave the meeting the *imprimatur* of history: "They sat with us last night at the Auditorium, the brooding shades of the Vigilantes. . . . The high resolve that consecrated their work sixty years ago, recrudescent, spoke from the lips of the younger generation. . . . Grim, stern, patriotic, the sons of the sires of 1856 pledged themselves to carry on in sacred trust the fair name of a great City that these men of an elder time cleared of the stain of dishonor and passed along to us unsullied and glorious, a golden escutcheon without a blotch. . . ."

However grim, stern, patriotic, or recrudescent the Law and Order Committee may have appeared that night, it subsequently engaged neither in armed rebellion nor in overt acts of vigilantism. It did not have to, for what it *did* do more thoroughly than at any other time in the city's history was coalesce the power, purpose, and resources of San Francisco's business element into a monolith against which labor, financially weak, fragmented into a dozen conflicting ideologies, and riven by the resulting struggles for power, found itself helpless. "There is no such thing as *peaceful* picketing," the head of the Law and Order Committee declared. "Picketing is an instrument of violence. It is un-American. It hurts the City by bad advertisement, leads to crime, and does labor no good." And in 1919, the citizens of San Francisco passed one of the most stringent anti-picketing ordinances in the country. "Radicalism has no place here!" cried the committee. And in 1920 the relatively militant Riggers and Stevedores Union was replaced by the employer-controlled Longshoremens Association of San Francisco and the Bay District. "These radical groups in organized labor are enemies of organized labor, enemies of the employer, enemies of society, and the enemies of the government itself," announced the Waterfront Employers Union. And in 1921, when the Sailors Union went on strike, its power was so completely shattered that in a matter of months its membership dropped from nearly seven thousand to fewer than three thousand. So it went: between 1921 and 1933, labor won not a single major strike, gained no greater wage increases than employers were willing in their charity to grant, and watched while all the hope that had been generated during the heady days of the Union Labor party was transmuted into the shriveled, bitter knot of what poet Langston Hughes, in a somewhat different context, called "the dream deferred."

The San Francisco of Progress: the streetcar circle at the foot of Market Street, about 1920—when Market Street was a four-track main stem.

ONE BY ONE, the best of the dreams had faded. In place of them now was Progress, and who could deny its benefits? It was Progress that made San Francisco one of the first cities in the country to own and operate its own street transportation system. In 1911, a bond issue was passed for the purchase of the Geary Street Railroad, and with similar bond issues over the next forty years all of the city's private streetcar and cable-car companies were absorbed into the network of the "Muni"—the Municipal Railway. Moreover, to facilitate the movement of streetcar and automobile traffic, the decade of the 1920s saw the construction of the ambitious Twin Peaks, Stockton, and Broadway tunnels, under the supervision of City Engineer Michael O'Shaughnessy.

It was Progress that brought city-owned water to San Francisco from the heights of the Sierra, though not without contention. In 1901, Mayor James Duval Phelan had appointed a committee of engineers to search for the most likely spot in the mountains for the construction of a dam. Of the several places that would have been feasible, the engineers recommended as the cheapest and easiest the Hetch Hetchy Valley of the Tuolumne River. Unfortunately, the Hetch Hetchy Valley lay within the boundaries of Yosemite National Park, created in 1890, and the notion of a dam there did not sit well with the members of John Muir's Sierra Club, many of whom were among the business and civic leaders of San Francisco. Citing the Hetch Hetchy Valley as the cheapest available source, the city repeatedly petitioned the Department of the Interior for permission to enter the park; John Muir and the Sierra Club repeatedly blocked the granting of such petitions, arguing that there were considerations beyond money at stake, among them the violation of the purposes and principles for which the park had been created and the certain destruction of a valley second in beauty and magnificence only to the Yosemite Valley itself. Time ran out for the conservationists in 1913, when the city petitioned Congress itself and secured passage of the Riker Act; President

The San Francisco of Progress: Lower Market Street in 1927.

Woodrow Wilson, more neatly attuned to the needs of Progress than his conservation-minded predecessors, Roosevelt and Taft, signed the bill on December 19. Work on the dam and the 156-mile aqueduct began in 1914 and after the interruption of World War I continued until 1934, when the first Sierra water was delivered to the Crystal Springs Reservoir south of San Francisco, and from there to the mains of the city. A little over a year after Wilson's signing of the Riker Act, John Muir died, his own dream undercut by economics. Today, contemplating the fact that the once-beautiful Hetch Hetchy Valley now lies buried beneath hundreds of thousands of acre-feet of water in an age that starves for parks and open space, one may indeed wonder: just what *did* San Francisco do with all that money it saved those many years ago?

It was Progress that built San Francisco's Civic Center, the only remnant of Daniel H. Burnham's vision of the perfect city—and a modified one at that. By 1930, three of the massive granite buildings in the complex just off Market Street had been built—with city funds and a good deal of city self-congratulation: the Public Library (1917), the Civic Auditorium (1915), and City Hall (1915), the last a more than worthy successor to the dismal, crumbling wreck that had preceded it. The Veteran's Memorial and the Opera House were both completed in 1932. (Sunny Jim dearly loved to point out to visitors that the dome of San Francisco's city hall was precisely sixteen feet, three inches higher than that of the national capitol in Washington; it was never shown whether Washington ever gave the matter much thought).

And it was Progress in the 1920s that erected more than a dozen skyscrapers whose modestly impressive heights gave definition to the downtown skyline of San Francisco for more than thirty years—among them the Pacific Telephone & Telegraph Building, the Sutter Building, Mills Tower, the Mark Hopkins Hotel, the Russ Building, the Shell Building, and the Standard Oil Building.

There was no question about it. Progress had shouted and built and conquered, but it was more a matter of steel and concrete than of spirit. If the citizens of the town could look around them and take some pride in the monuments to Progress they saw, they must also have known that this skyscraper San Francisco, this branch-office town, this San Francisco of Sunny Jim Rolph's gladhanded administration, of easy prohibition morality and freedom from labor strife, was neither the city that was nor the city that might have been. Thousands of them might have stood and watched, as Milla Logan watched, while the lights went out for the last time in the Panama-Pacific International Exposition of 1915, watched as a curtain descended behind which they would never again be allowed to see. "The night it went out, the Fair never looked lovelier," she remembered. "Every jewel in the Tower flashed for the last curtain call. Then a paralyzing dimness fell on the scene. The darkness drained the glow from the domes and palaces, bleeding them slowly to death. The walls turned cold and stiff. The last feeble lights gasped and then there was a dark void where a few minutes ago there had been a vision."

San Francisco women after their own kind of progress: a suffragette gathering in the Women's Pavilion of the Panama-Pacific International Exposition, 1915.

Sunny Jim and the Harmonics of Affluence. . .

In an age that was positively awash with nicknames for its public figures, it seems only appropriate that James "Sunny Jim" Rolph, Jr. should have succeeded P. H. "Pin Head" McCarthy as mayor of San Francisco in the November elections of 1911. It was appropriate in other ways, too, not the least of which was the fact that Rolph, more precisely than any other mayor before or since, mirrored the character of San Francisco as it rose from the ashes and dedicated itself to the pursuit of the happy dollar. There were some hard times to face after 1911—the Preparedness Day bombing of 1916, the First World War, the Swine Flu epidemic of 1918, and the rash of strikes that broke out after the war—but the city's brotherhood of business weathered them all and entered the 1920s ready to harvest the fruits of a surely endless prosperity.

At the head of the parade of affluence was Sunny Jim, the drum major of progress, dressed to the nines, persistently affable, an apparently permanent grin fixed on his cherubic face, ready and willing to present himself at any and all occasions, whether reviewing the troops on their return from war, saluting the men of the navy, getting sworn in as captain of the "Good Ship San Francisco" by the Chamber of Commerce, or comparing chapeaux with his eastern counterpart, Jimmy

"Beau James" Walker, mayor of New York. He was perhaps the most enthusiastically *public* of all the city's mayors.

And the most harmonious. One of his earliest acts as mayor was to appoint James Woods, manager of the St. Francis Hotel, as chairman of the board of police commissioners in 1912, and in a newspaper interview Woods outlined what he thought the job would entail: "I think I know what Mayor Rolph expected of me. . . . I think he wants to avoid extremes in the administration of the Police Department, and that will be my aim, too. . . . I think that Mayor Rolph wants me to do for the city what I have done for the St. Francis Hotel . . . but above all, it is essential that we should have a harmonious board; a board whose members are harmonious and which is in harmony as a whole with the chief of police and with the mayor. And it is essential that the chief of police should be in harmony with the mayor."

Harmony, indeed, and the city it produced was nicely outlined by Edward F. O'Day in his *Town Talk* in 1915: "No closed town. A lid of course, but a lid like the lid of Pandora's box, letting out some of the joys as well as some of the glooms; not a lid tightly hammered down as the smug-faced Puritans would have it. No open town, and yet no closed town." And so it was that for more than ten years Tessie Wall, the most successful madam of the uptown Tenderloin, was chosen as Queen of the Policeman's Ball; and so it was that every year on this auspicious occasion she made her grand entrance on the arm of the mayor of San Francisco, James Rolph, Jr. More than their taste in hats separated San Francisco's Rolph and New York's Jimmy Walker; Sunny Jim was the one who didn't get caught.

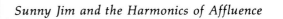

SUNNY JIM LIKED TO BE MAYOR OF SAN FRANCISCO. . . . It was an age of boom and ballyhoo and no one was better at it than Rolph. Campaigning was no chore to him; it was an avocation, a delight, and he would cheerfully get himself up in any outlandish costume, place himself in any unlikely setting, clutch any number of children, and attend any number of peculiar functions in his successful nineteen-year pursuit of the almighty vote. In an era almost two generations before the search for charisma through television, Sunny Jim knew precisely what he was doing.

THE SPORTING LIFE, PART I: Rolph was not notably athletic, but he had his moments. One of these came every spring, when he not only threw out the first pitch on opening day at old Seals Stadium, but actually *pitched* the first pitch. Another Rolph interest is documented by the scene below, an interest further substantiated by a story Sally Stanford—the heiress-apparent of Tessie Wall—recorded in her autobiography. On one occasion in the late 1920s, the story goes, New York newspaper cronies Gene Fowler and Bugs Baer converged on San Francisco, putting up in the St. Francis Hotel. After being entertained the evening long by Mayor Rolph, Fowler and Baer confessed to a certain sense of boredom. What did they want to see? Rolph inquired. Rummaging around in his mind, Fowler came up with what he felt was an impossible request. A cockfight, he replied. Less than an hour later, Fowler and Baer did in fact witness a cockfight. In their room at the St. Francis Hotel. On the carpet.

THE SPORTING LIFE, PART II: Rolph's skill as a swordsman was legendary in his time, and therefore accepted fact. Whatever truth there may have been in it, Rolph never went out of his way to avoid the company of the tender sex—although it is not likely that even Rolph would have essayed a pass at Marion Davies, a very close friend of William Randolph Hearst. Rolph is shown with her at the right during a Hollywood premiere in 1927. It is interesting to note that the photograph was sent out by its wire service with the following message: "Note to all Hearst editors: The wrinkles in Miss Davies' pants are to be air-brushed out. Also, no mention is to be made of the medals on Miss Davies' chest."

A NEW DECADE . . . A DECADE NOT AT ALL
SUNNY. . . . Early in 1930, near the end of his final
term as mayor, Rolph took on a rare mood of stern
purpose in order to encourage San Franciscans to
do their duty by the census report of that year. He
might have been mayor forever, but he had been
bitten by a larger ambition by then, going on to be
elected governor of the state later in the year. In
1934, barely started on his campaign for reelection,
beset by age and economic problems beyond his
experience or understanding, he was stricken by a
heart attack. In 1934, Sunny Jim, like Emperor
Norton before him, died with his times.

Scab, *a somber rendering by Maynard Dixon that suggests all the dark and disturbing elements of San Francisco's life turned loose by the economic collapse called the Great Depression.*

Chapter XI

OF CREEPING BEARS AND THE DRUMS OF WAR

IT WAS NOT AS IF there had been no warning. There had been several, in fact. Ever since the recession of 1924 and the collapse of the great Florida land boom of 1925–26, an increasing number of financial prognosticators had been pointing with alarm to the pitfalls of loose money and easy credit. While Secretary of Commerce in 1925, Herbert Hoover had consistently declaimed against speculation in stocks and early in 1929, as president, warned the Federal Reserve system that sooner or later it would have to stem the flow of money being siphoned into Wall Street by ordering its member banks to cease making speculative loans. In San Francisco, A. P. Giannini paid attention, even if the Federal Reserve did not. His Bank of Italy, started in 1904 with a capital of $150,000, had joined with the Bank of America, based in Los Angeles and New York, and a holding company called the Transamerica Corporation, and by 1929 had grown to become one of the largest and most prestigious financial institutions in the country, with 485 branch banks and assets in excess of $1 billion. Even before Hoover's warnings, Giannini had ordered his banks to keep speculative loans to a minimum, and he steadily advised other bankers to do likewise. The equally influential Colonel Leonard P. Ayres, economist for the Cleveland Trust Company, predicted the coming of a "creeping bear market" in March 1929—this at a time when the market was so bullish it amounted to a general stampede. Roger W. Babson, the investment counselor who had been predicting disaster since 1926, used even stronger and singularly prophetic words; on September 5 he declared "There is a crash coming, and it may be a terrific one, [involving] a decline of from 60 to 80 points in the Dow-Jones barometer."

In 1929, few were listening to such as Babson, Ayres, Giannini, and Hoover. The psychology of boom is built upon rising expectations, and for ten years following the war-to-end-all-wars the country had enjoyed the heady experience of watching the economy move from one plateau to another, each higher than the one before. No one seemed to notice that farm prices had not kept pace with inflation; that in spite of increased production, unemployment remained close to two million during the decade; that wages, like farm prices,

> **"Places are like people and must be surrounded by love. . . ."**

229

Fred Bell, a near millionaire in 1929, but in 1931 just another apple vendor peddling his fruit near Lotta's Fountain.

The placards carried by the members of this grim and wary Communist party parade of 1935 summarized the grievances of an entire age: Join the Communist Party, Free Tom Mooney, Stop Munitions Shipments, Waterfront Section Fights Company Unions, Boycott Hearst. . . .

were not on a par with price increases; that mortgage debt increased year by year; that all those goods being produced by all those industries depended for sales on a steadily expanding credit system that became flabbier the more it grew; that hundreds of the most entrancing investment opportunities—particularly in the oil industry and in real estate—were built on an inverted pyramid of undercapitalization. No, the man to whom most preferred to listen was economist Irving Fisher, who on October 16, 1929, announced that "stock prices have reached what looks like a permanently high plateau."

Eight days later the splendid wave of prosperity and speculation hit the beach with a fearful rumble, scattering financial wreckage along a suddenly lost and silent shore. The day was October 24, 1929, and it came to be called Black Thursday. It was followed by a Black Tuesday, a Black Wednesday, and a whole series of black days, weeks, months, and years, until by July 1933 the exchange boards of New York, Chicago, Denver, Los Angeles, and San Francisco showed the same dreadful figures: a drop of 80 percent in the value of stocks and a paper loss of more than $74 billion. The Gross National Product had fallen from $104 billion to $58 billion; more than eighty-five thousand businesses had crumbled into bankruptcy; and in 1932 alone more than fourteen hundred banks failed (only a few of Giannini's among them).

The disaster cut through the underpinnings of California's economy like a scythe. It was bad enough for the state's "real" industries, those turning out actual products: agricultural revenue, the keystone of the California economy, dropped from $750 million in 1929 to $327 million in 1932, and the oil industry, the second largest in the state, found itself producing more than two hundred thousand barrels a day above and beyond what a suddenly shrunken market demanded. For activities like real estate development, the Depression was nothing short of Armageddon, and thousands of businesses which had fed upon the bubbles of speculation—promoters and developers, banks, savings and loan associations, and construction firms—stumbled into receivership, accompanied by investigations into fraud, embezzlement, and the like. By 1933 more than a million people—nearly 20 percent of the state's population—were on state and county relief programs, including thousands and thousands of "Okies" and "Arkies," refugees from the sterile desperation of the Dust Bowl who cranked into California in their wracked and beaten flivvers looking for work that was not there. Few could see that light at the end of the tunnel which Sunny Jim Rolph had perceived in his 1931 inaugural address as governor: "All California needs right now to bring about . . . recovery is a spirit of confidence and quick response to courageous leadership; the state of mind which says, 'I will,' instead of 'I can not.' It is my wish to apply such leadership within my province. I wish to imbue the people of California with my own faith in California. I wish to begin my administration on a note of hope and confidence. Be prepared by holding such hope and confidence to follow my leadership into the bright days which I see just ahead." Angelo Rossi, who had succeeded Rolph as mayor of San Francisco, echoed the governor's sentiments, but rhetoric was a poor shield against joblessness and hunger, and the streets of the city, like those of the rest of the state and nation, were punctuated by all the images that have come down to us as a kind of grim folklore—the millionaire of the 1920s standing on the sidewalk near Lotta's Fountain with a trayful of apples for sale; the once successful broker huddled at the dark end of a Tenderloin bar slowly drinking himself to death (unlike those of his colleagues who sought death more directly); the children and old women scrounging through garbage cans in the alleys behind restaurants; the bread-and-soup lines that wound sullenly and silently around the blocks south of Market; the shell-shocked faces in the crowded waiting rooms of employment offices; the knots of men who stood on the corners of downtown intersections, rushing up to stopped automobiles and offering to clean windshields for a dime, a nickel, a penny; the anger on the faces of those who gathered in rallies to condemn the "bosses," working out the passions of an inchoate frustration.

For millions of Americans and thousands of San Franciscans, the Depression was hell, and no amount of the gentle nostalgia which we so often lay upon the 1930s is enough to obscure that fact. Yet the descent into hell led to awareness, for like a man stricken suddenly blind, groping about in the darkness of his home in an effort to re-establish the outlines of his life by touch, the city was now forced by circumstance to define, seriously, its own meaning—indeed, to question whether it *had* meaning. That smug reliance upon all the comforting assurances of a documented past that had carried the city through the years following the earthquake and fire was no longer enough. The old definitions no longer seemed to work. New ones had to be found, and in its haphazard, vague, and sometimes violent search for them between the beginning of the Depression and the end of World War II, the city returned to a task it had all but abandoned more than a generation before: the gathering and fitting together of the pieces in the puzzle of an idea called San Francisco.

WHEN ON JANUARY 7, 1939, an aging Tom Mooney was released from San Quentin prison and allowed to lead a victorious parade up Market Street, waving his arms and accepting the applause of the masses on the crowded sidewalks, he was a man who walked free in a world whose history had passed him by. The bloody site of the bombing that had caused his imprisonment in 1916 had long since been obliterated by the massive sandstone-and-brick headquarters of the Southern Pacific Railroad, and even Mooney's name, so long a talisman for organized labor, had been superseded by another. Alfred Renton Bridges—"Harry" Bridges—was a wiry, hawk-faced, taciturn, and frequently moody Australian, whose tough-minded and singularly effective organizing abilities had been instrumental in leading San Francisco's labor movement out of the closet in which it had been trapped since 1919 and into a position of strength and security which it would never again relinquish.

Bridges had come from Australia to San Francisco as a seaman in 1920, liked what he saw, and—like many of his countrymen ever since the unhallowed days of the Sydney Ducks—had promptly jumped ship. After fewer than three years of shipping out on various freighters, he settled down to work as a stevedore on the San Francisco waterfront. It was here that he encountered the curious workaday habits of the Longshoremens Association of San Francisco and the Bay District, the so-called "Blue-Book" union (after the color of its membership books) formed in 1919 to take the place of the militant International Longshoremens Association and thoroughly dominated by the Waterfront Employers Association. Among other things which Bridges experienced in the union and did not like were the "shape-up" system, which required that all longshoremen gather at the various docks each morning to form a pool out of which gang bosses would choose each day's working contingent; the consequent existence of "star gangs," men selected to work on a regular basis, often as the result of a kickback to the gang boss; the "speed-up" system, which encouraged gangs to compete with one another in breaking and loading cargo, a practice that resulted in frequent injuries and occasional deaths; and

A gray and paunchy Tom Mooney marches triumphantly up Market Street, January 7, 1939. He was a martyr, and, like most, was not an easy man to like, even in his cell at San Quentin. "For years I had one great ambition," San Francisco Sheriff Daniel Murphy is reported to have said at one point. "Now I have two. The first remains to free Tom Mooney. The second is to kick his ass into the Bay."

The perils of reckless cycling in Golden Gate Park, ca. 1935.

This scene mystifies and perversely fascinates. All we seem to know about it is that it was shot sometime in 1933 near the corner of Third and Market. Why is the policeman pointing? What is that thing? What is going on here?

the fact that paychecks could only be cashed at certain local speakeasies for a discount of 10 or 15 percent, that fee to be split between the bar owners and their bootleggers.

Throughout the 1920s there was little that Bridges or any other worker could do about such conditions. Although revived and rechartered with the American Federation of Labor in 1924, the old, traditionally militant International Longshoremens Association was not recognized by the San Francisco Labor Council and for the rest of the decade was almost memberless and totally powerless. By 1930, the situation had changed dramatically. Tonnage in all Pacific Coast ports had dropped at least 25 percent and in some places by as much as 40 percent; hundreds, then thousands, of casual laborers found themselves getting no work at all, and even the dutiful star-gang members of the employer-dominated union saw their average *weekly* pay plummet to only $10.46—below subsistence even for that time. Suddenly not even steady work was enough to offset the brutal disadvantages of membership in the Longshoremens Association of San Francisco, and the ranks of the rival ILA began to swell.

In June 1933 the inaugural edition of a mimeographed newspaper called the *Waterfront Worker* appeared. One of its editors was Harry Bridges, and if he did not write its first editorial himself, it accurately reflected his views on the kind of union the waterfront needed: "The *Waterfront Worker* and the organized group of stevedores on the principal docks [who] will publish it stand solidly for the organization of such a union. It must be built by US, the stevedores, right here on the docks. Already a start has been made by the organization of small groups of reliable men on the main docks. . . . As they grow, they will more and more organize and lead the fight on each dock against short-timing, pay for all traveling time, against the slave-driving and abuse of certain bosses, and the whole system of petty graft and bribery on the 'front. . . . In the course of the fight for these small demands, we will organize and train ourselves, and we will lay the basis for a powerful union on the waterfront, capable of protecting the interests of all stevedores. Such is our policy." It was a manifesto and a battle cry, and the movement whose purpose it articulated was given hope from an unexpected quarter that same year when Congress passed, and President Franklin D. Roosevelt signed, the National Recovery Act, section 7a of which recognized, for the first time in American history, the right of employees "to organize and bargain collectively through representatives of their own choosing." Armed with federal sanction, the ILA accelerated its membership drive and by the end of the summer had all but gutted the old Blue-Book union. In September, it won acceptance by the San Francisco Labor Council and created a Pacific Coast District organization to encourage and aid ILA locals in other Pacific ports, with William J. Lewis at its head and Harry Bridges as one of its chief organizers. In October, the ILA struck the Matson Line which had fired four men for not carrying Blue-Book union cards. Arbitration by local NRA director George Creel gave the decision to the ILA and Matson was forced to rehire the dismissed men—and a book-burning ceremony was staged in front of the Matson dock, as hundreds of new ILA members stepped up to a large bonfire and tossed in their membership books from the Longshoremens Association of San Francisco. The company union was dead.

In the meantime, Bridges had been traveling up and down the coast, laying the groundwork for a convention of all Pacific locals of the ILA to meet in San Francisco. They did so on February 24, 1934, and in that convention made a number of demands on West Coast port employers: the creation of the six-hour day and the thirty-hour week; a minimum of $1.00 an hour and $1.50 for overtime; the closed shop; and the elimination of the shape-up system and company-controlled hiring halls, delegating to the ILA itself the right and duty to assign all men to available work. The question of hours and wages, the convention declared, could be worked out through bargaining; the matter of hiring was non-negotiable. A strike deadline was set for March 7. Frantic effort on the part of NRA arbiters managed to stall a walkout for two months, but when it became clear to the leaders of the ILA that no agreement was in sight, a coastwide strike vote was called on May 7. It was approved by an overwhelming majority, and on May 9, 1934, the largest maritime strike in the history of the United States up to that time began, as twelve to fifteen thousand men refused to show up for work in Seattle, Bellingham, Tacoma, Aberdeen, Astoria, Gray's Harbor, San Francisco, Oakland, Stockton, San Pedro, and San Diego, tying up hundreds of ships and leaving thousands of tons of cargo to rot or rust on docks and in holds. One by one, other maritime and related unions joined in the strike—the Marine Workers Industrial Union, the International Seamens Union, the Association of Machinists and Boilermakers, Marine Radio Operators, Masters, Mates, and Pilots, Marine Engineers, Inland Boatmen, and finally even the ultraconservative Teamsters Union.

Nothing moved, reluctant negotiations dragged on sonorously and fruitlessly, and for several weeks the most exciting incident in the strike was an internal dispute in the ILA that saw Harry Bridges emerge as the unchallenged leader of the union. Still, so long as the talks remained deadlocked, a street confrontation was inevitable. To that end, the Waterfront Employers Association, the San Francisco Chamber of Commerce, and the Industrial Association of San Francisco—genuinely active for the first time since the waterfront strike of 1919—made their preparations, initiating an increasingly virulent anti-strike campaign in the newspapers (led by William Randolph Hearst's *Examiner*), gathering a small army of strikebreakers, and laying the groundwork for police cooperation. Early in July, they announced that they would open the port on July 3. "We sent out an emergency call to all the unions in the city," Bridges later recalled, "and asked them to have a mass picket line down there that morning. That line extended the entire length of the waterfront. Police charged the line, and a few trucks got through. There were glaring headlines in the papers that the port was at last open. But it wasn't."

Independence Day was quiet, but on the morning of July 5, some five thousand pickets, half as many strikebreakers, and hundreds of police combined to produce what has forever after been known as "Bloody Thursday." It

Nostalgia in fog, midnight, sometime in 1939: the last "E" car prepares to leave the Ferry Building for its bedtime run. Is Sam Spade lurking somewhere in the shadows, ready to follow the elusive Brigid O'Shaugnessy?

Before the 1920s the last of San Francisco's old horsecars were hauled out to the dunes of Ocean Beach and abandoned. Gradually, imaginative indigents of one sort or another rescued them, converted them into homes, and put them together in what came to be known as Carbarn City.

One of the toy tanks of Governor Merriam's National Guard sent to put down violence during the General Strike of 1934. As it turned out, the tanks were never used, and the Molotov cocktail was invented in Spain two years later.

was sufficiently bloody, as Paul S. Taylor and Norman L. Gold reported in the September 1934 issue of *Survey Graphic:* ". . . hundreds of police and some thousands of pickets faced each other. The trucks of the Industrial Association began to move. The pickets were forced back, back, in an extended maneuver covering many blocks. Thousands of commuters from the East Bay jammed the viaduct and the sidewalks; clerks crowded to the windows of office buildings. As police drove strikers and sightseers up Rincon Hill, the pickets hurled bricks, and the police, at the cry of 'Let 'em have it,' threw tear-gas grenades. Here and there clubbing occurred as men and police clashed. Before the ILA halls fighting was more vicious. Inspectors of police, surrounded by angry strikers seeking to overturn their car, fired. Two men were killed. Police, horses, strikers, and spectators were wounded." At day's end, sixty-four strikers and spectators had been injured (thirty-one of them with gunshot wounds), and two strikers were dead, in the battle of Rincon Hill, and, citing interference with the state-owned Belt Line Railroad, Governor Frank Merriam sent in the National Guard, armed with light artillery, machine guns, and barbed wire.

On July 9, workers staged a massive funeral parade for the killed strikers, and on July 16, in a gesture of support and sympathy, virtually every union member in San Francisco and Alameda counties walked off the job in the most widespread general strike in American history, an exercise in power that "surprised, bewildered, gratified, or terrified and maddened the average citizen," according to Taylor and Gold. Only those grocery stores and restaurants given a union "permit" were allowed to remain open; trucks carrying food, hospital supplies, and other necessaries did so with placards that stated, "By Permission of the Strike Committee." Although no remarkable violence occurred, Governor Merriam added another two thousand National Guard troops and a contingent of small tanks to patrol the waterfronts in the two counties. By July 19, it became clear to the General Strike Committee (of which Harry Bridges was a member) that whatever public support the unions had gained on Bloody Thursday was being seriously undermined the longer the general strike continued; it was called off, and the Committee urged the ILA and the Waterfront Employers Association to submit their differences to federal arbitration.

Ironically, it was John Francis Neylan, William Randolph Hearst's personal attorney and, like his employer, an arch-enemy of everything Harry Bridges represented, who convinced the waterfront employers to submit to federal arbitration; everything else had been tried and had failed, he pointed out, and it was now time to get the goods moving again. The employers agreed, albeit reluctantly, and with the promise of arbitration, Bridges sent his men back to work on July 31. A little over two months later, the Federal Arbitration Board awarded Bridges and the ILA their primary demand: the control of all hiring through their own halls.

This decision, forged in violence though it was, stood as the greatest encouragement the labor movement in San Francisco had known since the formation of the Union Labor party in 1901. With both collective bargaining and arbitration accomplished and accepted facts by now, union organization was on the march: between 1934 and 1939, union membership in the city (and the state) increased by an incredible eight times, much of the growth coming with the active support, advice, and leadership of Harry Bridges and ILA organizers. In 1936, Bridges took the ILA itself out of the American Federation of Labor, renamed it the International Longshoremens and Warehousemens Union (ILWU), and joined it with John L. Lewis's growing Committee for Industrial Organization (later, the Congress of Industrial Organizations—the

[*Continued on page 242*]

During the perilous four days the General Strike Committee issued thousands of free meal tickets; by arrangement with cooperating restaurants, a man could get a meal when he got a break from the picket lines.

Good for One Meal at

Eagle Restaurant

I. L. A. Strike Relief Committee

Between hours of...... JUL 0 ....193..

Revolution in San Francisco . . .

San Francisco Chronicle
THE VOICE OF THE WEST

JULY 6, 1934

By Royce Brier

Blood ran red in the streets of San Francisco yesterday.

In the darkest day this city has known since April 18, 1906, one thousand embattled police held at bay five thousand longshoremen and their sympathizers in a sweeping front south of Market street and east of Second Street.

The furies of street warfare raged for hour piled on hour.

Two were dead, one was dying, 32 others shot and more than three score sent to hospitals.

Hundreds were injured or badly gassed. Still the strikers surged up and down the sunlit streets among thousands of foolhardy spectators. Still the clouds of

Strike Violence. Firemen attempt to extinguish flames of overturned truck.

tear gas, the very air darkened with hurtling bricks. Still the revolver battles.

As the middle of the day wore on in indescribable turmoil the savagery of the conflict was in rising crescendo. The milling mobs fought with greater desperation, knowing the troops were coming; the police held to hard-won territory with grim resolution.

It was a Gettysburg in the miniature, with towering warehouses thrown in for good measure. It was one of those days you think of as coming to Budapest.

The purpose of it all was this: The State of California had said it would operate its waterfront railroad. The strikers had defied the State of California to do it. The police had to keep them off. They did.

Take a San Francisco map and draw a line along Second street south from Market to the bay. It passes over Rincon Hill. That is the west boundary, Market is the north of the battlefield.

Not a street in that big sector but saw its flying lead yesterday, not a street that wasn't tramped by thousands of flying feet as the tide of battle swung high and low, as police drove them back, as they drove police back in momentary victory.

And with a dumfounding nonchalance, San Franciscans, just plain citizens bent on business, in automobiles and on foot, moved to and fro in the battle area.

Don't think of this as a riot. It was a hundred riots, big and little, first here, now there. Don't think of it as one battle, but as a dozen battles.

It started with a nice, easy swing just as great battles in war often start. The Industrial Association resumed moving goods from Pier 38 at 8 A.M. A few hundred strikers were out, but were held back at

S. F.'s finest hurrying to scene of action in yesterday's riot.

Man flees pursuing officer.

Brannan street, as they had been in Tuesday's riot, by the police.

At Bryant and Main streets were a couple of hundred strikers in an ugly mood. Police Captain Arthur de Guire decided to clear them out, and his men went at them with tear gas. The strikers ran, scrambling up Rincon Hill and hurling back rocks.

Proceed now one block away, to Harrison and Main streets. Four policemen are there, about 500 of the mob are on the hill. Those cops looked like fair game.

"Come on, boys," shouted the leaders.

They tell how the lads of the Confederacy had a war whoop that was a holy terror. These boys, a lot of them kids in their teens, came down that hill with a whoop. It sounded blood-curdling. One policeman stood behind a telephone pole to shelter him from the rocks and started firing with his revolver.

Up the hill, up Main, came de Guire's men on the run, afoot and the "mounties." A few shots started whizzing from up the hill, just a scattering few, with a high hum like a bumble bee.

Then de Guire's men, about 20 of them, unlimbered from Main and Harrison and fired at random up the hill. The down-plunging mob halted, hesitated, and started scrambling up the hill again.

Here the first man fell, a curious bystander. The gunfire fell away.

Up came the tear gas boys, six or eight carloads of them. They hopped out with their masks on, and the gas guns laid down a barrage on the hillside. The hillside spouted blue gas like the Valley of the Ten Thousand Smokes.

Up the hill went the moppers-up, phalanxes of policemen with drawn revolvers. The strikers backed

sullenly away on Harrison street, past Fremont street. Suddenly came half a dozen carloads of men from the Bureau of Inspectors, and right behind them a truck load of shotguns and ammunition.

In double quick they cleared Rincon Hill. Ten police cars stuck their noses over the brow of the hill.

Noon came. Napoleon said an army travels on its belly. So do strikers and police, and even newspapermen.

Now it is one o'clock. Rumors of the coming of the soldiery fly across the town. The strikers are massing down at the foot of Mission and Howard streets, where a Belt Line freight train is moving through.

Police massed there, too; the tear gas squads, the rifle and shotgun men, the mounties. Not a sign of machine guns so far. But the cops have them. There's plenty of talk about the "typewriters."

There they go again into action, the gas boys! They're going up the stubby little streets from the Embarcadero to Steuart street, half blocks up Mission and Howard. Across by the Ferry Building are thousands of spectators.

Boom! go the gas guns, boom, boom, boom!

Around corners, like sheep pouring through a gate, go the rioters, but they don't go very far. They stop at some distance, say a half block away, wipe their eyes a minute, and in a moment comes a barrage of rocks.

Here's the hottest part of the battle from now on, along Steuart street from Howard to Market. No mistake about that. It centers near the I.L.A. headquarters.

See the mounties ride up toward that front of strikers. It's massed across the street, a solid front of men.

Ready for gas and disaster.

Ben Metz escorted to patrol wagon.

*Officers hustle rioting striker away
from action and into custody.*

Take a pair of opera glasses and look at their faces.
They are challenging the on-coming mounties. The
men in front are kneeling, like sprinters at the mark.

Clatter, clatter, clatter come the bricks. Tinkle goes
a window. This is war, boys, and this Steuart street
between Howard and Mission is one of the warmest
spots American industrial conflict ever saw.

The horses rear. The mounted police dodge bricks.

A police gold braid stands in the middle of the
street all alone, and he blows his whistle. Up come
the gas men, the shotgun men, the rifle men. The
rioters don't give way.

Crack and boom! Sounds just like a gas bomb, but
no blue smoke this time. Back scrambles the mob and
two men lie on the sidewalk. Their blood trickles in a
crimson stream away from their bodies.

Over it all spreads an air of unutterable confusion.
The only organization seems to lie in little squads of
officers hurrying hither and yon in automobiles. Sirens keep up a continual screaming in the streets. You
can hear them far away.

Now it was 2 o'clock. The street battle had gone on
for half an hour. How many were shot, no one knew.

Now, it was win or die for the strikers in the next
few hours. The time from 2 o'clock to 3 o'clock
dragged for police, but went on the wings of the wind
for the strikers. An hour's rest. They had to have that
one hour.

At 3 o'clock they started again, the fighting surg-
ing once more about Steuart and Mission streets.
Here was a corner the police had, and had to hold. It
was the key to the waterfront, and it was in the
shadow of I.L.A. headquarters.

The rocks started filling the air again. They crashed
through street cars. The cars stopped and citizens
huddled inside.

Panic gripped the east end of Market street. The
ferry crowds were being involved. You thought again
of Budapest. The troops were coming. Soldiers.
SOLDIERS IN SAN FRANCISCO! WAR IN SAN
FRANCISCO!

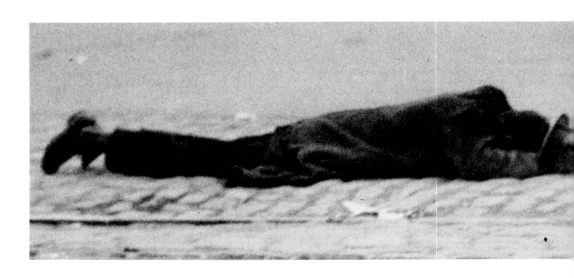

Bystander Wounded. Edward Hodges, 69, shot in hand. With reporters.

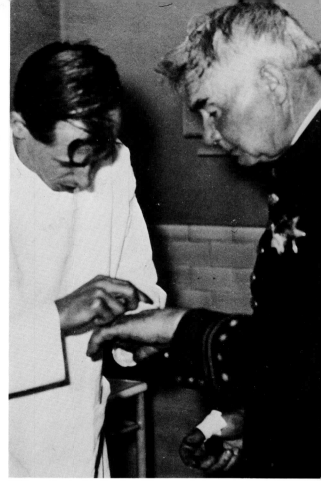

Officer Gavin McCarthy, 57, attended at emergency aid station for injured hand.

Strike Injuries. Many strikers hurt and wounded during yesterday's violence.

Battle at Rincon Hill.
Police use gas bombs to
scatter waterfront strikers.

Riot Deaths. Howard Sperry and Gene Olson, shot on Mission Street, July 5. Sperry rushed to hospital, but died. Olson, shot in leg, will recover. Nicholas Bordoise, waiter, was killed elsewhere in city yesterday. Strikers marked off spot of Sperry's death with flowers.

CIO). By 1939, membership in the ILWU had grown to more than fifty thousand men. If the union member benefited from this sudden resurgence of strength, so too did the Democratic party in San Francisco, which for nearly twenty years had run a poor second to the Republicans. In 1934, for example, San Francisco's Democratic vote for Upton Sinclair in his unsuccessful bid for the governorship had accounted for only 38.9 percent of the city's total vote. Four years later, nourished by the growth of the predominantly Democratic union labor movement, that voting percentage had leaped to 53.4 percent and contributed significantly to the election of Culbert Olson as governor—not coincidentally the man who pardoned Tom Mooney as one of the first acts of his administration. The hope of a unionized San Francisco, so long a bitter, unrealized dream, had become reality.

Which is not to say that the corporate powers-that-were had given up on Harry Bridges. In a fifteen-year campaign that would, in the words of United States Supreme Court Justice Frank Murphy, "stand forever as a monument to man's intolerance of man," the Seattle department of the U.S. Immigration Service, the police departments of Los Angeles, San Francisco, and Seattle, the San Francisco and California chambers of commerce, the *San Francisco Examiner*, and the Associated Farmers of California joined in a systematic effort to have Bridges deported as an undesirable alien, claiming that he was a member of the Communist party and therefore dedicated to the overthrow of government by force and violence. Although he consistently denied membership in the party, Bridges was vulnerable on the point, for he more than once candidly admitted that he had called upon Communist support in various labor activities, and did not apologize for the fact; what is more, while he had twice applied for American citizenship, neither application had ever been acted upon—a kind of punishment, Bridges maintained, for his union organizing. In spite of his denials and in spite of the fact that the San Francisco head of the Immigration Service declared that the evidence against him was shot through with inaccuracies and blatant Red-baiting, the Seattle department, with questionable legality, forced a deportation hearing at the Government Immigration Station on Angel Island in July 1939, Judge James Landis, dean of the Harvard Law School, presiding. After months of testimony, Landis ruled that "The evidence . . . establishes neither that Harry R. Bridges is a member of nor affiliated with the Communist party of the United States." It was not the end. In 1941, another deportation hearing was held; this decision went against Bridges, but was unanimously reversed by the Board of Immigration Appeals; *that* decision was reversed in May 1942, by Attorney General Francis Biddle, who ordered Bridges deported, and only recourse to the Supreme Court kept him in the country—even though he was forbidden throughout World War II to go anywhere near the waterfront and the workers he represented. In 1946, he was finally granted citizenship, but that did not deter his opponents. In February 1950 he was brought to trial on the charge that he had perjured himself when taking the oath of citizenship by declaring that he had never been a member of the Communist party. During that trial he was forced to explain, for perhaps the hundredth time, why he would have been "a fool" ever to have joined the Communists: "When I was asked to join the party, I declined. One reason was that I knew that all alien members of the party were subject to the process of deportation. I was no fool. But that was not necessarily the main reason. The waterfront spokesmen, the organizers for the Communist party and other groups, were putting out programs that were utopian, idealistic, revolutionary—but they offered no answer to our immediate problems. . . .

Taken just before the verdict came in on his perjury trial in 1950, this may be one of the rarest photographs in existence: it shows Harry Bridges laughing right out loud.

So I didn't see any need for the Communist party and I had enough sense to see that it would subject me to deportation. That was the reason it was kissed off."

He was acquitted, and his opponents and the government finally gave up the campaign. Today, as an appointed member of the San Francisco Port Commission, the head of one of the largest and most powerful unions in the United States sits cheek-by-jowl and in generally friendly concourse with such corporate representatives as Cyril Magnin. Yet each July 5, the anniversary of Bloody Thursday, is a contractual holiday for the members of the ILWU; Harry Bridges may forgive, but he does not forget.

T HE 1934 WATERFRONT STRIKE and its aftermath was by no means a purely local affair. It was, after all, not just in the port of San Francisco, but in every major port on the Pacific Coast that workers went on strike in May 1934, and it was not just the city of San Francisco, but the cities of Berkeley, Oakland, and Alameda that were affected by the general strike that followed in July. If various chambers of commerce, industrialists, and newspapers throughout the Bay Area decried what they saw as a massive conspiracy against all that was right and good and progressive, by their very accusations they gave tacit recognition to something very important: if nothing else, the strike had been a dramatic object lesson in the reality of regional interdependence. Economically, if not politically, the Bay Area was becoming a single metropolitan unit in which individual city and county segments were tangled in an increasingly complex web of mutual interests. If San Jose steadily enlarged its city limits, creeping into the orchards and truck farms of the Santa Clara valley, it had a measurable effect on the nature of produce marketing in the stalls and warehouses of San Francisco's Davis and Clay streets; if a San Francisco bank expanded its investments in East Bay industries, it had a measurable effect on the quality of life of hundreds, sometimes thousands, of people in and around those industries; and so it went as the "Bay Area" grew.

Not that the cities and counties of the Bay Area immediately coalesced in a movement to assure cooperation with one another; for the most part, they continued to function as if they were so many independent Balkan states. While the notion of regional planning had rumbled around ever since the earthquake and fire of 1906, it was not until 1925 that anything significant was done about it. That year, the Commonwealth Club hosted a conference of sundry minuscule city and county planning commissions, and at its end the conference put together a Regional Plan Association, with Senator James Duval Phelan as the chairman of its ways and means committee and Frederick W. Dohrmann, Jr., as its director. (Along with Phelan, Dohrmann had been one of the founders of the Association for the Improvement and Adornment of San Francisco in 1904.) Dohrmann's instincts and intentions were unquestionably excellent. "Places," he declared in one of many speeches, "are like people and must be surrounded by love in order to lift them to a level at which the citizens will do more than merely live and make a living." But love, he found, was not enough without public support, and that was not forthcoming; in 1928, after nearly four years of fruitless campaigning and the expenditure of thousands of dollars of his own money, Dorhmann closed up the offices of the Regional Plan Association. The idea was revived briefly in 1931 and again in 1935, but each time withered for lack of support from either the business community, the political community, or the public at large. Civic bickering and the squabble of business competition remained the order of the day.

July 14, 1931, 5:30 P.M. —commute hour for the Sausalito and Berkeley car ferries of the Northwestern Pacific and Southern Pacific transport systems. The tiny lineup at the right center of the picture was what was known in those days as a traffic jam. The car ferries offered other marks of a civilized life, including railroad coffee and corned-beef and roast-beef hash and eggs for the morning run, and a suitably wide variety of more relaxing refreshments during the evening.

Bernard Zakheim (seated) and an assistant working on the plans for a mural in Toland Hall of the San Francisco State Hospital, 1937. Murals that have aged remarkably well enlivened such other public buildings as Coit Tower, the casino of Aquatic Park (now the San Francisco Maritime Museum), and the main and Rincon Annex post offices—all of them financed by the Works Progress Administration.

The Golden Gate in about 1932, as photographed by Ansel Adams. It was this prospect which caused novelist Katherine Fullerton Gerould, among others, to agitate against the idea of putting up a bridge: "When you have one of the most romantic approaches in all geography, why spoil it? Let the landowners of lovely Marin County stew in their own juice. Make the Sausalito ferry a 'floating palace'; beguile the half-hour journey with every vulgar pleasure; subsidize the commuters, if necessary; but in the interest of your own uniqueness, dear San Francisco, do not bridge the Golden Gate."

Still, there were some aspects of regional interdependence which could not be ignored. Chief among these was transportation, and central to the question of transportation was the matter of bridges. By 1930, three privately financed Bay Area crossings had been constructed: the San Mateo and Dumbarton bridges across the southern arm of San Francisco Bay, and the Carquinez Bridge across the Carquinez Strait to the north. Two points on which everyone seemed able to agree were that two more crossings were needed—one connecting San Francisco with Oakland or Alameda, the other connecting the city with Marin County—and that these bridges should be built in the public interest and with public funds. This was, it should be remembered, the golden age of American engineers and of the massive public projects which they designed and constructed, a tradition that continued right through the pit of the Depression with such enterprises as the TVA, Grand Coulee Dam, the Boulder (Hoover) Dam Project, and the Central Valley Project. Even the less spectacular efforts of the Works Progress Administration—with its parks and playgrounds, its street and highway improvements, its sidewalk layings, its support of local painters and sculptors for the ornamentation of the walls and façades of public buildings, and its sponsorship of local writers to produce the finest series of state and city guides ever published—had accustomed the public to the visible expenditure of public money, and only the most unregenerate mossbacks could be heard muttering darkly about "socialism."

The Marin crossing to the north had been the dream since 1917 of engineer Joseph Strauss, a "five-foot giant" and sometime poet whose vision of a bridge matched the aspirations of the poetry he occasionally scribbled in the margins of his engineering drawings. Ignoring the abjurations of others that the powerful tides would destroy any foundations he could lay, Strauss wanted to build his bridge smack across the Golden Gate itself from Fort Point to the Marin headlands. By 1924, he had completed a preliminary design for the bridge, a monolith combining steel truss and suspension characteristics—unquestionably impressive but with all the grace of a railroad bridge. (Fortunately, the design was later modified into its present form by Strauss's subordinates, engineer Clifford Paine and architect Irving F. Morrow.) The supervisors of San Francisco and Marin counties were suitably awe-stricken, and submitted the engineer's plans to the War Department for the necessary approval. That was forthcoming in December 1924, and the two counties began laying the groundwork for the creation of a public agency capable of financing the project. It was more easily announced than done, for opposition to the idea developed on several fronts: from ferry and railroad interests who justifiably feared what an automobile bridge would do to their enterprises, from engineers

and geologists who refused to believe that the bridge could be built at all, and from traditionalists who deplored the alteration of the landscape ("The Golden Gate," one newspaper advertisement read, "is one of nature's perfect pictures—let's not disfigure it.") Finally, in December 1928, under the authority of the state's Bridge and Highway District Act of 1923, bridge proponents were able to put together the Golden Gate Bridge and Highway District, composed of the counties of San Francisco, Marin, Sonoma, Napa, Del Norte, Mendocino, and Humboldt. (All of Humboldt County and part of Mendocino County later withdrew from the project.) On November 7, 1930, the voters of the district went to the polls and approved a bond issue of $35 million by a majority of 145,057 to 46,954, although further litigation delayed the beginning of construction until January 1933.

The dream of a central crossing from San Francisco east to Oakland had, in one sense, been around for nearly sixty years. Like many people possessed of an outsized dementia, "Emperor" Joshua A. Norton frequently displayed a flash of antic wit so close to gentle mockery that it made one wonder whether the old boy had not been pulling the collective leg of San Francisco for years. One such occasion was his ambitious edict of 1873, which forecast the future in startling fashion: "Now, therefore, we, Norton I, Emperor of the United States and protector of Mexico, do order and direct . . . that a suspension bridge be constructed from . . . Oakland Point to Yerba Buena [San Francisco], from thence to the mountain range of Sausalito, and from thence to the Farallones. . . ." While no one seemed to agree that a bridge thirty miles out to the Farallon Islands was a matter of pressing necessity, there were few willing to argue that a connection between San Francisco and Oakland was not needed—in fact, inevitable. The question of how the bridge might be built, however, was not settled until 1929, when the state legislature passed a law that designated the governor, the lieutenant-governor, the director of the State Department of Public Works, the director of the State Department of Finance, and the chairman of the California Highway Commission as the California Toll Bridge Authority, empowered to direct the State Department of Public Works to build toll bridges with financing through the sale of revenue bonds. And the question of where the bridge might be built was not settled until 1930, when the federally appointed Hoover-Young San Francisco Bay Bridge Commission, a reflection of the national interest in the development of the greatest harbor on the Pacific Coast, determined that a route from Rincon Hill to Yerba Buena Island and from there to Oakland was not only the most feasible but the cheapest of several alternatives; as Mark L. Requa, chairman of the commission, put it, "The Almighty apparently has laid out this route for the bridge." In May 1933, without notable further help from the Almighty, construction of the central crossing began.

On November 12, 1936, the San Francisco–Oakland Bay Bridge was opened to traffic, while "cannons roared, bombs burst in air, sirens and whistles shrieked, and massed thousands of enthusiastic citizens at the east and west approaches of the great structure blasted the welkin with their cheers," according to a somewhat overwrought pamphlet issued by the California Toll Bridge Authority. Within a little over one hundred hours after its opening, an estimated one million people had traveled over the bridge in two hundred fifty thousand automobiles, trucks, and buses. Six and a half months later, on May 25, 1937, the "harp of steel," the Golden Gate Bridge, was opened to similar fanfare and the steady thud of the feet of two hundred fifty thousand pedestrians who walked across it the first day. The response of Joseph Strauss to the

Most notable among those in this collective mug shot of the designers of the Golden Gate Bridge is Joseph B. Strauss, the "five-foot giant" who appears third from the left in the front row of the picture, and the splendid-looking gentleman in the rear, Andrew C. Lawson, former dean of the College of Mining of the University of California and consulting geologist for the project.

The beginning of construction on the Golden Gate Bridge, 1933. In the stream is the U.S.S. Constitution—"Old Ironsides" —on one of her tours; the structure in the foreground is Fort Point, built in 1861 to keep out predatory frigates.

completion of the second of the two most dramatic monuments to regional-state-federal cooperation in American history, since he *was* Joseph Strauss, was to compose a poem:

At last the mighty task is done;
Resplendent in the western sun,
The bridge looms mountain high;
Its titan piers grip ocean floor,
Its great steel arms link shore with shore,
Its towers pierce the sky. . . .

High overhead its lights shall gleam;
Far, far below, life's restless stream
Unceasingly shall flow;
For this was spun its lithe fine form,
To fear not war, nor time, nor storm,
For fate had meant it so.

Opening day on the Golden Gate Bridge, May 27, 1937. Most people walked, but these girls were the first (and perhaps last) to scoot across on rollerskates.

The response of San Francisco, since it was San Francisco, was to throw a party and invite the world. As early as 1933 there had been those urging that San Francisco should hold a world exposition, that eternal psychological antidote to hard times, and as the towers of the two great bridges indeed pierced the sky, the idea took on momentum. With the creation of an exposition company and the promise of nearly $4 million from the Works Progress Administration, the creation of a 400-acre artificial island on a tidal flat just north of Yerba Buena Island began in February 1936. Almost precisely three years later—after a seven-day warm-up called "Fiesta Week"—the Golden Gate International Exposition opened for business on the former mudflat now called Treasure Island, complete with temples, halls, and concourses presumably patterned after Mayan, Incan, Malay, and Cambodian examples, a 400-foot Tower of the Sun topped with a gilded "rising Phoenix," a carnival strip called the Gayway in those more innocent times, Sally Rand's Nude Ranch (not so innocent), and the traditional collection of exhibitions having to do with technological progress and the manifest benefits of the free enterprise system.

From late February 1939 to late September 1940—with a four-month interruption—the Treasure Island fair entranced and diverted Bay Area citizens worn down by ten years of worry, financial uncertainty, and periodic violence. Yet, like its predecessor, the Panama-Pacific International Exposition of 1915, the Golden Gate International Exposition opened and operated not only to the sounds of celebration, but to the chilling thunder of war in a distant land, a sound that no amount of carnival noise could obscure. Another world was coming to an end, and the citizenry knew it, according to the recollections of Richard Reinhardt in his *Treasure Island: San Francisco's Exposition Years:* "On the final night . . . several thousand guests stayed on, by invitation, after the public gates were locked. Huddled together in the wind, they stared around them in anticipation and dismay. For several months they had sensed a growing guilt about the Exposition. Fun was out of fashion. It was time now to end the foolishness and turn to other things. Yet they longed to save some trace of Treasure Island in their minds, some mark of faith in the endurance of beauty, the recurrence of joy, the consolation of laughter. The fair had been a sedative, of course, a tranquilizer for a frightened generation; we had understood this and accepted it with gratitude. We welcomed our brief oblivion and clung to

our illusive innocence as long as the spell would last. In a world consumed by rage, there would be no further respites, no more innocent islands."

THE END OF ONE WORLD, the beginning of another: "All that could be heard as the Depression ended," social historian Robert Goldston has written, "was the summons of the steady drummer; a continuous rolling of the drums now, ever louder, ever nearer." The citizens of San Francisco and the Bay Area had reason enough to pay closer attention than many in other parts of the country. As early as 1924, the War Department had declared the San Francisco Bay Region one of the three principal strategic areas, or "nerve centers," on the Pacific Coast—in other words, a target. Over the next fifteen years the department steadily added to the military facilities already in the Bay Area—among them the San Francisco Presidio, Forts Mason, Miley, and Funston, the Mare Island shipyards, and the Benicia Arsenal—with an army base on the western shore of the bay at Oakland, a navy base on Alameda, Hamilton Air Force Base in Marin County, and Moffet Field near San Jose. Even Treasure Island had been promised before the fair's closing to the navy for yet another base.

All of this gave San Franciscans food for thought as they, like most Americans, scanned the front-page war bulletins of their daily newspapers and gathered around their radios in the evening to listen to crackling, static-ridden reports from across the Atlantic, particularly the growly voice of Edward R. Murrow: "This . . . is London." One by one, European nations fell to the inexorable colossus of Nazi Germany: Norway and Denmark in April 1940; the Netherlands, Belgium, and Luxembourg in May; France in June. And across the Pacific, the Japanese invaded Indochina and swept down the Malay Peninsula, capturing Singapore on February 15, 1941. Finally, the inevitable: on December 7, 1941, shortly before 8:00 A.M. Hawaii time, more than one hundred carrier-based Japanese planes and a number of submarines launched a surprise assault on the U.S. Pacific Fleet anchored at Pearl Harbor. At its end the attack had destroyed or irreparably damaged ten major American ships and severely damaged eight more. The Americans lost 177 warplanes, most of which never got off the ground; 4,303 men were killed or missing in action, and 1,272 wounded. On December 8 the United States declared war on Japan and three days later extended the declaration to include Germany and Italy.

San Francisco's response to the attack on Pearl Harbor was a kind of bemused fatalism, an attitude perhaps endemic to the only American city to have more than once been completely destroyed. That attitude did not sit well with Lieutenant-General John L. DeWitt, head of the Western Defense Command. On the evening of December 13, 1941, having misinterpreted a radar blip, DeWitt ordered the city's first air-raid alert. It was a dismal failure; offices, businesses, bars, and homes by the hundreds remained lit in violation of the blackout, and thousands of people reacted to the sound of sirens by walking around in the streets, their curious gazes on the night sky. The next day, DeWitt called the city's Civil Defense leaders before him and addressed them in no uncertain terms: "You people do not seem to realize we are at war. So get this: Last night there were planes over this community! They were enemy planes! I mean Japanese planes! . . . Your blackout was completely ineffective. Why bombs were not dropped, I do not know. It might have been better if some bombs had been dropped to awaken this city. I never saw such apathy. . . . Unless definite and stern action is taken to correct last night's

Installing the Twin Peaks air raid siren, December 18, 1941—a necessary precaution, one supposes, but few San Franciscans ever paid much attention to its unearthly howling during drills and false alarms.

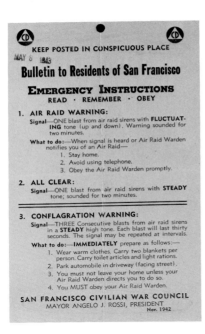

KEEP POSTED IN CONSPICUOUS PLACE

MAY 5 1943

Bulletin to Residents of San Francisco

EMERGENCY INSTRUCTIONS
READ · REMEMBER · OBEY

1. AIR RAID WARNING:

Signal—ONE blast from air raid sirens with **FLUCTUAT-ING** tone (up and down). Warning sounded for two minutes.

What to do:—When signal is heard or Air Raid Warden notifies you of an Air Raid:—
1. Stay home.
2. Avoid using telephone.
3. Obey the Air Raid Warden promptly.

2. ALL CLEAR:

Signal—ONE blast from air raid sirens with **STEADY** tone; sounded for two minutes.

3. CONFLAGRATION WARNING:

Signal—THREE Consecutive blasts from air raid sirens in a **STEADY** high tone. Each blast will last thirty seconds. The signal may be repeated at intervals.

What to do:—**IMMEDIATELY** prepare as follows:—
1. Wear warm clothes. Carry two blankets per person. Carry toilet articles and light rations.
2. Park automobile in driveway (facing street).
3. You must not leave your home unless your Air Raid Warden directs you to do so.
4. You MUST obey your Air Raid Warden.

SAN FRANCISCO CIVILIAN WAR COUNCIL
MAYOR ANGELO J. ROSSI, PRESIDENT
Nov. 1942

A portrait of "the enemy." In 1943, photographer Dorothea Lange photographed one of the thousands of native-born Japanese-Americans who were herded up and given the inside room of the badlands on the curious theory that only they—not German-Americans or Italian-Americans—were insidious enough to pose a threat to the security of the nation.

deficiencies, a great deal of destruction will come. If I can't knock these facts into your heads with words, I will have to turn you over to the police and let them knock them into you with clubs. Bombing is bound to come to San Francisco if the war continues. Don't be jittery. Learn to take it. You've got to take it. And if you can't take it, get to hell out of San Francisco now—before it comes!" Abashed, the Civil Defense people promised to do better next time, but in fact, San Francisco's adherence to blackout rules and air-raid alerts remained sporadic at best for the rest of the war.

The Bay Area's first legitimate casualties of war, as it turned out, were not the result of Japanese bombs, but of American intolerance and self-feeding insecurity. Between January and May 1942, Thailand, Burma, much of Malaya and Indonesia, and the Philippines fell to the sweep of the Japanese. While the string of conquests mounted, stories began to circulate that the attack on Pearl Harbor had been made possible only by the collusion—direct or implied—of Hawaii's one hundred sixty thousand Japanese, and Californians were soon regarding their own ninety thousand resident Japanese with increasing suspicion. Hearsay gained the weight of documented fact: Japanese farmers were plowing and planting their fields in the shape of arrows pointing at military targets; Japanese fishermen were in reality enlisted men and officers in the Imperial Navy; Japanese field hands were militiamen; Japanese gardeners, household workers, laundrymen, butchers, bakers, and candlestick-makers were actually intelligence agents in a vast espionage network that blanketed the state, financed by Tokyo through Japanese banks and other businesses. Almost immediately, a cry was raised for the outright removal of Japanese from the Pacific Coast, typified by the passionate eloquence of the *San Francisco Examiner*'s columnist, Harry McLemore: "Herd 'em up, pack 'em off and give them the inside room of the badlands. Let 'em be pinched, hurt, hungry, and dead up against it." His desires, if not his words, were echoed by a growing collection of organizations and politicians, including the state Chamber of Commerce, the American Legion, the Native Sons of the Golden West, state Attorney General Earl Warren, and Governor Culbert Olson.

For a while, Lieutenant-General DeWitt resisted the idea, muttering, "An American citizen, after all, is an American citizen." By the end of January 1942, responding to increasing pressure, he had changed his mind, reporting to the War Department in Washington that "The Japanese race is an enemy race and while many second and third generation Japanese born on American soil, possessed of American citizenship, have become 'Americanized,' the racial strains are undiluted. . . . There are indications that [many of] these are organized and ready for concerted action at a favorable opportunity. The very fact that no sabotage has taken place to date is a disturbing and confirming indication that such action will be taken"—surely one of the most astonishing non sequiturs in the annals of military jargon. And so it was done: on February 19, 1942, President Franklin D. Roosevelt signed Executive Order 9066, authorizing Japanese removal. Under the direction of the War Relocation Authority, the Bay Area's approximately twenty thousand Japanese were ordered with others in the west to leave their homes and businesses with no more personal belongings than they could carry on their backs, stuff under their arms, or hold in their hands, were herded into "assembly centers" (locally, the Tanforan Race Track in San Mateo County), and after weeks and sometimes months of waiting were transshipped to "relocation centers" from Tule Lake in northern California to Jerome, Arkansas. Housed in crowded, jerry-built barracks surrounded by barbed wire and armed guards, the evacuees may not have been hungry, but they were most certainly pinched and hurt and dead up against it—and most of them remained so until well after the Battle of Leyte Gulf in October 1944 (which destroyed the Japanese Navy), in one of the least justified and most shameful episodes in American history.

In the end, however, it was neither the imminence of enemy attack nor the almost heartless disruption of a good portion of its community that did the most violence to the social and economic life of the Bay Area—it was the very *machinery* of war. Not since the Gold Rush itself had the region had to do so much with so many in so short a time as during World War II, a maddened and maddening time that stretched every resource of government, transportation, and industry to something very near the breaking point.

Consider the problem. Between December 1941 and the end of the war in August 1945, 23,389,000 tons of war materiel and 1,644,243 military personnel passed through the Golden Gate. Scores of major industries sprang into being or expanded dramatically in the same period with the infusion of the Bay Area's share of the $35 billion in federal money that poured into California. Chief among these industries, of course, were the great ship building yards: the government-owned yards at Mare Island, the General Engineering and Drydock Company and the Union Iron Works in San Francisco, the Bethlehem and Western Pipe and Steel Company yards in South San Francisco, Marinship in Sausalito, the Moore Drydock Company in Oakland, the Bethlehem Steel Company Shipbuilding Division in Alameda, and, most notably, the Kaiser-owned Todd-California Shipbuilding Company in Richmond, whose huge yards alone turned out nearly five hundred Liberty cargo-carriers, those ugly but reliable "rustbuckets" that provided the war effort with its most efficient line of supply. And with industry came labor, complete with families. In 1941, the number of wage earners employed in Bay Area industry was 101,000; by April 1943, the peak of wartime production, that figure would swell to 269,000. They came from everywhere, but thousands came from the farms, fields, and plantations of the South, black people who read such advertisements as "Help Wanted!!! Male or Female, Young or Old, Experienced or Inexperienced," packed their belongings, and headed West, settling in the Western Addition and Hunters Point districts of San Francisco and in available portions of Oakland, Richmond, Vallejo, and Sausalito.

Even had it not been wartime, even had the cities and counties of the Bay Area not abdicated the notion of serious regional planning more than ten years before, such an influx would have tested the best efforts to meet the newcomers' needs. As it was, the game was never more than one of "catch-up" in which no one emerged the victor. The shortage of lumber and other supplies

For more than three years, the crowded yards of the Marinship complex north of Sausalito contributed their share of the hundreds of Liberty ships slapped together during the war.

Four of the more than 10 million soldiers, sailors, marines and other warriors in the struggle against fascism sleep it off in the lobby of a San Francisco hotel in 1943; there was nowhere else for them to go. These and other frustrations were worked off with violent enthusiasm on V-J Day, August 16, 1945, during which, among other events, the Winged Victory monument of the Native Sons of California was topped with a flag and festooned with combatants (following page).

meant that only crowded, cheapjack housing units could be constructed, units that started crumbling almost the minute a family moved in. Wartime necessities made it impossible to expand or even keep in decent repair existing transportation facilities, much less develop new ones. Electric and telephone lines remained months behind demand. New water lines took months to construct, and even then water stayed in short supply throughout the war. Sewers ruptured. Schools were overcrowded and understaffed. It was, in short, an incredible mess, a lunatic caricature of urban development, and it would remain so until well after the end of the war.

The Bay Area greeted the news of Japanese surrender with a relief that bordered on hysteria. On the night of August 16, 1945, San Francisco's Market Street erupted in a riot of celebration that saw the smashing of windows and street lights, the looting of stores, scores of fist fights, at least one woman standing on the sidewalk dressed only in an unbuttoned pea coat, and others struggling feebly as they were carried off into alleys to be raped. Coming in off the street during the middle of it all, the *Chronicle's* Stanton Delaplane noted that "There must be a lot of casualties. A few minutes ago I noticed that both of my hands had blood on them and I don't know where it came from." It was well after midnight before local and military police were able to sweep the street clean of revelers, clean out the bars, and haul away those unable to navigate.

A considerably more elegant commemoration of war's ending had taken place even before the ending itself, when in April, May, and June of 1945, representatives of all the "free nations of the world" met in San Francisco's Veteran's Memorial Building to draft the charter of a new world organization, one that it was hoped would not go the way of the old League of Nations. It was to be called the United Nations, and San Francisco, led in its effort by Walter A. Haas, chairman of the United Nations Permanent Headquarters Committee of the San Francicso Chamber of Commerce, put in an immediate bid to become home town of the world. The decision went instead to New York, but when Haas wrote to Paul C. Smith, editor of the *Chronicle,* thanking him for his support even though they "had failed in our objective," Smith refused to capitulate: "Someday the United Nations will emerge into the full flower of world federal government—or it will collapse into the final chaos of our civilization. I choose to think it will be the former because I haven't the dull-witted courage to contemplate the latter. If it is the former, this region of the world is the most logical capital for the greatest junta in world history—regardless of essentially temporary decisions such as the locating of a 'permanent' site in a vertical property on a Manhattan lot. . . . We have not yet 'failed in our objective.' Such a failure can ensue only from a lack of determination to develop the kind of community, a bay region, and a state which ultimately will fulfill requirements of a world government."

Smith's reply—however unreliable a prediction it turned out to be—was a cry of hope, of new possibility, an echo from the best aspirations of four generations of history. It was a declaration that out of the wreckage of time and war it might still be possible to build a life and a world whose name would be tomorrow.

No Foundation . . .

Drunken man, south of Mission, 1933.

In the time of your life, live—so that in that good time there
shall be no ugliness or death for yourself or for any life your life touches.
Seek goodness everywhere, and when it is found, bring it out of
its hiding place and let it be free and unashamed.

These words begin the prologue to William Saroyan's *The Time of Your Life*. His writer's eye found goodness and strength in a landscape of weariness and despair during the depression years in San Francisco, and his play—set in a Pacific Street saloon and published in 1939—documents the patient innocence of the human animal. Photographer Dorothea Lange saw that same strength and patience in somber images that yet speak well of the light of hope in the generation that preceded us. On the following pages, we offer a portrait fashioned from the words of Saroyan and the images of Lange.

*Migrant family
in Great Central Valley, 1936.*

OFFICER KRUPP: They're all guys who are trying to be happy—trying to make a living, support a family, bring up children, enjoy sleep. Go to a movie, take a drive on Sunday. They're all good guys, so out of nowhere comes trouble. All they want is a chance to get out of debt and relax in front of a radio while Amos and Andy go through their act. What the hell do they always want to make trouble for? I been thinking everything over, Nick, and you know what I think?

NICK THE BARTENDER: No. What?

OFFICER KRUPP: I think we're all crazy. It came to me while I was on my way to Pier 27. All of a sudden it hit me like a ton of bricks. A thing like that never happened to me before. Here we are in this wonderful world, full of all the wonderful things—here we are—all of us, and look at us. Just look at us. We're crazy. We're nuts. We've got everything, but we always feel lousy and dissatisfied just the same. . . . Every once in a while I catch myself being mean, hating people just because they're down and out, broke and hungry, sick or drunk. And then when I'm with the stuffed shirts at headquarters, all of a sudden I'm nice to them, trying to make an impression. On who? People I don't like. And I feel disgusted. I'm going to quit, that's all. Quit. Out. I'm going to give them back the uniform and the gadgets that go with it. I don't want any part of it. This is a good world. What do they want to make all the trouble for all the time?

Migrant workers on the road, 1935.

Policeman and demonstrators, 1935.

ARAB: No foundation. All the way down the line.

OFFICER KRUPP: What?

ARAB: No foundation. No foundation.

OFFICER KRUPP: I'll say there's no foundation.

ARAB: All the way down the line.

OFFICER KRUPP: Is that all he ever says?

NICK THE BARTENDER: That's all he's been saying *this* week.

OFFICER KRUPP: What is he, anyway?

NICK THE BARTENDER: He's an Arab, or something like that.

OFFICER KRUPP: No, I mean what's he do for a living?

NICK THE BARTENDER: What do you do for a living, brother?

ARAB: Work. Work all my life. All my life, work. From small boy to old man, work. In old country, work. In new country, work. In New York. Pittsburgh. Detroit. Chicago. Imperial Valley. San Francisco. Work. For what? Nothing. Three boys in old country. Twenty years, not see. Lost. Dead. Who knows? What. What-not. No foundation. All the way down the line.

Lineup to file claims for unemployment insurance, 1938.

HARRY THE COMEDIAN: Can you use a great Comedian?

NICK THE BARTENDER: Who, for instance?

HARRY THE COMEDIAN: Me.

NICK THE BARTENDER: You? What's funny about you?

HARRY THE COMEDIAN: I dance and do gags and stuff. . . .

NICK THE BARTENDER: All right. Get funny.

HARRY THE COMEDIAN: Now I'm standing on the corner of Third and Market. I'm looking around. I'm figuring it out. There it is. Right in front of me. The whole city. The whole world. People going by. They're going somewhere. I don't know where, but they're going. I ain't going *anywhere.* Where the hell can you go? I'm figuring it out. All right, I'm a citizen. A fat guy bumps his stomach into the face of an old lady. They were in a hurry. Fat and old. *They bumped.* Boom. I don't know. It may mean war. *War.* Germany. England. Russia. I don't know for sure. . . .

NICK THE BARTENDER: All right, comedian. Lay off a minute.

HARRY THE COMEDIAN: Nobody's got a sense of humor any more. The world's dying for comedy like never before, but nobody knows how to *laugh.*

Park bench in Portsmouth Square, 1933.

Employment office waiting room, 1934.

ELSIE THE NURSE: Hello, Dudley.

DUDLEY THE YOUNG MAN: Elsie.

ELSIE THE NURSE: I'm sorry. So many people are sick. Last night a little boy died. I love you, but—

DUDLEY THE YOUNG MAN: Elsie, you'll never know how glad I am to see you. Just to *see* you. I was afraid I'd never see you again. It was driving me crazy. . . . I know. You told me before, but I can't help it, Elsie. I love you.

ELSIE THE NURSE: I know you love me, and I love you, but don't you see love is impossible in this world?

DUDLEY THE YOUNG MAN: Maybe it isn't, Elsie.

ELSIE THE NURSE: Love is for birds. They have wings to fly away on when it's time for flying. For tigers in the jungle because they don't know their end. We know *our* end. Every night I watch over poor, dying men. I hear them breathing, crying, talking in their sleep. Crying for air and water and love, for mother and field and sunlight. We can never know love or greatness. We *should* know both.

DUDLEY THE YOUNG MAN: Elsie, I love you.

ELSIE THE NURSE: You want to live. *I* want to live, too, but where? Where can we escape our poor world?

DUDLEY THE YOUNG MAN: Elsie, we'll find a place.

ELSIE THE NURSE: All right. We'll try again. We'll go together to a room in a cheap hotel, and dream that the world is beautiful, and that living is full of love and greatness. But in the morning, can we forget debts, and duties, and the cost of ridiculous things?

DUDLEY THE YOUNG MAN: Sure we can, Elsie.

ELSIE THE NURSE: All right, Dudley. Of course. Come on. The time for the new pathetic war has come. Let's hurry, before they dress you, stand you in line, hand you a gun, and have you kill and be killed.

KILLER THE WHORE: Nick, what the hell kind of a joint are you running?

NICK THE BARTENDER: Well, it's not out of the world. It's on a street in a city, and people come and go. They bring whatever they've got with them and they say what they must say.

White Angel bread line, 1933.

The flowering of the Haight-Ashbury, in the mid-sixties, the emergence of San Francisco as the home of causes lost and won, is summed up in this poster of the period—which is still carried home by tourists from Dubuque and beyond.

Chapter XII

THE DIMENSIONS OF POSSIBILITY

THE CENTRAL FACT IN THE postwar history of the world had its practical beginnings in Gilman Hall, an otherwise unremarkable building on the Berkeley campus of the University of California. It was in Gilman Hall that Ernest O. Lawrence considered Albert Einstein's theory of the interchangeability of matter and energy, the researches of Enrico Fermi, and much else, and then with the help of such assistants as J. Robert Oppenheimer constructed the world's first cyclotron in 1931. It was a cyclotron that enabled Lawrence to transmute ordinary uranium into plutonium in Gilman Hall on February 23, 1941. And it was plutonium that became the critical ingredient in the making of the world's first nuclear fission bomb in the laboratories of Los Alamos, New Mexico, in 1945.

"Prove to us that it really is progress. . . ."

On the morning of July 16, 1945, just twenty days after delegates had signed the charter of the United Nations in San Francisco, the device was detonated from the top of a steel tower in the desert 120 miles southeast of Albuquerque. Oppenheimer, director of the Los Alamos laboratory, was there, and what he experienced as years of theory were translated into the flash and thunder of the Atomic Age caused him to recall two passages from the *Bhagavad-Gita:* "If the radiance of a thousand suns were to burst into the sky, that would be the splendor of the Mighty One," and, "I am become Death, the shatterer of worlds. . . ."

Oppenheimer read death in the fire of that morning, and went on to become one of the leading opponents of nuclear weapons. Lawrence and others read national survival in that fire, and with the backing of the federal government went on to carry the new age in all its possible directions—to the hydrogen bomb, to nuclear-powered submarines and aircraft carriers, to the creation of the Lawrence Radiation Laboratory in the hills above Berkeley and a similar complex in the Livermore Valley, to the construction of nuclear-fueled power plants and desalinization plants, and such linear accelerators as the two-mile-long facility at Stanford University.

Progress, it was called, yet behind it like a shadowed curtain lay the threat

Old men, old boats, old stories of older and possibly better times: an afternoon scene at Fisherman's Wharf in 1962.

of destruction—sudden destruction, as in the explosion of war, or slow destruction, as in the creeping stain of nuclear poisons. Hence the paradox under which we all have lived for more than thirty years, and it is significant that this paradox began in the Bay Area. For if the nuclear dilemma the Bay Area helped create became the definitive symbol of the age, the dilemma itself nourished the growing conviction that a world balanced at the lip of an abyss necessarily required some changes in the rules of the game which had brought it there— and, again, it was in San Francisco and the Bay Area that this halting, often vague, sometimes violent, revolution in thought was most forcefully expressed. San Francisco had begun its headlong career as a reflection of all the diverse hopes that energized a still young America; for most of the thirty years that followed World War II, it mirrored all the foibles and failures of the very dream which had given it birth.

W
ITH THE EXCEPTION of potential nuclear annihilation, there seemed to be little justifiable reason for complaint, much less rebellion. Movement and growth were, somehow, progress, were they not? More had always been better, had it not? And San Francisco and the Bay Area most definitely moved and grew in the postwar years; what is more, freed of the restrictions of war and encouraged by an economic boom that defied tradition, they managed to face and satisfy those needs for housing, services, and transportation whose demands had eluded solution during the war.

Between 1940 and 1950 the population of the Bay Area increased by 947,014; during the decade of the 1950s, an average of nearly one hundred thousand people a year were added, until by 1960 the region's population exceeded four million, almost double what it had been in 1940. Housing units proliferated to enclose the multitude—"Doelgervilles" in the Sunset and Westlake districts of San Francisco, and "dingbats" (as they were called in the building trades) or "ticky-tacky" (as song-writer Malvina Reynolds called them) in a lookalike spread that inundated major portions of Alameda, Santa Clara, San Mateo, and Contra Costa counties.

Between 1950 and 1960 the officials of building departments in the cities and counties of the Bay Area issued permits for nearly three hundred thousand dwellings. Freeways—the Bayshore, the Eastshore, the Lick, the Embarcadero, the Nimitz, highways 24, 280, 580, 680, and 101—lanced into the heart of urban centers and eventually laced all the subcommunities together. Beginning with San Francisco's Stonestown in 1952, retail shopping and service centers blossomed, until by 1960 there were twelve scattered from the Corte Madera Center in Marin County to the Village Fair in Santa Clara County. Industry, although naturally slacking off in shipbuilding, continued to boom. Between 1945 and 1950, the Bay Area gained nearly five hundred manufacturing concerns, and through the 1950s and on into the 1960s industries continued to multiply, fed by a steady influx of federal money for research and development in electronics and aeronautics. Salaries managed to keep one step ahead of inflation, increasing by as much as 400 percent from 1940 to 1960. Scores of new primary and secondary schools were constructed and colleges and universities expanded as thousands of ex-servicemen took advantage of the provisions of the G.I. Bill.

Westward-seeking Americans, Francis Parkman had written more than a century before, were "driven by an insane desire to better their condition in life." For most citizens of San Francisco and the Bay Area—not the Blacks, or

An afternoon's lounge in front of the Bay Hotel on lower Sacramento Street before the Golden Gateway project shoveled the Bay Hotel and all its neighbors into the dustbin of history. Where did these old boys go?

the Chicanos or most of the Asians—the postwar years gave answer to desire. Here, it seemed at last, was everything the generation of the Depression years had wanted so desperately: homes, education, opportunity, jobs, security, prosperity. For white-collar and blue-collar worker alike a new lifestyle was, if not already attained, surely just around tomorrow. It was called "California Living"—affluent, consumptive, credit-oriented, extremely mobile, and leisurely self-indulgent in a kind of minor-league sybaritism—a way of life that in its purest physical comforts surpassed anything the common man had ever before enjoyed, one for which (so the conviction ran) man had endured all the long centuries of his pilgrimage.

Yet there were snakes of doubt in this particular Eden. Prosperity, in the view of some, had brought with it not only jobs and comforts, but a dreadful homogeneity whose cottony presence threatened to smother the diversity that had given America its greatest strength. David Reisman wrote of *The Lonely Crowd* and William S. Whyte, Jr., of *The Organization Man* in sociological treatises heavy with footnotes and laden with research, and a rash of more popular books followed them, documenting the fact that a growing number of Americans were beginning to wonder if they had not sold their birthrights for a mess of security. Some local citizens were quickly forced to realize that there was, in fact, a direct connection between security and conformity—at least in the political sense. California and the Bay Area, like the rest of the United States, entered the postwar years hamstrung by an unreasoning terror of communism. "Americanism" and "un-Americanism" became the issues of the day, and were fully and cheerfully exploited by politicians. Nationally, Senator Joseph McCarthy announced with shaking gray jowls his intention to ferret out Communists wherever he found them, and the House Un-American Activities Committee, founded in 1941, seemed to have become the most powerful committee in the Congress. In California, a young Richard M. Nixon began his long and colorful political career by defeating liberal Jerry Voorhis in the congressional race of 1946, largely on the strength of his charge that Voorhis was "one of those who front for un-American elements, wittingly or otherwise," and four years later went on to defeat Congresswoman Helen Gahagan Douglas in the Senate race of 1950—again, by repeated charges that Douglas's voting record in Congress had followed, point by point, "wittingly or otherwise," the Communist party line. And the state's own Committee on Un-American Activities, headed by Assemblyman Jack B. Tenney and later by State Senator Hugh M. Burns, began looking for any Communist influences the energetic Nixon might have missed.

Early in 1949 the state committee zeroed in on the University of California, whose students and faculty had been known to engage radical speakers from time to time. Moreover, the committee was not certain that the university was doing all it should to weed out subversive elements among its employees. Chairman Tenney proposed a state constitutional amendment that would take the responsibility of insuring the loyalty of university employees out of the hands of the university's board of regents and give it to the legislature. To counter this move, the university responded by offering to devise a more thorough loyalty oath than that required of all state employees (and which the university's staff had already signed). The offer was accepted by the committee, and after a closed board of regents meeting in March, which authorized the action, university President Robert G. Sproul announced in May that all employees on all eight campuses of the university—from janitors to administrative heads—would be required to sign a new loyalty oath by July 1

One of the most popular of the city's many bocce-ball courts reposed near Aquatic Park on the northern waterfront before Eastman Kodak decided to erect its local building on the spot, obliterating another quiet landmark from the past.

Mile Rock Lighthouse off Land's End, now reduced to a helicopter platform, another signpost of the city's life done in by the dictates of expediency.

or face dismissal. The oath proposed was thorough and specific, requiring the signer to declare that he or she did not "support any party or organization that believes in, advocates, or teaches the overthrow of the United States government, by force or by any illegal or unconstitutional methods," and was later amended to include the statement, "I am not a member of the Communist party."

Vigorous protest immediately ensued, so vehemently that President Sproul then reversed himself, asking the regents to rescind their decision. He found support from Governor Earl Warren, who pointed out that any Communist worthy of the label would "take the oath and laugh." Nevertheless, the regents refused to change their stand, led by John Francis Neylan (who, it will be remembered, had engineered a compromise in the waterfront strike of 1934) and Lawrence Mario Giannini, president of the Bank of America. Debate continued for more than a year, during which time twenty-seven professors resigned in protest and forty-seven from other schools who had been invited to join the faculty refused to accept, making the reasons for their refusals a matter of public record. Finally, in August 1950, the regents dismissed thirty-two non-signing employees. The employees fought back in the courts, and on April 6, 1951, Justice Paul Peek of the Third California District Court of Appeals ordered that they be reinstated, declaring that "equal to the danger of subversion from without by means of force and violence is the danger of subversion from within by the gradual whittling away and the resulting disintegration of the very pillars of our freedom." In October 1952, the state supreme court overturned Justice Peek's decision, but at the same time *also* ordered the employees reinstated—not on the grounds of disintegrating freedom, however, but because the statewide Levering Oath (passed by the legislature in 1950 and containing much of the same language of the university oath) superseded the oath required by the university regents. Even though they had won their point (more or less), only sixteen of the non-signers returned to teach at the university. As the decade of the 1950s wore on, the fearfully intense emotions that had given birth to the affair generally dissipated, yet a residue of doubt remained, as historian John Caughey—himself one of the non-signers—wrote in 1967: "Within the university the oath controversy certainly left resentments and scars. It may be questioned whether faculty voice in crucial determinations is as effective as it was from 1925 to 1949. The larger imponderable is what would have resulted from complete and quiet submission to the oath requirement."

COMPLETE AND QUIET SUBMISSION. . . . The remarkable fact, finally, was not that thirty-two people put their jobs on the line for principle, but that out of the thousands of employees of the university *only* thirty-two did so—surely one of the most accurate measures we have of the temper of those years. Apathy, it was called, and if the loyalty oath controversy might be said to represent apathy at the highest end of the social scale, then the lowest end of that scale was represented by a collection of practicing nihilists who had gathered loosely amid the ancient bars and restaurants of San Francisco's North Beach. When they called themselves anything all, they called themselves the "Beat Generation," and if they had a philosophy, it was the philosophy of vacuum expressed by one of their own: "I DON'T KNOW. I DON'T CARE. AND IT DOESN'T MAKE ANY DIFFERENCE." The man who authored that declaration of indifference was novelist Jack Kerouac, who also had given a name to the emotional state which it defined, calling it "a kind of beatness." Kerouac had come by his own beatness honestly enough. Rejected by the Navy during World War II as a potentially schizoid personality, he had joined the Merchant Marine and spent most of the war on the deadly Murmansk run. Returning to New York City after the war, he settled in the environs of Columbia University and Greenwich Village, determined to become a writer. Soon he found himself at or near the center of a coterie of like-minded poets and novelists who gathered regularly at the West End bar to comfort one another in their exile from the world of the city's intellectual establishment; among them were John Clellon Holmes, William S. Burroughs, Seymour Krim, Allen Ginsberg, and Gregory Corso—and, around them, a growing circle of those whose names would never escape anonymity. Sickened by the continuing frustrations (and hard winters) of life in New York, many— including Kerouac, Ginsberg, and Corso—drifted west to San Francisco in the early 1950s, most of them inspired by no more specific a sense of purpose than that expressed by one of the anonymous ones some years later: "We were worried about the Bomb. I didn't want to be in New York when it landed. And I wanted to ball a little before it did. And there was this terrible, dragging conformity. Everyone getting married and moving to the suburbs and tithing their lives to General Motors. Everything in group. All 'we' and no 'I.' So I cut out."

What they found by cutting out to San Francisco was a sort of bohemian tradition that still spanned the generations, defying earthquake, fire, two wars, and a depression. The Montgomery Block itself had survived the earthquake and fire and in the "Monkey Block" and elsewhere San Francisco had seen an impressive number of writers and artists scattered through the years, coming and going, staying until death or obscurity claimed them, moving in, around, up and out, or just out—painters like Xavier Martinez, Maynard Dixon, Bernard Zackheim, Victor Arnautoff, Ray Boynton, Charles Howard, Dorr Bothwell, Emmy Lou Packard, Robert McChesney, and Byron Randall; photographers Ansel Adams, Imogen Cunningham, and Dorothea Lange; sculptors Ralph Stackpole, Ruth Cravath, Adeline Kent, Sargent Johnson, Robert Howard, Mary Erckenbrack, and Beniamino Bufano; writers Idwal

The city of the Fifties—the new Fifties—when the canyons of the town were not so deep that they obscured the light and life that enlivened its streets and defined its meaning. This was the city of which columnist Charles McCabe was speaking: "I think it may be truly said, in this century, that if you are tired of Frisco you are tired of life."

Jones, Sadakichi Hartmann, Charles Caldwell Dobie, Kathleen Norris, Muriel Rukhuyser, Kenneth Rexroth, Miriam Allen deFord, Dashiel Hammet, Robin Kinkead, John Steinbeck, and William Saroyan. If these and the hundreds like them could no longer cluster in "Papa" Coppa's (which never reopened after the earthquake and fire), there was always the Bologna up on the Montgomery Street slope of Telegraph hill around the 1920s, and after it a half-dozen places where good food, good wine, and—most important of all—credit might be had. If Duncan Nicols's Bank Exchange did not survive Prohibition in 1919, it was not difficult to find accommodating speakeasies in the San Francisco of Sunny Jim Rolph, and after Prohibition's repeal in 1933 such spots as the New Pisa, Gino and Carlo's, and the upstairs saloon of the redoubtable Izzy Gomez at 848 Pacific Street carried on the bohemian lifestyle. (It was Gomez, it is reliably reported, who began to worry that his saloon, perhaps the most disheveled in the city, was attracting too many tourists and slumming socialties; turning to newspaperman Neil Hitt one night, the moon-faced Gomez inquired, "Neil, do you suppose if I sprinkled some sawdust around I could make this place look like a dive?") And if only a handful of the whole pantheon of hopefuls ever achieved work of lasting merit or national reputation—well, that, too, was a part of the San Francisco tradition.

After the war, surviving even the death of Izzy Gomez in 1944, the city's artistic life continued to enjoy sparkling good health. A discussion group called the Anarchist Circle was formed, and sprightly radicals of one stripe or another filled the air with talk. Under Ruth Whit and Robert Duncan a Poetry Center was established at San Francisco State College, featuring readings by such local people as William Everson (Brother Antoninus) and such national luminaries as W. H. Auden. Lawrence Ferlinghetti, poet, entrepreneur, and publisher, opened the City Lights Bookshop in the ground floor and basement of a building near the corner of Columbus and Broadway—the first all-paperback bookstore in the United States and a way-station, debating center, informal poetry workshop, contact point, and mail drop-off for the *literati*. North Beach restaurants and bars doubled as art galleries, chief among them No. 12 Adler Place, the Black Cat, and the Iron Pot, whose menu included the following statement: "Notice to tourists: For Bohemian atmosphere, go to Bohemia. The male customers who need a haircut are not artists. The paintings and prints displayed here are for sale. Limit: one dozen to a customer. But don't ask the help to explain them to you. They don't understand them, either." Henri Lenoir, a former chorus boy ("No, No, Nanette") and lingerie salesman, opened a bar called Vesuvio's just across the alley from the City Lights Bookshop, and to demonstrate a finely honed sense of history, placed the door of Izzy Gomez's defunct saloon on the wall above the mirrors and glasses of his own establishment. "All in all, I guess you could really say that the place was jumping from the end of the war to 1955," Kenneth Rexroth recalled in Bruce Cook's *The Beat Generation* (1971). "So you see, when the Beats came here . . . they hit all this stuff that had been bubbling away in San Francisco, and it sort of exploded them. They never heard of anything like this."

In addition to Kerouac, Ginsberg, and Corso, the most noteworthy Beats by then included Gary Snyder, Michael McClure, Philip Lamantia, Phil Whalen, Bob Kaufmann and Lew Welch among the poets; Byron Hunt and Robert LaVigne among the painters; and Neal Cassady, who neither wrote nor painted, but simply lived out a life that defined the best and worst of what the Beats saw as their meaning. The occasion of their "explosion" was a 1955 poetry reading at the Six Gallery when Allen Ginsberg, like Walt Whitman,

The dapper and ebullient Henri Lenoir, servitor to the limberlost of the Beat Generation. He is seen here in 1962, surrounded by all the trappings of Vesuvio's when it was still a place where poets could discourse on the wisdoms of Ginsberg and Corso. Directly above and behind Lenoir is a photograph of Izzy Gomez, and behind that is the door of his defunct saloon of 848 Pacific Street. The door, like so much else from that place in time, has since disappeared.

opened his barbaric yawp and read *Howl*, a two thousand-word poem he had written in a matter of hours while under the influence of peyote, amphetamines, and dexedrine. Innocent of meter, rhyme, structure, or grammar, and uncommonly specific (for the time) in its language, *Howl* possessed an awesome intensity and the kind of raw power normally associated with rockslides; this was not merely free verse, but verse unchained and running amok, and it was an immediate local success, giving birth to what Rexroth came to call the "San Francisco Renaissance." The poem, the renaissance, and the Beats achieved more than local success the following year, when a British edition of Ginsberg's *Howl and other Poems* was seized by the San Francisco Customs Office on the grounds of obscenity and when Lawrence Ferlinghetti was almost simultaneously tried and acquitted on obscentiy charges for publishing the book in this country. The Ginsberg sensation was followed in 1957 by the publication of Kerouac's *On the Road*, a nearly formless celebration of the wanderings of its hero, Moriarty (Neal Cassady), and a book that did to prose what *Howl* had done to poetry: "The only people for me are the mad ones, the ones who are mad to live, mad to talk, mad to be saved, desirous of everything at the same time, the ones who never yawn or say a commonplace thing, but burn, burn, burn like fabulous yellow roman candles exploding like spiders across the stars and in the middle you see the blue centerlight pop and everybody goes 'Aww!'"

To the astonishment of the critics (most of whom panned them unmercifully), both books enjoyed splendid sales. For all their artlessness, it seemed, Kerouac and Ginsberg had stirred up something dark and disenchanted in a generation's psyche, a fermenting stew of anomie and rejection. Two years after publication of *On the Road*, the little cult of the Beats in North Beach had become a genuine subculture that swarmed with young men and women who patterned their lives on characters out of the Kerouac novel, mouthed the indictments of American society that laced Ginsberg's poetry, and fumbled with vague mysticisms and the Zen Buddhism then being promulgated by Alan Watts and others.

Like motes of dust in a sunbeam, these footling rebels meandered through North Beach, "an open-air, come-and-go mental hospital," in and out of the Coffee Gallery and Tea Room, the Spaghetti Factory, The Place, the Cafe Trieste, the City Lights Bookshop, Vesuvio's, the Co-Existence Bagel Shop, and Mike's Pool Hall. Living on faith, hope, handouts, and an occasional check from home, they lived in calculatedly squalid "pads," drank prodigious quantities of wine, indulged in marijuana and sometimes heroin, and experimented with freewheeling heterosexuality, homosexuality, and bisexuality. They listened to Bob Seider, Sonny Rollins, Dave Brubeck, and Gerry Mulligan blowing modern jazz at the Cellar, the Blackhawk, and the Jazz Workshop. When they wrote, which was not often, it was in puerile imitation of the Kerouacs, Ginsbergs, Snyders, and McClures; when they talked, which was often, it was frequently in the sort of disconnected phrases recorded in a *Chronicle* feature story in 1958: "Life is a drag, man. Really a deathly drag. Oh, man! I mean like. . . . Well, a drag, man. . . . Well, if you don't *know*. . . . Everything's all hung up, man. Rugged, you know? Well, you gotta feel it, man. You gotta feel that it's a drag to know it. Then, when you know it, you're cool. And it's a drag and it doesn't make any difference." To some, they were living reminders of the shallow and ersatz qualities of so much of American life; to others, cliché-ridden automatons mindlessly pursuing life to the ultimate nihilism of death. "They have carried their rebellion from society past the end," Herbert

Pierre Monteux, director of the San Francisco Symphony, shown above playing with the San Francisco String Quartet in 1950. For nearly two generations of San Franciscans, "Papa" Monteux was the very sound of the city.

Robert McClay's "Beat Madonna," one of the liveliest and—some had it—most outrageous works ever produced by the Beat Generation's handful of working artists. The times were still simple enough to be offended by such irreverence.

Gold wrote in *The Nation*. "Excising from their innards the cant of a mass culture, these fierce surgeons have also badly cut up their humanity. They are cool. Now they blow nothing but the miseries." Those with enough talent or psychic energy survived; those without them did not, including Kerouac himself, leader of the unled, whose life burned out quietly in a Florida bungalow in 1967. In 1975, Mark Green, one-time bartender of the Co-Existence Bagel Shop and one of the survivors, penned a reflection on the Beats as sad in its own way as Mark Twain's elegy to the lost young men of 1849. "For me," Green wrote, "the world I was in was, and still remains, a poetic symbol of limbo, searcher's purgatory. I have a theory that the artists of each generation, like Orpheus, have to make the trip through hell in order to perceive. Most of my generation in North Beach never came out. Many of my friends died in their twenties or thirties or wound up in jails or mental institutions. Most of the survivors in North Beach are still in that emotional moment in time."

EVEN FOR THE SURVIVORS, the Beat Generation was a fearfully short-lived phenomenon, perhaps consumed by its own intensity, perhaps done in by overexposure in the media that followed its antics with such goggle-eyed fascination. Never an integrated movement, nor even what might be called a philosophy, it had sputtered out by the early 1960s, its few remaining practitioners the object of idle curiosity, its bars and clubs the province of tourists. Aside from their sparse literary efforts, which certainly roused the ire of the traditionalists, the Beats had inspired more amusement and disdain than fear and loathing from the world outside; they had not actively *challenged* the system, after all, they had merely chosen to ignore or lampoon it. But even as the Beat Generation began to fade from sight another generation was developing, one destined to reject not only the uneasy comforts of conformity but the nihilism of the Beats, and once again it was in San Francisco that the world gained a hint of what this new direction might be.

In 1960 the House Un-American Activities Committee, on one of its frequent fact-finding junkets, elected to hold closed sessions in the chambers of San Francisco's City Hall. In the lexicon of the committee, such hearings were purely routine, but to its great surprise—and the surprise of city officials—scores of short-haired, neatly dressed students, most of them from the University of California and San Francisco State College, demanded access to the hearings, crowding the halls of Sunny Jim's pride and joy and giving out with cries of "Witch-hunt!" and "Inquisition!" or, among the better-read, "Star-chamber proceedings!" A flabbergasted city government, devoid of experience in the handling of any kind of student disorder that did not have to do with beer-busts or panty-raids, sent in the police department with fire hoses and nightsticks. Many students, themselves inexperienced in such matters, resisted. These were washed off their feet, beaten, dragged out of the building, thrown into paddy wagons, and hauled off to jail. Dozens of students were injured; one policeman suffered a heart attack.

Reaction to the City Hall riot of 1960 ranged from stunned disbelief to charges that the incident had been nothing less than a Communist plot to discredit and frustrate the efforts of the House Committee on Un-American Activities. More reasoned observations saw it for what it was: apathy was giving way to militant conviction among the student young, who were now ready not only to question old values but to challenge them directly. Such students had grown hungry for causes; their political and social beliefs became

Students greeting the House Un-American Activities Committee with placards, catcalls, and fist-waving on the floor of the rotunda of City Hall, 1960. The police soon greeted the students with billy clubs and fire hoses.

a sometimes confused amalgam of Jeffersonian democracy, Marxist-Leninism, and good old-fashioned American anarchy, with touches of Transcendentalism, Zen Buddhism, and Ghandian fervency thrown in. They were determined to Do Something, Change Things, Shake Up the Establishment. And so they did—and soon. Filled with a myriad of causes and the need to promulgate them, student organizers in Berkeley set up booths and tables on a narrow strip of land near the southern edge of the University of California campus at the beginning of the fall semester, 1964. Responding to a number of complaints from some Berkeley citizens, the university administration decided to dust off and enforce an old rule that prohibited political recruitment on the campus—a tactical error of monumental proportions. The students rebelled, labelled their rebellion the "Free Speech Movement," and proceeded to engage the system head-on. After several days of mass demonstrations and speeches in which their demands were ignored by the school's officials, more than eight hundred students crowded into Sproul Hall, the university's administrative center, sat down, and refused to move for a day and a night. Governor Edmund Brown then ordered state, local, and campus police to move them out, and over a period of several hours nearly every one of the eight hundred students was physically picked up, carried out of the building, and arrested—the largest mass arrest in the state's history. The conviction rate was equally impressive: in a later mass trial, 578 of the students were convicted of trespassing and several of resisting arrest.

In the eyes of the authorities, of course, the "sit-in" tactic was reprehensible, but not even they could effectively deny that the principle—that the largest university in the world should *encourage* rather than suppress the free expression of ideas—was respectable. Responding to that fact, the university's faculty immediately passed resolutions to the effect that the administration should not attempt to hamper political advocacy or regulate its content, and perhaps in response to *that*, the administration ultimately relaxed its rules. Thereafter, the Berkeley campus and its environs became a kind of "free-thought" center for the dissemination of student and non-student political opinion across the state and, indeed, across the nation. Gradually, this center and others—most of them similarly connected with college campuses—began to develop what came to be called the counterculture, with its own set of mores (including sexual mores), its own press (the *Berkeley Barb, Rolling Stone,* etc.), and its own language. And, like the Beat Generation before it, this generation had its own music—called "rock." Though influenced markedly by country-western traditions, by the rock-and-roll that preceded it, and most notably by the songs written and sung by the Beatles, much of this music was developed or refined in San Francisco by such groups as the Jefferson Airplane, and exerted a powerful influence on the patterns of popular music in the country. It was, according to some, the Bay Area's first significant contribution to the cultural life of America, since the region had yet to develop a distinctive art or literature.

To most of the "straight" world, the counterculture was a single, amorphous, threatening mass movement. It was by no means so simple an affair, yet it can be said that it did break down into two general movements, one essentially political, the other psychological; one would change the system, the other, the souls of those who ran it. The latter was made up of those who came to be known collectively as the hippies, whom some considered the spiritual descendents of the Beat Generation. While they later scattered in enclaves and communes throughout the Bay Area, the state, and the nation, the psychologi-

Soviet Premier Nikita Khrushchev in Longshoreman's Hall in 1960. There were still a few left who could be heard muttering about Harry Bridges and his alleged Communist party connections at the time of this innocent visit.

cal home of the hippies between 1965 and 1970 was the "Haight," an older neighborhood that bordered the long strip of Golden Gate Park known as the Panhandle. For as long as they retained their innocence, the hippies displayed a surpassing gentleness and undeniable charm. They adorned themselves (male and female alike) with flowers and jewelry and clothes that shouted with colors. They gave of themselves with astonishing openness, and shared unstintingly. They strove to become childlike. They spoke of love and of the joy of trees and animals and all growing things. Above all, they spoke of their conviction that in order to know oneself and others, it was far more important to *feel* than to think, and that the search for feeling was an inward journey. "That's where love comes from," Peter Mackaness, director of the Hip Job Co-op, declared (in *Voices from the Love Generation,* by Leonard and Deborah Wolf). "You become lovely and loving and full of love when you cop out to who you are, and what you are. And like who you are is a thousand faces, it's just many, many things, but what you are is always eternal and absolute, and real, and that is the ultimate reality you can tune in to. And that's what we're all doing here in the Haight. And that's our manhood, our humanity, that's what we are."

Drugs pointed the way. All drugs, but most of all LSD—lysergic acid diethylamide—the psychedelic sacrament in a high mass for the mind. The commitment to drugs was a religion as much as anything else, and its priest was a former Harvard psychologist by the name of Timothy Leary, who by his own count had taken LSD more than five hundred times. And if Leary was the priest of this drug culture, his most visible acolytes were Allen Ginsberg, that refugee from the Beat Generation, and novelist Ken Kesey, whose Merry Pranksters assaulted the eyes and sensibilities of the straight world in a rainbow-colored bus driven by none other than Neal Cassady. "Turn on, tune in, and drop out," Leary and his followers said. And so the hippies did, with spectacular enthusiasm, even when LSD was declared illegal in 1966, even when "bummers" and "bad trips" left their minds blown of coherence, even when some of them died of their distorted dreams. With a splendid insouciance they pursued their visions, sure that they were leading the way to a brave new world, indifferent to police harassment, drug busts, the spread of disease and malnutrition.

While the hippies explored the dark of their interior landscapes, the political arm of the movement—the New Left, it was called—went about its own business. Often fragmented and confused, the movement found one issue on which most of its parts could agree: the Vietnam War. Beginning with a massive "teach-in" on the war on the Berkeley campus in the spring of 1965, the New Left increasingly coordinated its efforts in an attempt to force an end to the conflict. In October 1965, the Vietnam Day Committee organized a mass march from the Berkeley campus to the Oakland Army Base on the edge of San Francisco Bay, vaguely intent on shutting it down; police turned them back at the Oakland city line, and the following day a similar attempt was inexplicably broken up by the motorcycle gang called the Hell's Angels. That was the beginning, and over the next six years violence swept over and through the Bay Area (and the country), with marches, demonstrations, riots, tear-gas assaults, sit-ins, lie-downs, police beatings and shootings, burnings, bombings, and mass arrests of questionable legality.

It was a head-on challenge to the system; it was traditional, it was very American, and it was inevitably and sometimes savagely violent as the authorities responded, as they always had, with a vigor that often bordered on hysteria. And it spread to other areas, other lives, other causes. On the Univer-

Landscapes exterior and interior: Hippies in Golden Gate Park during one of the last expressions of the best they had in them—the Summer of Love in 1967. They were on The Path and were righteous and loving and true . . . for a time.

sity of California campus, Black activist Eldridge Cleaver led demonstrations in an attempt to force the Board of Regents to let him teach "Social Analysis 139X: Dehumanization and Regeneration in the American Social Order," again without success. On the campus of San Francisco State College, the Black Students Union demanded the creation of a Black Studies Department, with teacher-scholar Nathan Hare at its head, and followed up with a long and violent strike finally ended by the tactical squad of the San Francisco police with the liberal application of tear gas, Mace, and riot clubs. On both campuses the Third World Liberation Front demanded the creation of Third World colleges, and demonstrated in support of the idea. Disorganized racial violence cropped up in San Francisco in 1966 and 1967—dim but disruptive echoes of the Watts riot of 1965 in Los Angeles. In Oakland, Cleaver, Bobby Seale, and Huey Newton formed the Blank Panthers, a paramilitary organization verbally aggressive in its conviction that Black was not only beautiful, but better, and would prevail.

Scorning a request from Eugene McCarthy that it put its full effort behind him in the presidential election of 1968, a more militant element of the New Left created the Peace and Freedom party and in dim lofts in San Francisco's warehouse district rancorous debates on policies and programs wore on late into the night (and many of those present went on to get a taste of their own blood during the horror of the Chicago convention later that year). In the spring of 1969, street people and police in Berkeley clashed in a struggle over a small plot of university-owned land dubbed "People's Park," a conflict that resulted in the shotgun killing by police of James Rector, a student watching the action from a rooftop; within hours, Berkeley was invaded by more than five hundred Bay Area police and units of the National Guard, and for the next two weeks the town was an occupied city, until on May 30, twenty-five thousand people representing a broad spectrum of the Bay Area's population marched through Berkeley in protest, an act that finally convinced Governor Ronald Reagan to withdraw his occupation troops. Later in 1969, a group of militant Indians "captured" the abandoned federal prison on Alcatraz Island, christened it "Indian Land," and remained until their peaceful removal more than a year later. And in 1970, Marin County's Frank Lloyd Wright-designed courthouse saw blood and heard gunfire when three Black prisoners on trial for the alleged murder of a prison guard produced guns and kidnapped the judge in an escape attempt which saw all four killed by gunfire.

It was as consistently violent and disruptive a period as any in American history, and nowhere more consistently so than in San Francisco and the Bay Area. At times, it seemed that the savagery would never end, that it could only lead to one long apocalyptic struggle between the forces of light and darkness (and who belonged to which was entirely a matter of interpretation). Yet the ultimate conflict never came. Increasingly, the New Left lost cohesion, and as early as 1971 students on the Berkeley campus talked of the old New Left of the 1960s and debated the causes for its decline. Bobby Seale reformed some remaining Black Panthers into a political party and ran, unsuccessfully but remarkably, for mayor of Oakland. Tom Hayden, one of the principal leaders of the New Left, married actress Jane Fonda and later announced his Democratic candidacy for Senator from California. In Berkeley, enough radicals were elected in 1972 to completely dominate the city council, an event which resulted neither in the subversive disaster the city's conservative element had predicted nor the revolutionary breakthrough the radicals had expected. In San Francisco, Nathan Hare became editor and publisher of *The Black Scholar*, an academic journal quite as staid as any other. Eldridge Cleaver, in exile in Paris,

Hard hats, gas masks, and bayonets protect the president's residence on the Berkeley campus of the University of California during the People's Park riots of May, 1969.

went into the rag trade, producing a line of men's pants that featured impressive codpieces, and later returned to the country and surrendered to the authorities.

The more mystical branch of the movement suffered its own decline. After a "Human Be-In" held in Golden Gate Park in January 1967 (largely organized by Allen Ginsberg) and the "Summer of Love" that followed it that same year, the Haight saw its own sweet culture begin a slide. The San Francisco police began a systematic campaign to cut off the traffic in marijuana and LSD, while some of the faithful turned increasingly to amphetamines, cocaine, and eventually to heroin—and with heroin came the Mafia. Prices skyrocketed, and theft and vandalism spread to such a degree that most of the shops in the district boarded up their storefronts or went out of business. Prostitution—male and female alike—blossomed like a hothouse rose. Muggings, burglaries, and generalized street violence proliferated, and in despair hundreds of those who could no longer tolerate the scene fled to other parts of the city and the state, many of them to countryside communes, leaving a raw distillate of those more in tune with the new environment. Allen Ginsberg retired to his farm in upstate New York; Ken Kesey, after leading the authorities on a sometimes farcical year-long chase to evade a charge of marijuana possession, turned himself in, pleaded nolo contendere, served his time, and disappeared to his farm in Oregon; Neal Cassady was found dead beside a Mexican railroad track in 1968; and Timothy Leary, convicted and jailed for possession of marijuana, escaped from prison, fled to Europe, renounced the use of LSD, was recaptured, and returned to the United States to begin informing on his various drug contacts and fellow users.

The movement had not died, as some claimed, but it was clear that it had changed—how and to what degree, no one seemed to know with certainty. Historian Walton Bean, in his highly orthodox 1973 history of California, declared that the movement "had collapsed largely from its own weaknesses, excesses, and general counter-productiveness." It is significant that in his last phrase Bean utilized one of the cant Maoist terms so much of the New Left had loved. The simple fact was that the movement had been changed by a process as old in America as violence itself: it had been absorbed, as all rebellions in the country's history had been absorbed. What the New Left had wanted was revolution; what it got was accommodation, the inexorable "winding down" and eventual end of the war in Vietnam, and the superficial "radicalization" of government on just enough levels to blunt the cutting edge of revolt. What the hippies had wanted was the transformation of the Protestant Ethic to a Morality of Universal Love; what they got was the Esalen Institute, Gestalt therapy, encounter groups, middle-class communes, corporation-sponsored sensitivity-training clinics, an entertainment industry that appropriated their music and a fashion industry that appropriated their clothes.

In a very real sense, then, the movement declined because it had in fact altered the system—by no means completely, but substantially. On June 18, 1970, Louis B. Lundborg, chairman of the board of the Bank of America, got up and addressed the Rotary Club of Seattle, Washington. Lundborg was not exactly a dispassionate observer; just a few days before, the Isla Vista branch of his bank had been burned by rioting students from the Santa Barbara campus of the University of California. He was not dispassionate, but he was wise, and his remarks indicated the depth to which the movement's goals and attitudes had penetrated. "There is a new value system emerging in this country," he said. "For generations we have been mouthing the cliché, 'You can't stand in the

Cult become commerce: As the hippy persuasion faded as a movement, it slipped with astonishing ease into such curious expressions of grace as the Renaissance Pleasure Faires held each summer in the woods of Marin County.

way of progress.' Now there is a new generation that is saying, 'The hell you can't.' That generation—and an increasing number of its elders—are saying, 'Prove to us that it really is progress.' In a sense, that is the essence of everything that is stirring and boiling and seething. Thoughtful people in increasing numbers are asking about one thing after another, 'Is it really progress—progress for the human condition?' What they say they want doesn't sound so different, you know, from what our founding fathers said they wanted.''

WHILE THE YOUNG PEOPLE were "stirring and boiling and seething," calling into question all the tenets of conventional morality and politics, an even broader spectrum of people was beginning to question the value of a system that had created a physical world that threatened to strangle in its own excesses, or collapse of its inadequacies. The issue at hand was one having to do with the definition of the quality of life, and in its resolution San Francisco and the Bay Area became a principal battleground in a fifteen-year conflict that made up in polite fervor what it lacked in open violence.

Working boats at Fisherman's Wharf in 1961. There are fewer boats, now, and fewer crabs and fish and fishermen, and there are those who claim that one of the oldest—and surely most romantic—of the city's many trades is dying out.

The roots of the conflict—like the phenomena of the Beat Generation, the student wars, the Black revolt, and the hippies—lay in what had happened to the Bay Area during and after the war. What had happened, of course, was growth, uncontrolled growth, although government had made some fumbling efforts in the direction of control. In 1944, the Bay Area Council (then called the Bay Region Council) had been patched together by a group of businessmen to consider the problems and prospects of growth; a purely voluntary organization, with little funding and almost no professional planners among its membership, the council's performance over the next several years caused city planner Mel Scott (among others) to complain in 1958 that "The record of attempted cooperation among the cities and counties of the Bay Area raises almost as much doubt as it does hope concerning the possibility of metropolitan government." A step considerably further in that direction was taken in 1961, when the state legislature created the Association of Bay Area Governments (ABAG), funded primarily through the U.S. Department of Housing and Urban Development and small local taxes, described as "a voluntary council of local governments formed to solve regional problems through cooperative action of cities and counties," and quite as effective as that description would suggest. Although its membership came to include seven counties, eighty-five cities, and twenty-seven "cooperating agencies," from the Bay Area Air Pollution Control District to the Redevelopment Agency of the City and County of San Francisco, although its staff included an impressive number of city and regional planners, and although this staff issued a remarkable number of reports over the years on everything from transportation to parkland acquisition, ABAG was powerless to do anything but advise and proselytize. Bay Area governments remained almost wholly free of regional control, with consequences that had an increasingly visible and deplorable effect on the environment.

The more visible those consequences became, the more concerned the public became, and in the 1960s a grassroots movement to preserve and protect the environment exploded into a major force that crossed political, class, and generational lines as have few others in the history of the United States—and nowhere was it more active than in San Francisco and the Bay Area. The Sierra Club, the conservation organization founded in San Francisco by John Muir in 1892, grew in membership from just under twenty thousand in 1960 to more

The Bay of San Francisco, the region's most eloquent legacy. "God took the beauty of the Bay of Naples," New York Mayor Fiorello La Guardia once said, "the Swiss Alps, the Hudson River Valley, rolled them into one and made San Francisco Bay."

than one hundred thousand by 1970, largely through the efforts of its executive director, David Brower. (Ousted from the club during an internal dispute in 1969, Brower organized Friends of the Earth, which became an equally militant watchdog for the environment.) In 1961, also in San Francisco, Alfred Heller founded California Tomorrow to bring to the public "a greater awareness of the problems we must face to maintain a beautiful and productive California," and its quarterly journal, *Cry California,* under the editorship of William Bronson, launched an all-out assault on the "land-wreckers," ranging from the State Division of Highways to the Army Corps of Engineers. In the late 1960s, a group of environmentally concerned young people got together in Berkeley to establish an ecology center for the dissemination of information and to function as a base for direct action against environmental problems; the Berkeley center was quickly followed by one in San Francisco, and then by forty-five centers scattered across the country and tied together under the aegis of the Ecology Center Communications Council.

Like waves from a storm, the energy of what had become known as the Ecology Movement ("Green Power!") spread throughout the state and country. Locally, one of the earliest and most immediate concerns was the gradual disappearance of San Francisco Bay itself. For more than a century, ever since Gold Rush entrepreneurs began dumping crates of tea and tobacco into Yerba Buena Cove, the cities and counties that ringed the Bay had been filling it in for port facilities, roads, marinas, airports, bridge approaches, and housing developments, until by 1960 nearly 40 percent of the original Bay had been filled—and in that year alone an additional thirty-two "sanitary land-fill" projects were under way. Against this backdrop, the city of Berkeley in 1962 announced plans to fill in some four thousand acres of city-owned tidelands, an act which more than any other awakened the region's citizens to the fact that San Francisco Bay, *their* Bay, one of the most splendid geographical sites in the world, was well on its way to becoming little more than a turgid shipping canal. The result was the "Save-the-Bay" movement, and *its* result was the creation of the Bay Conservation and Development Commission (BCDC) by the state legislature in 1965, designed as an interim organization until a comprehensive Bay plan could be developed and in the meantime empowered to "issue or deny permits, after public hearings, for any proposed project that involves placing fill in the Bay or extracting materials from the Bay."

Under the chairmanship of *Sunset* magazine publisher Melvin Lane, BCDC worked—it worked so well, in fact, that in 1969 the legislature recreated it into a permanent organization with even greater regulatory powers, the politicans ignoring for once those industrialists, real estate developers, and ambitious city managers who brought out and waved the tired bloody shirt of Socialism. And in many instances, the politicians continued to ignore them, taking the energy of the ecology movement and shaking it down into committees, debates, investigations, and bills, a remarkable number of which became translated into law. Among the locally important conservation victories between 1965 and 1975 were not only the creation and preservation of BCDC, but the effective stalling of the Peripheral Canal, a state project that would have diverted as much as 80 percent of the flow of the Sacramento River from its natural watercourse; the blocking of the San Luis Drain, a Bureau of Reclamation project that would have dumped pesticides and agricultural wastes into the Sacramento–San Joaquin Delta and ultimately the Bay; the passage of Proposition 20 in 1972, which created the California Coastline Commission, an agency patterned directly after BCDC; the creation of the Golden Gate National Recreation Area in 1973, a 36,000-acre complex of parks and open space tied together under the supervision of the Department of the Interior; and in 1975 the suspension of plans by the Army Corps of Engineers to build a major dam on Warm Springs Creek in Sonoma County. The thrust of progress had been diverted—not enough, surely, but significantly—from an attitude of careless exploitation to one of cautious preservation.

Within San Francisco, the movement was even more directly involved with the idea of the quality of life, for it was sharpened by almost continuous exposure to the honing edges of steel and concrete. At issue was the question of what kind of city San Francisco was going to be. World War II and the postwar years had not merely presented the city with a set of unanticipated problems, they had effectively altered the patterns of generations. If the Bay Area as a whole had gained nearly five hundred industrial concerns between 1945 and 1950, San Francisco had lost nearly two hundred, as companies fled for the wide open spaces and lower taxes of suburban industrial parks. After industry went much of the city's general retail merchandising, on the reasonable theory that the seller goes to the market, the market does not come to the seller—and most of the market now lived in suburban developments. Even the city's port suffered a decline, as Oakland and Richmond, blessed with greater space and a quicker perception of technological change, gradually took over more and more of the Bay's shipping, particularly in the handling of container ships with their huge pre-packed containers, loaded and unloaded by shoreside cranes (and in spite of the highest of hopes, the decline was not appreciably reversed in 1969 when the city persuaded the legislature to transfer ownership and operation of the port from the state, which had operated it since 1856, to the city under its own Port Commission). The city's population dropped steadily, the biggest loss in the middle-income, blue-collar working class; between 1950 and 1960, San Francisco—unlike any other major city in the country—witnessed a decline in its population, from 775,000 to 742,000, and by 1970 it had gone down to just over 715,000.

Increasingly, the city was becoming the Bay Area's office town, a center of generalized paper-shuffling among banking, brokering, and insurance firms, with side excursions into highly specialized retailing, communications, wholesaling, printing, conventioneering, and tourism "industries." Its labor force was largely white collar, and it commuted; by 1970, more than three hundred thousand people a day were streaming into the city, spending their nine or ten hours, then returning to their suburban homes. Most of them came via bridge and freeway in automobiles, but by 1975 ten or fifteen thousand were coming in the electric railroad cars of BART (Bay Area Rapid Transit District), a system begun in 1962, financed by a three-county, $800 million bond issue, and designed specifically to handle peak-hour commuting. The concept of "highest use" (literally, as well as economically) was applied more and more as a rationale for new construction; on the hills, older homes and apartments were torn down and replaced by high-density high-rise buildings, and in the downtown area older, "less efficient," office buildings (some of them called skyscrapers in their day) were razed and on their sites *real* skyscrapers poked into the air, among them the Wells Fargo building (43 stories), the Security Pacific Bank building (45 stories), the Transamerica Pyramid (48 stories), and the Bank of America building (52 stories); between 1960 and 1975, seventeen buildings of twenty or more stories had been built in the downtown area, and eight more were either planned or under construction by the end of 1975. Reflecting the highest-use concept, the city's major redevelopment projects

The Trinidad Bean & Elevator Co. building at the corner of Front and Vallejo streets in 1961. The wonderfully obscure sign is gone, but the structure lingers on, its sandstone doorway dating from the boom of the 1850s.

An editorial comment amid the new ruins of the Yerba Buena redevelopment project, 1972.

begun in the late 1950s—the Western Addition project, the Golden Gateway project, and the Yerba Buena project—stripped away thousands of older homes and low-rise buildings, with plans for hotels, tall middle-income residential complexes, towering office buildings, and, in the case of the Yerba Buena project, a sports arena and convention center (although by 1975 Yerba Buena had not yet progressed beyond the planning and acrimony stage).

To some, the changing face of the city was not only inevitable, but right and proper. "As a practical matter," insurance executive Roger Lapham, Jr., was quoted as saying in the *San Francisco Bay Guardian* in 1968, "you can't have 18 different banking and insurance centers. You have to concentrate them with all the various services around them. The people who run these centers want all their services, the people they work with—advertisers, attorneys, accountants—around them. It's a complete part of the way we do business in this country." When it was pointed out that at least some San Franciscans objected to the "Manhattanization" of the city, Lapham replied, "Then let 'em go someplace else. But don't keep complaining about it, because that's what is *going* to happen, and nobody can stop it."

There were those willing to try—some, in fact, had been trying for years, convinced that San Francisco's ready capitulation to those interests promoting high-density development and all that came with it was destroying all that the city possessed of life, light, and charm. Sometimes organized, sometimes not—and sometimes positively *dis*organized—these cityside conservationists kept up a running battle with what they saw as untrammeled and almost completely undirected change. In 1959, they protested the destruction of the Montgomery Block for a parking lot, and lost, but that same year so deluged the State Division of Highways with protests that it was forever discouraged from completing its planned extension of the Embarcadero Freeway to the Golden Gate Bridge. In 1962, they protested the demolition of the Fox Theatre on Market Street for a high-rise office complex, and lost, but that same year the Junior League of San Francisco began a painstaking survey of all buildings in San Francisco, San Mateo, and Marin counties worthy of preservation for their historical or architectural value; the results of the survey were published in 1968 as *Here Today: San Francisco's Architectural Heritage*, a book that gave the ammunition of information to the city's Landmarks Preservation Advisory Board. At about the same time, the residents of Russian Hill saw the rise of the Fontana Towers (East and West), an apartment complex that cut off their view of the Bay "like a Chinese wall," organized their outrage, and managed to persuade the San Francisco Planning Commission and Board of Supervisors to impose strict (but by no means inviolate) height limitations in the area to prevent another such development. Height limitations were sub-

"STOP THEM FROM BURYING OUR CITY UNDER A SKYLINE OF TOMB-STONES" shouted the headline of a full-page advertisement in the San Francisco *Chronicle* and *Examiner* in October 1970, the opening gun in a vigorous anti-high-rise campaign on the part of dressmaker Alvin Duskin and the San Francisco Coalition.

sequently applied to many other areas of the city, most dramatically in the waterfront region north of the Ferry Building, an area held to a limit of forty feet. In 1965, the residents of the Haight-Ashbury district—hippies and non-hippies together—rose up to protest the announced intentions of the State Division of Highways to build the Panhandle Freeway, a crosstown artery that would have damaged Panhandle Park, destroyed hundreds of Victorian homes, and sliced away a good-sized chunk of Golden Gate Park itself. After a two-year campaign on the part of the Haight-Ashbury Neighborhood Council, enough of the rest of the city's residents were persuaded against the project that they simply rejected the offer of $180 million in federal highway funds in a ballot initiative. Muttering darkly, the rarely defeated planners of the division called San Francisco "the worst highway bottleneck in America" and diverted the federal funds to Southern California, where they would be appreciated. Eight years later, the much-touted convention center of the Yerba Buena project was given a bitter setback by opponents. For years, development had been held up by dressmaker Alvin Duskin and the San Francisco Coalition, among other citizens and organizations, who demanded that funds for low-cost housing be provided in the project, that minority workers be guaranteed a high percentage of available jobs in its construction, and that before all, the citizens of San Francisco be given a chance to vote on the whole thing. In May 1975, a suit to force this last condition was sent to the State Supreme Court for a decision on its validity; the court found it valid, and project planners, faced with the prospect of months, perhaps years, of court proceedings, declared the center dead.

Skirmishes large and small, won and lost, in the continuing struggle for a definition of San Francisco. . . . In 1970, however, perhaps the largest and most definitive skirmish took place. Early that year, the United States Steel Corporation proposed that it build an office tower on a site just south of the Ferry Building; the tower would be 550 feet tall, just slightly higher than the pylons of the Bay Bridge. The height limitation in that area was 175 feet. Undaunted by this inconvenience and given the enthusiastic support of Port Commissioner Miriam Wolfe, Mayor Joseph Alioto, the San Francisco Chamber of Commerce, the San Francisco Labor Council, and the Downtown Businessmens Association, U.S. Steel put pressure on the San Francisco Board of Supervisors to change the height limitation to accommodate its building. Opposition developed from San Francisco Tomorrow, Alvin Duskin and the San Francisco Coalition, columnist Herb Caen, the *San Francisco Bay Guardian*, the Telegraph Hill Dwellers, and the Citizens Waterfront Committee, an extemporaneous organization of individuals not otherwise affiliated. Proponents argued that high-rise buildings eased the burden of property tax on

A photographic comment in the Haight-Ashbury district, 1959.

By far the most effective device in the Duskin advertisement of October 1970 were these two photographs, the one on the far left taken in 1958, the one immediately left from the same spot in 1970. "What can you do to stop it?" the advertisement asked, and more than ten thousand citizens clipped coupons and sent them to City Hall.

homeowners; opponents pointed out that between 1950 and 1970 property tax assessments in the residential areas of the city had increased an average of 196 percent, while those in the downtown, high-rise district had increased only 67 percent. Proponents argued that high-rises generated income in local retail sales, restaurant business, and related services; opponents admitted that, but maintained that the increased costs of police, fire, and sanitation provisions more than offset generated income; proponents argued that high-rises made more jobs available, both in construction and in staffing after completion; opponents argued that the construction jobs were dominated by white workers, doing little for the minority job situation in the city, and that most of the construction workers and the staffs that followed completion were commuters; proponents argued that only high-rises were economically feasible under modern conditions; opponents replied that they were also firetraps and earthquake hazards, and wondered whether there was a rational price on human life. In December 1970, after months of debate, demonstrations, propaganda, and newspaper editorials, the Board of Supervisors voted to retain the 175-foot limit, thus killing the U.S. Steel Tower "dead and double-dead," in the words of the *Bay Guardian*'s environmental editor, Robert Jones.

Any notion that the victory over U.S. Steel indicated a citywide revulsion over the very idea of high-rise development was negated the following year, however, when a Duskin-sponsored ballot proposition to set a 70-foot height limitation throughout the city was soundly defeated. San Francisco was not ready for open revolution yet, it seemed, but there remained the possibility of rebellion here and there. One such, perhaps the littlest rebellion of all, centered around a small waterfront bar and restaurant in the summer of 1973.

The place was the Eagle Cafe, a building that had stood on the corner of Powell and Jefferson streets since its construction as a waiting room and ticket office for the McCormick Steamship Company in 1911. In 1928, after McCormick vacated the space, one Joseph Andreotti took over the building and converted it into a restaurant, and after the repeal of Prohibition in 1933 added a bar. That was the Eagle Cafe, and that was all it ever was. After Andreotti's death in 1947, his son Evo and a cousin, Daniel Andreotti—together with their wives, Josephine and Albina—stepped in to operate the place, which continued to cater to longshoremen, bus drivers, teamsters, the brakemen, oilers, and engineers of the Belt Line Railroad, office workers from nearby buildings, and a scattering of writers, artists, and "street people" who appreciated good food and honest drinks at reasonable prices and an atmosphere supremely tolerant of all the shapes and foibles of the human condition. In May 1973, the Eagle Cafe, which had operated on a month-to-month lease for thirty-five years, was presented with an eviction notice by the Port Commission, which had decided to raze the building so that the property on which it stood could be utilized for "development."

The response was immediate. Customers organized "The Friends of the Eagle Cafe," circulated a petition which gathered more than a thousand signatures within two weeks, called in the press, television, and radio, and bearded the Port Commission in its Ferry Building den on June 11, 1973, when a representative of the Friends of the Eagle Cafe maintained that the enterprise represented something important to the life of the city: "The value of the Eagle Cafe derives not so much from specific architectural or historical virtues . . . but from the quality of life which it both represents and nurtures, a sense of the unaffected gusto which has always been a hallmark of the San Francisco waterfront." The Port Commission, somewhat taken aback, took two weeks to reach a decision, and when it did surprised perhaps even itself: it voted unanimously to extend to the Eagle Cafe and the Andreotti family a guaranteed fifteen-year lease.

THERE MAY BE THOSE WHO would claim that the story of the Eagle Cafe was no more than a footnote to San Francisco history, one infinitely less significant that the rise and fall of the U.S. Steel building. Perhaps. But something should be considered here: The Eagle Cafe, a rickety and weather-beaten old saloon, possessed of almost no architectural charm and only marginal historic value, was saved not by the full (or even substantial) weight of San Francisco's preservationist and conservationist establishment, but by a purely ad hoc collection of people who had no axe to grind save that of affection for a way of life that cut close to the heart of what it meant to them to be San Franciscans; and it was an official city body, the San Francisco Port Commission, a singularly unsentimental gathering of merchants, lawyers, laborites, and bureaucrats, who listened to that murmur of affection and gave it the stamp of approval. One cannot imagine such a thing happening in any other city in the United States, and it stands as a particularly telling illustration of the dimensions of possibility that still remained in San Francisco as it approached its two hundredth year.

San Francisco had not solved its problems—indeed, it was not even close to solving them. It endured city-wide strikes, clamoring charges of political corruption, crime, a crippled and fumbling school system, the failure of planning, and the dismal specter of municipal bankruptcy—just as every urban complex in America. Yet it could also take hope for the future. In thirty years, San Francisco had gone from the dull acceptance of things-as-they-were to the sometimes violent rejection of the conventional. And now, perhaps, it could synthesize the best of both. It would never have a better opportunity, for in many respects it was 1849 all over again; in no other region in America did there exist such a combination of human talent, energy, imagination, and money, and in no other area did there exist such a natural arena for the expression of the best they could produce. San Francisco was still a city of hills and wind and water; still a city of style, grace, wit, and the splendid provincialism that provided a sense of place in a placeless world; still a city with the antique courage to tolerate the different without hysteria—"a century-old thread of humanism," columnist Herb Caen once called it, "that comes of being thrown together with all kinds of people on a tiny spit of land at the western edge of a continent." Two generations before Caen, poet Gelette Burgess remarked that "Time alone can tame the town, rob it of its nameless charm, subdue it to the Commonplace. May time be merciful—may it delay its fatal duty till we have learned that to love, to forgive, to enjoy, is but to understand."

Time had not yet done its work. If San Francisco was very lucky—and very, very careful—perhaps it never would.

Something of Value . . .

KARL KORTUM

So what's new? . . . The American penchant for tearing down for the sake of building up hit San Francisco with ever-increasing force in the 1960s and '70s. Back in the '50s, the loss of pleasant landmarks could be written off with a rueful sigh as the price of progress. Then the price started going up. The wholesale destruction in the Western Addition redevelopment looked more and more like a mistake as new apartment blocks of low quality but high rent replaced good buildings that might have been renovated. And if the planned improvements in the cityscape were of doubtful value, the unplanned operation of speculative fad was more often than not downright obnoxious. "Progress" was becoming as popular as the plague to increasingly large elements of the populace.

What had happened? For one thing, people were finding that the real amenities of urban living were compounded of a multitude of details, all sorts of little things that could have no place in a flat, dead, homogenized architecture that leveled all distinctions of people and place. For another, the ambience of the city *was* being damaged, and the loss was more than nostalgic. A marvelous cast-iron bank front, a modest ornamental railing that had been a builder's stock item back in the 1890s . . . thousands of details were being lost to the senses. More and more, San Franciscans were coming to see value in saving what is good, or pleasant, or distinctive. And we were learning that there was very tangible economic value in the supposedly intangible, that economic arguments need not always be won by anybody who was prepared to slap together something new.

KARL KORTUM PHOTOS

KARL KORTUM PHOTOS

SHOW AND TELL. . . . The Freeway Revolt that has since spread to most civilized enclaves in the nation began in San Francisco as the Embarcadero Freeway marched past the Ferry Building toward some undetermined connection with the Golden Gate Bridge. No sooner was the monstrously negative impact of this structure apparent to everybody than the highway engineers set into motion the next phase that would connect up everything and turn San Francisco into a freeway paradise to match Los Angeles.

Opposition to the Golden Gate and Panhandle freeways started large and by 1966 was overwhelming. The new links were not built. The Embarcadero Freeway stands with its stub-ends hanging out, waiting to be torn down.

While millions from the public treasury were being poured into the concrete elevated highway to nowhere, private thousands invested here and there in restoration and renovation paid handsomely and Victorian rows that escaped the wrecking claw appreciate in value even while the middle class, it is said, deserts the city.

BANCROFT LIBRARY PHOTOS

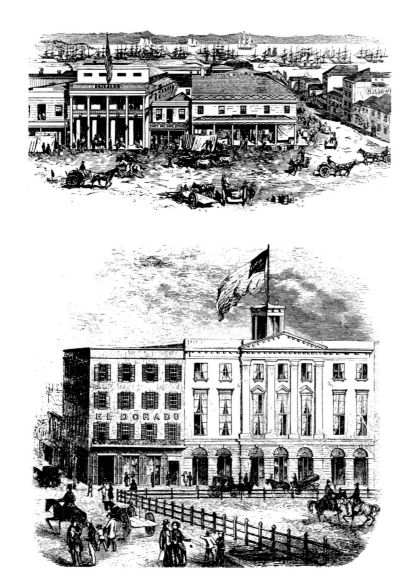

PORTSMOUTH SQUARE: A STUDY IN PARK MISMANAGE-
MENT . . . The one-time Plaza of Mexican Yerba
Buena has never been much of a park, but it *was* the
heart of the first town, and one would think it deserved a better fate than to be treated as an annex to
an unusually grotesque Holiday Inn. It was a dusty
little square when Daniel Coit made his drawing of it
at the outset of the Gold Rush, a scene of awesome
bustle and exchange a single wild year later. In the
scene of the late 1850s, it was the seat of civic government. When Muybridge photographed
Portsmouth Square in the early 1870s, it looked like a
small-town courthouse park.

In more recent memory, the noble Hall of Justice
(on the site of the old Jenny Lind Theater and corner
hotel) dominated the Kearny Street side, with its
outriding gaggle of bailbond storefronts and cheap
lunch counters. The upper side of the Square nestled
into Chinatown, and the park itself was the outdoor
living room of the Chinese community. In our times,
the Plaza has been maimed by becoming the roof of
an underground garage; then the City Fathers sold off

the Hall of Justice to the famous Memphis quick-sleep chain, which had the effrontery to suggest anchoring a concrete bridge in the middle of the remaining park! They found enough influence with the promotion-minded city government to get away with the gag. It never *was* a big plaza, but big thinking has managed to cut its useful park area by about half.

Losing the Seawall—and more.

. . . With the destruction of the famous Montgomery Block to provide a building site for Transamerica's idea of a pyramid the Seawall Warehouse became the oldest remaining structure of any size or significance dating from the boom years of the Gold Rush. Built in 1853 by Adams & Co., the huge California express and banking firm, it was for many years owned by William T. Coleman, head of the great vigilance committee of l856. Clipper ships and Downeasters lay alongside the Seawall and unloaded their cargoes through its row of close-spaced arches. With a number of other fine brick structures of a not much later date, the Seawall escaped the 1906 fire and inconspicuously performed its function until the whole area right under Telegraph Hill began to look like a nifty speculation.

Something called North Waterfront Associates put together the property package that ultimately led to the destruction of the Seawall and several other buildings more valuable than their successors. But the intended successor of all these buildings was "The $100 Million San Francisco International Market Center," a scheme so ugly and damaging to the public interest of the entire Telegraph Hill-North Waterfront area that a citizenry aroused by such experienced agitators for historical and environmental values as Jean and Karl Kortum turned enough heat on to turn the project off.

But not before the historic Seawall was lost. In the words of *The San Francisco International Market Center* news sheet, "Henry Adams, president of the Market Center, hit the first demolition blow with a golden pick ax, surrounded by leaders of the furniture, floor covering, and interior design professions. These key men and women had been invited to a festive holiday luncheon when the demolition ceremony surprise was revealed."

Adams's vandalism has been covered up by a peculiarly tacky apartment building. But at least the building's dimensions are acceptable—and the people who fought at Fort Seawall will organize again when they see another Henry Adams start to work. The man with the balloons is Karl Kortum, scourge of the Chamber of Commerce and the Building Trades Council.

Aquatic Park: A plan makes its point at Ghirardelli Square. . . . The development at Aquatic Park of a unique urban environment that is everywhere acclaimed one of the leading attractions of San Francisco owes almost nothing to the political, bureaucratic, investment, and development interests of the city—the people that we usually look towards for civic leadership in such large affairs. Rather, it is the still uncompleted vision that Karl Kortum presented to Scott Newhall of the San Francisco *Chronicle* in 1949.

Kortum wanted to develop a maritime museum in the unused Aquatic Park Casino, a W.P.A. legacy to the city. At the same time, he saw the magnificent old brick blocks surrounding the Casino as structures to be preserved for lively public use and he saw the whole complex as a popular attraction to both rival and complement Fisherman's Wharf.

With the support of the *Chronicle*, the maritime idea worked out. The museum opened in 1951 and Kortum's promotion of the State of California's maritime park got underweigh with the purchase of the West Coast lumber schooner *C. A. Thayer* in 1957. The state park opened in 1962, at the rebuilt Hyde Street Pier, with the great Haslett Warehouse building adjoining the pier slated to become the finest transportation museum in the country. A dusty parking lot at Hyde and Beach streets became the present Victorian Park with its cable car terminus.

But even the best expressed and most practical vision of real scope is apt to elude the grasp of many of the public and private authorities who shape our environment, and there were setbacks for the development even as its potential became obvious. Eastman Kodak bulled through its program for a blockhouse of no corporate importance that destroyed the traditional bocce ball park setting at the western connection to Fort Mason. Much worse, the grand Fontana Building, a structure with as much economic potential as the best of the biggest San Francisco restoration-developments of the last few years, came down to provide a footing for the gross Fontana Apartments—the celebrated "Chinese Wall" twin structures which gave San Franciscans a taste of what they were going to see all along the North Waterfront if they weren't careful. In no time at all, the views and property values of thousands of people could be irreparably damaged by the successful speculations of a few.

Even while the State Maritime Park was proving itself one of the great exhibitions of its kind in the world, the state dragged its feet about turning the Haslett purchase into a museum, dickered with a developer who dressed up the top two floors into trendy offices, and tried to set up the sale of the building to the best bidder—just as though the state parks system were a plain red-blooded speculator who had run short of quick cash. Only stopgap legislation introduced by such enlightened legislators at the state and federal level as George Moscone and Philip Burton has from year to year saved the building bought as the home of the great historical museum that San Francisco needs and deserves.

Yet losses and setbacks can be offset by determination and vision. The crown jewel of the Aquatic Park setting, the Ghirardelli chocolate factory, came up for grabs in 1962. (For sheer terror, see an architect's pipe dream at right.)

It was more than an anxious year later that William Matson Roth, a man of civic virtue, private wealth, and insight into the values of vision, announced the creation of Ghirardelli Square to a press that gave the news as big a play as some shopping mall might get. It cost a great deal, but what is $5 million? Or the $18 million invested by now? Or the countless millions running through the cash boxes of San Francisco merchants—there and thereabouts and elsewhere—now and until the bricks crumble? What it *is:* putting money into something of value.

Ghirardelli Square *won* the dream of Aquatic Park. But it did not finish it. Asked by a reporter from the *Winston-Salem Sentinel* how he got to be such a visionary, Roth replied, "It's a business deal." Translated into what should become Boardroom English, Roth was saying that there is sound money in amenity, that profit can be generated by ambience and association.

Ghirardelli Square has served as a model to thoughtful investors who see the results, but they often miss the point of the Aquatic Park aesthetic: that Ghirardelli Square would be hanging out there all by itself were it not for the Maritime Museum and the old ships at Hyde Street, the Victorian Park and the promised museum in the Haslett that give people a focus and a purpose and a sense of uncommercialized value. Every planner and promoter who has seen at least the first light should ponder carefully: "There has got to be more than eat and buy."

MORLEY BAER

Fort Point to the Ferry Building. . . . *a time to get it all together.*

In the wake of the Freeway Revolt, the most colorful mayor of San Francisco since Sunny Jim concluded his inaugural address with a civic invitation to greatness: "Join with me in a grand urban coalition . . . in a relentless effort to ignite a flame in the breast of this city, a fiery spirit of adventure, that soars beyond the ordinary." With such words Joseph L. Alioto brought down the house on the eighth of January, 1968. Eight years later, the most visible monument to the soaring spirit of adventure is an overbuilt skyline, a trivialization of progress that is most charitably assigned to cultural lag.

"Make no little plans," advised Daniel Burnham—a thoroughly practical visionary. The plans of the last decade have not all been little from the investment standpoint, but they have been little by any standard that goes beyond the limited vision of building contractors. San Franciscans are sick of "plans" that will not make the city a better place. Hence the huge Yerba Buena redevelopment remains a vacant expanse, waiting for a vision that Alioto could not generate.

It would be appropriate to offer here, in this appraisal of San Francisco, an imaginative solution to the Yerba Buena miscalculation. But we prefer to suggest a concept that is already a long way towards realization, a plan that can be accomplished comparatively easily but

Fort Point

The Palace of Fine Arts   MORLEY BAER

with much more dramatic—and profitable—results to the city than anything apt to happen south of Market. Indeed, the Fort Point to the Ferry Building proposal, which seemed breathtaking in scope when we talked about it more than ten years ago in the course of writing *Here Today,* has piece by piece been fitting itself together as the result of the efforts of several groups and many individuals, each doing their own good work for their own limited purposes. Today, only failure to see the whole and its possibilities can result in mistaken developments that will vitally damage what can be the greatest waterfront scenes in the world, an ever-present joy to the citizen and a tourist attraction beyond comparison.

Ten years ago all of this waterfront was in public ownership, as it is today, but then the various authorities controlling it had little in common interest. Now, Fort Point to Aquatic Park is all firmly committed to park purposes and the Port Authority's thoughts for monstrous building complexes between Fisherman's Wharf and the Ferry Building (such as the grotesque Ferry Port Plaza) have been shrinking toward more human scale.

What is needed at this time is a sense of general purpose in the

The North Waterfront in the 1880's: the Old Ferry Building at right, Fort Point at left.

development of the North Waterfront. This public purpose can be identified in several key elements:

——The great and potentially great public museums that provide focal points along the Waterfront—Fort Point, the Palace of Fine Arts, the San Francisco Maritime Museum, the Old Ships of the State of California, the *Balclutha,* and above all the undeveloped Haslett Building must be given greater public funds, based on the realization that they all together form a tremendous public attraction and serve a vital public need.

——There must be a public committment to opening up the vistas of the bulkhead line between Fisherman's Wharf and the Ferry Building, so that San Francisco and the Bay again become one grand environmental unit. When the obsolete piers are removed they must not be replaced by a new Chinese wall of development.

——The first step in realizing the general goal of a waterfront for people is to install an attractive transportation system that will tie together the sweep of the North Bay margin and give the public an idea of what it has and can have. *Continued on page 294*

The Haslett building

Fisherman's wharf a generation ago

Alongside the seawall in the 1880's

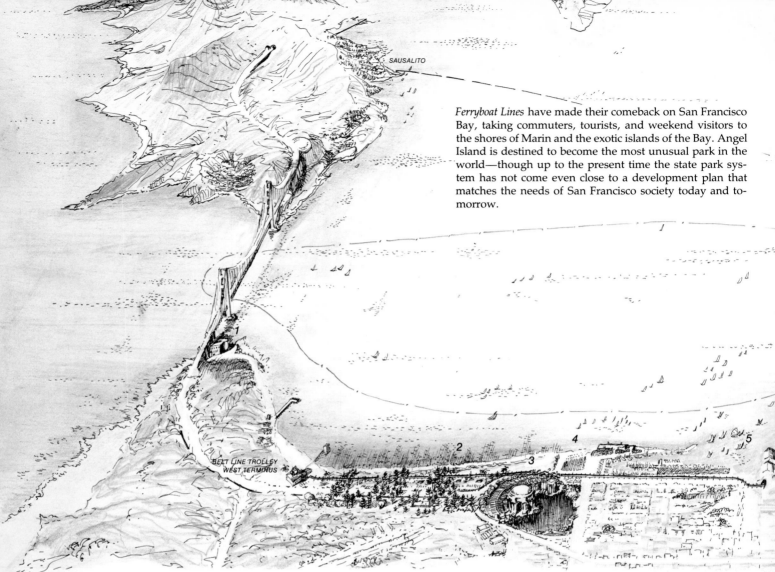

Within the illustration:

SAUSALITO

Ferryboat Lines have made their comeback on San Francisco Bay, taking commuters, tourists, and weekend visitors to the shores of Marin and the exotic islands of the Bay. Angel Island is destined to become the most unusual park in the world—though up to the present time the state park system has not come even close to a development plan that matches the needs of San Francisco society today and tomorrow.

BELT LINE TROLLEY
WEST TERMINUS

A tour from the Golden Gate to the Foot of Market

1—FORT POINT, the most important historic monument of its kind in the West and the oldest really big structure of the Pacific Slope, is the natural anchor and attraction of the western end of San Francisco's historic and scenic waterfront. Its tiers of massive arched gun-bays provide a magnificent architectural opportunity for the museum of the Army of the West that is at present only a glimmer of what it may become when a Belt Line Trolley finally connects it to the Aquatic Park-Fisherman's Wharf tourist center and the Ferry Building. (*Present development level—25%. Present use level—10%*)

2—THE BEACH, stretching from the delightful Victorian Coast Guard Station (which should house a small museum) to the Marina, is San Francisco's true aquatic park. As the new Golden Gate National Recreation Area develops this Bay front, the potential of this heretofore overlooked strand will become apparent. The beach itself should be extended inland and planted with pines and cypress to frame the Bay and break the wind in picnic areas. (*Present development level—0%. Present use level—0%.*)

3—THE PALACE OF FINE ARTS is a fine romantic setting for the Exploratorium experience. The delightful and educational visual experiments have been put together on the barest shoestring. Given a place on the Belt Line Trolley, many more people will have the opportunity of grasping physics through perceptions. (*Present development level—35%. Present use level—30%.*)

4—MARINA GREEN. The only place presently given to the people of San Francisco where they can fully grasp the unity of the Bay and its near and distant shores. (*Present development level—97%. Present use level 97%.*)

5—FORT MASON. Black Point is the surprising connection between the sweep of the curving beach to the west and the intensive Aquatic Park-Ghirardelli Square-Fisherman's Wharf complex to the east. Its intimate gardens and secret vistas, well-kept lawn and historic residences are a delightful contrast in scope—but of potentially grand outlook. Is demolition the only solution to its sturdy but unsightly piers? (*Present development level—10%. Present use level 2%.*)

6—AQUATIC PARK. A waterfront scene—still unfinished—that is already a landmark to urban planners of the world. A triumph of imaginative cooperation between non-profit and private enterprise on a human scale. Requires further development of the State Park and Haslett Building Museum that join it to Fisherman's Wharf.

7—FISHERMAN'S WHARF. The enhancement of the fishing industry, and removal of the view-destroying Pier 45, are necessary to the preservation and enhancement of San Francisco's world famous tourist center. Never mind "good taste"—let's have more marine activities and views. (*Present development level–65%. Present use level 65%.*)

8—THE NORTH FRONT PIERLINE from Fisherman's Wharf to the Ferry Building is a low-rise "Chinese Wall" representing an engineer's grandfather's idea of what a neat-looking waterfront should be. With a couple of exceptions the present piers are either obsolete or actually in advanced decay. The need for a new passenger-ship terminal should be met with a scheme for berthing parallel to the bulkhead, with a minimum of buildings to obscure the sight of the cruise ships and the Bay. Warren Simmon's plan for a marina project including Piers 37 through 41 has been shown here, but much more detailed consideration must be given to low-level view from background areas—perhaps the planned pier is at the wrong angle. Study it.

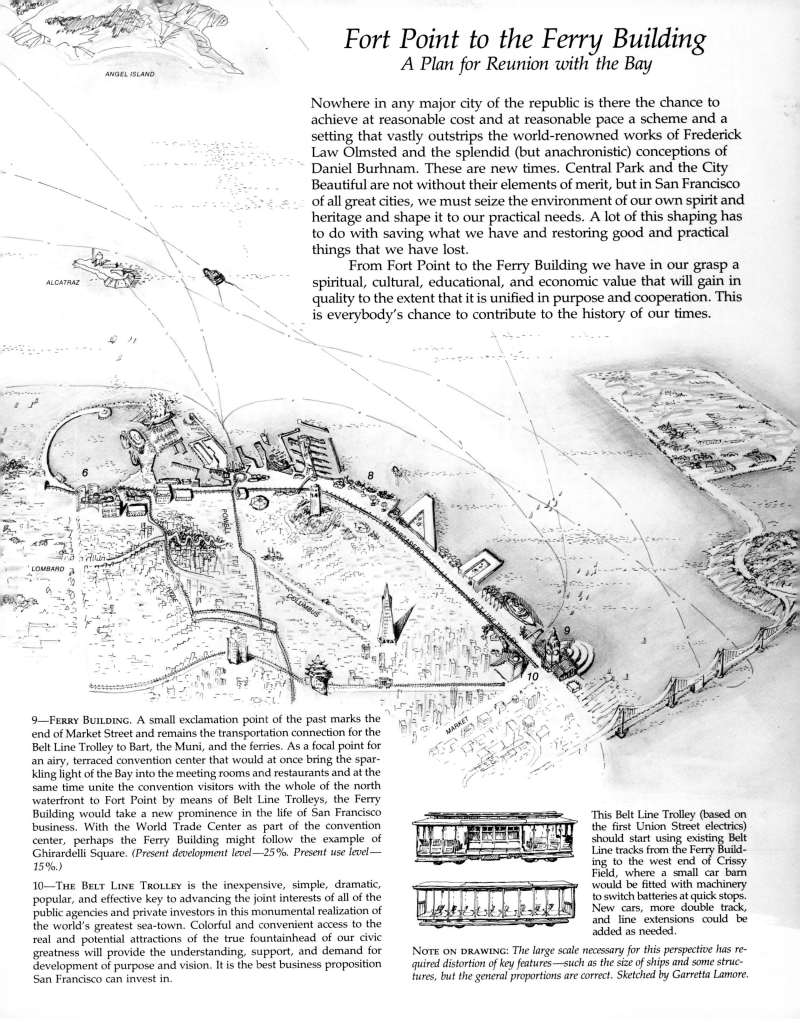

Fort Point to the Ferry Building
A Plan for Reunion with the Bay

Nowhere in any major city of the republic is there the chance to achieve at reasonable cost and at reasonable pace a scheme and a setting that vastly outstrips the world-renowned works of Frederick Law Olmsted and the splendid (but anachronistic) conceptions of Daniel Burhnam. These are new times. Central Park and the City Beautiful are not without their elements of merit, but in San Francisco of all great cities, we must seize the environment of our own spirit and heritage and shape it to our practical needs. A lot of this shaping has to do with saving what we have and restoring good and practical things that we have lost.

From Fort Point to the Ferry Building we have in our grasp a spiritual, cultural, educational, and economic value that will gain in quality to the extent that it is unified in purpose and cooperation. This is everybody's chance to contribute to the history of our times.

ANGEL ISLAND

ALCATRAZ

LOMBARD

POWELL

HYDE

COLUMBUS

EMBARCADERO

BELT LINE TROLLEY

MARKET

9—FERRY BUILDING. A small exclamation point of the past marks the end of Market Street and remains the transportation connection for the Belt Line Trolley to Bart, the Muni, and the ferries. As a focal point for an airy, terraced convention center that would at once bring the sparkling light of the Bay into the meeting rooms and restaurants and at the same time unite the convention visitors with the whole of the north waterfront to Fort Point by means of Belt Line Trolleys, the Ferry Building would take a new prominence in the life of San Francisco business. With the World Trade Center as part of the convention center, perhaps the Ferry Building might follow the example of Ghirardelli Square. (*Present development level—25%. Present use level—15%.*)

10—THE BELT LINE TROLLEY is the inexpensive, simple, dramatic, popular, and effective key to advancing the joint interests of all of the public agencies and private investors in this monumental realization of the world's greatest sea-town. Colorful and convenient access to the real and potential attractions of the true fountainhead of our civic greatness will provide the understanding, support, and demand for development of purpose and vision. It is the best business proposition San Francisco can invest in.

This Belt Line Trolley (based on the first Union Street electrics) should start using existing Belt Line tracks from the Ferry Building to the west end of Crissy Field, where a small car barn would be fitted with machinery to switch batteries at quick stops. New cars, more double track, and line extensions could be added as needed.

NOTE ON DRAWING: *The large scale necessary for this perspective has required distortion of key features—such as the size of ships and some structures, but the general proportions are correct. Sketched by Garretta Lamore.*

To implement these goals several steps should be considered right now.

1. A NEW BREAKWATER FOR FISHERMAN'S WHARF is an important step in preserving and enhancing the fishing industry, without which the Wharf will become an increasingly hollow tourist attraction. The Army Engineers' plans, years in development, are too limited and must be reworked into a concept which includes the removal of most of Pier 45, the most visually disastrous structure on the whole waterfront.

2. ON THE NORTH FRONT PIERLINE the need for a new passenger-ship terminal should be met with a scheme for berthing parallel to the bulkhead, with a minimum of buildings to obscure the sight of cruise ships and the Bay. Warren Simmon's plan for a marina project including Piers 37 through 41 must be given thoughtful consideration; he has steadily improved it, but it still has such unfortunate features as the entirely wrong garage structure in the entirely wrong place. Finally, the city or its Port Agency should find a formula to share the fantastic unearned increase in private property values that must be the inevitable outcome of opening up the waterfront.

Time to start moving   RANDOLPH BRANDT

MUNI PHOTO

When the Ferry Building was the hub

3. THE FERRY BUILDING will again be a great San Francisco landmark when the freeway is torn down. The city should consider building the convention center it wants out over the Bay behind the building or nearby—but this should not be the giant complex we think we need. It should be a place that enhances the meeting of the city and the Bay, the small and medium-sized meetings that are the main stuff of conventions, a place of terraces and restaurants and the vistas that bring conventioneers to San Francisco. A huge new auditorium can indeed be built somewhere in the Yerba Buena redevelopment; other facilities, like Brooks Hall, the Opera House, and Civic Auditorium, are up the street, at the Civic Center. All these convention amenities and necessaries (including the hotels) are tied together by BART, the new Muni subway, and eventually by an extension of the waterfront trolley suggested below. In a city with the intimate scale of downtown San Francisco, it should not be necessary to pack convention facilities in a single place.

4. THE BELT LINE TROLLEY, extending from the Ferry Building to a Crissy Field terminus, a short walk from Fort Point, will give immediate focus and impetus to the enhancement of the waterfront. Battery-powered cars, much like the original cable cars in appearance, with plenty of outside seating, can start by using the existing Belt Line tracks. The system will almost immediately become one of the most popular rides in the world and will develop and improve under the real pressure of patronage rather than as the result of wishful thinking and large initial capitalization.

Just as the Belt Line Trolley can be instituted for less money than it would take to extend the Powell Street cable line three blocks into the heart of Fisherman's Wharf, so the whole Fort Point to the Ferry Building concept implies comparatively modest thinking in all its elements and no requirement for sudden and gigantic capital investment. Its essence lies in protecting what we have in our grasp and moving into the future with a sense of purpose.

Something of value is at stake.

Picture Credits

Letters of Gold, pp 39–53: All lettersheets are from the Honeyman collection and general collections of the Bancroft Library.

The Perfect Likeness of a Legend, pp 66–81: From original daguerreotypes in the Bancroft Library, with the exception of p. 68 (San Francisco Maritime Museum), p. 71 (George Eastman House), p. 79, bottom left (Society of California Pioneers).

The City of the Sixties, pp 106–115: All photos are from a possibly definitive set of Muybridge stereo cards (untouched since the photographer packaged them in the 1870 s) that turned up in the archives of the San Francisco College for Women several years ago and now reside in the Bancroft Library.

The Chinese Must Go!, pp 124–129: *Wasp* cartoons from the California Historical Society. Photographs from the Genthe Collection, California Palace of the Legion of Honor.

On the Loose in the Eighties, pp 140–149: This essay in white-collar life is entirely from the personal album of Frank B. Rodolph, a professional photographer of Oakland and San Francisco during the 1880 s. The Rodolph album is in the Bancroft Library.

At the End of Our Streets are Spars, pp 160–167: All of these photographs are the work of "The Emerald Gang," yachtsmen and leaders of the amateur photographic society of Northern California in the late '80s and '90s. The plates, made by William Betts Oliver, owner of the *Emerald*, wound up in the Bancroft Library; work of other friends and members is in the Shaw Collection, San Francisco Maritime Museum.

The City that Was, pp 174–183: The fine nitrate negatives comprising the Muhlmann Collection are in the San Francisco Maritime Museum.

Gone in Three Days, pp 190–199: No single photographer covered the 1906 disaster in all its phases. Page 190, Bear Photo Service. Page 191 (top) Bancroft Library; (bottom) William Bronson, Palace of the Legion of Honor, Bancroft Library. Page 192: Bancroft Library; California Historical Society, *American West*. Page 193: California Palace of the Legion of Honor. Page 194: Bancroft Library. Page 195: San Francisco Maritime Museum. Page 196: (top) author's collection; (bottom) *American West*. Page 197: (top) Palace of the Legion of Honor; (bottom) James Leonard Collection. Pages 198–99: San Francisco Maritime Museum; page 199 (top) Bancroft Library.

Saloon Politics, pp 209–211: Page 209, San Francisco Public library. Pages 210–211, San Francisco Maritime Museum.

Sunny Jim and the Harmonics of Affluence, pp 219–227: All are news photographs of the period from the collections of the San Francisco Public Library.

Revolution in San Francisco, pp 235–241: All news photographs are on deposit in San Francisco Public Library.

No Foundation, pp 251–257: Page 251, Dorothea Lange. Page 252, 253, Dorothea Lange, Oakland Museum. Page 254, Dorothea Lange. Page 255, San Francisco Public Library. Pages 256, 257, Dorothea Lange, Oakland Museum.

Something of Value, pp 278–294: All photos are from Karl Kortum and the San Francisco Maritime Museum except page 282 (Bancroft Library) and 289 (Morely Baer).

A Site Without a City—8, 10, 11, 12 Bancroft Library; 13, 14, 15 author's collection; *Destiny's Village*—16 Bancroft Library; 18–26 author's collection; 26 (bottom) Bancroft Library; 27–29 author's collection. *The Actual Metropolis*—30–38 author's collection. *Let Each Man Be His Own Executioner*—54 Bancroft Library; 56–65 author's collection. *The Dictatorship of the Bourgeoisie*—82 Bancroft Library; 84 author's collection; 84–85 S. F. Maritime Museum; 86–87 author's collection; 88–89 Bancroft Library; 90–93 author's collection. *Thirty Days from Wall Street*—94 author's collection; 96 (top) Bancroft Library; 96 (bottom) Sutro Library; 97 California Historical Society; 98–99 California State Library; 99 author's collection; 100–102 Bancroft Library; 103 Oakland Museum; 104 author's collection; 105 California State Archives. *The Trade Winds of Time*—116 author's collection; 118 (top) Bancroft Library; 118 (bottom) Huntington Library; 119 Title Insurance and Trust Co.; 120 Wells Fargo History Room; 121–122 Society of California Pioneers; 123 Bancroft Library. *On the Altar of the Golden Calf*—130 California Historical Society; 132 S. F. Maritime Museum; 133 (top) Bancroft Library; 133 (bottom) author's collection; 134 (top) Bancroft Library; 134 (bottom) California Historical Society; 135–137 California Historical Society; 138 Bancroft Library; 139 S. F. Maritime Museum. *Portrait of a Memory*—150 author's collection; 152 (top) Bancroft Library; 152 (bottom)–153 Stanford University Museum; 154 Bancroft Library; 155 (top) Los Angeles County Museum; 155 (bottom) S. F. Maritime Museum; 156 S. F. Public Library; 157–159 author's collection; 159 (bottom) S. F. Maritime Museum. *The Inheritors*—168 author's collection; 170 (top) Los Angeles County Museum; 170 (bottom)–171 author's collection; 184 author's collection; 185 (top) Bancroft Library; 185 (bottom) S. F. Maritime Museum; 186 (top) author's collection; 186 (bottom) Bancroft Library; 187–189 S. F. Maritime Museum. *Diminishing Returns*—200 courtesy Howell-North Books; 202–203 S. F. Maritime Museum; 204 (top) author's collection; 204 (bottom) S. F. Maritime Museum; 205 *S. F. Chronicle*; 206 J. S. Holliday; 207–208 Bancroft Library; 212 (top) Bancroft Library; 212 (bottom) S. F. Municipal Railway; 213 Huntington Library; 214 S. F. Maritime Museum; 215 Bancroft Library; 217 S. F. Maritime Museum; 218 California Historical Society. *Of Creeping Bears and the Drums of War*—228–230 Library of Congress; 231 Bancroft Library; 232 S. F. Public Library; 233 S. F. Maritime Museum; 234 (top) S. F. Public Library; 234 (bottom) Eagle Cafe; 242 S. F. Public Library; 243 S. F. Maritime Museum; 244 S. F. Public Library; 245 S. F. Maritime Museum; 246 Scrimshaw Press; 247 Department of Defense; 248 Dorothea Lange; 249 S. F. Public Library. *The Dimensions of Possibility*—260–261 Karl Kortum; 262–263 S. F. Maritime Museum; 264–266 author's collection; 266 (bottom)–267 S. F. Public Library; 268–270 author's collection; 271 S. F. Maritime Museum; 272 Richard Conrat; 273 Karl Kortum; 274 S. F. Maritime Museum; 277 Joan Parker.

Index

Acknowledgements

This book is the expression of the dream of J. S. Holliday, who began work with me on the project in 1962. In his association with *American West* and the California Historical Society, Jim has supported, and often made possible, the work of both Tom Watkins and myself.

Nearly all of the materials for this book that should be credited must be credited to the great old timers of the California history business. Lawrence Kinnard and W. H. Hutchinson sought to produce good students of history in both of us. John Barr Tompkins worked with us to best express the quality of the collections of the Bancroft Library, and his help and enthusiasm have been more than vital to this work. Robert H. Becker (of the Bancroft Library), Helen Giffen (of the Society of California Pioneers), Gladys Hansen (of the San Francisco Public Library), and Irene Simpson Neasham (of the Wells Fargo History Room), contributed both the resources of their institutions and their generous expertise.

We finally credit Karl Kortum, whose life has been dedicated to the perfection of our city, and note in passing that life and action mean more than words or lists of credits.

—R. R. OLMSTED

PRINTING: Graphic Arts Center, Portland
BINDING: Lincoln & Allen Co., Portland
PAPER: Centura Dull
TYPESETTING: Aldus and Palatino by Holmes Composition
A great deal of patience was required of
Alex Georgiadis, indexer, Dan Gridley, who helped tremendously,
and John Beyer, who designed it.

John Wodehouse Audubon, son of the famous artist-naturalist, joined the California Gold Rush to cure a lingering malaise, a popular idea of the times being that a rigorous trip through the American West would surely toughen the body and heal the spirit. Homesick and lonesome, he spent a miserable Christmas Day of 1849 in San Francisco in which he remarked on the total absence of female companionship but failed to mention in his diary that the center of town burned up the night before. Only a few fragments of his drawings were saved, among them, this vignette of mining life and San Francisco which bears the legend, "Rain, rain, and more rain . . ."